American
Its History, 1650-1850

America Writes
Its History, 1650–1850

The Formation
of a National Narrative

JUDE M. PFISTER

June, 2014

To: Nancy & Byron,
Hope you are both well. Look forward
to seeing you soon —

Love,
[signature]

McFarland & Company, Inc., Publishers

Jefferson, North Carolina

LIBRARY OF CONGRESS CATALOGUING-IN-PUBLICATION DATA

Pfister, Jude M.
    America writes its history, 1650–1850 : the formation of a national narrative / Jude M. Pfister.
      p.   cm.
    Includes bibliographical references and index.

    ISBN 978-0-7864-7921-4 (softcover : acid free paper) ∞
    ISBN 978-1-4766-1448-9 (ebook)

    1. United States—Historiography.   2. Historians—United States.
3. United States—History—Study and teaching.   I. Title.
E175.P46 2014
973.072—dc23
                                        2014016956

BRITISH LIBRARY CATALOGUING DATA ARE AVAILABLE

Cover art: Gilbert Stuart, *George Washington*, oil on canvas, 60" × 96", 1797 (White House)

Printed in the United States of America

McFarland & Company, Inc., Publishers
  Box 611, Jefferson, North Carolina 28640
    www.mcfarlandpub.com

To
my wife,
Miriam

Table of Contents

......

Acknowledgments

• • • • • •

First acknowledgment must go to the cultural resources staff at the Morristown National Historical Park for their unfailing dedication to the preservation of the resources that made this work possible. Joni Rowe, Sarah Minegar, Krystal Poelstra, Stephanie Dougherty, and Bruce Spadaccini all function under less than ideal conditions in the herculean task of trying to ensure one of the largest, arguably one of the most significant, archival collections within the National Park Service is curated for the benefit of current and future generations of visitors and scholars. I am truly inspired by their work and devotion and I thank them for their assistance and support in this work.

I want to thank Randy Turner, former superintendent of Morristown National Historical Park for his encouragement and commitment to the cultural resources program. I wish also to acknowledge Jill Hawk, another former superintendent of Morristown National Historical Park. Also, I wish to thank the Washington Association of New Jersey and especially Alan Shaw. The late Lloyd W. Smith was a true scholar in every sense of the word, whose vision and dedication brought about the nation's first national historical park and whose rare book and manuscript collection was the inspiration for this work. Debbie Van Buren, as always, proved yet again through her keen observation of telling America's story why she is such a valuable public historian. Thanks are also due to Joan Loveless, formerly of the Papers of John Mar-

shall; and to Michele Lee, Special Collections Librarian at
Mount Vernon. Mary Claffey, of the Massachusetts Historical Society, assisted with an obscure John Adams quote for
which I am grateful. Thanks are due as well to two anonymous readers who provided many suggestions and thoughtful
critique. Even with help, errors of judgment, omission, inclusion, or interpretation may remain in a final manuscript. In
the case of this particular study, those that occur are the
author's and he takes full responsibility for them.

Special posthumous thanks to the preservationists with
the National Park Service who have for eighty years maintained the collection built by Lloyd W. Smith and the Washington Association of New Jersey. The collection has been
referenced many times in the course of the research for this
work, and the author drew extensively from the magnificent
first editions housed at the park library. These editions
include works by John Marshall, Jared Sparks, Mercy Otis
Warren, Ebenezer Hazard, Thomas Prince, David Ramsay,
John Adams, Washington Irving, Jeremey Belknap, Samuel
Smith, and many others. Without the inspiration provided
by this wonderful collection this work would have been
much more difficult.

Preface

......

The work before you is an overview of a topic that has been discussed around the periphery in academic studies but never attempted as a full treatment for the nonspecialist. This is a topic that has fascinated the author for nearly two decades; working as a public historian has provided glimpses of what can only be termed historical illiteracy in some members of the public. This is not to say they don't know the highlights of American or even world history; no, what is so disturbing is the lack of awareness of what exactly history is. What does history do? Where does it come from? Once written, can it ever change? It wasn't until the author had access to a magnificent collection of historical writings that he was able to finally start to pursue some of these questions in a cogent way. In the largest sense, this work is a meditation as to how American history is taught and perceived. The author has no plan or course of action to offer per se to change the sorry state of historical literacy other than to suggest approaches or perspectives in historical education—from grade school through college and beyond—and how these can and should help ameliorate the crisis of historical awareness facing our nation.

History is a process, not a destination. History, to be honest history, must challenge, engage, and, at times, anger the reader. The figurative outlines of historical study should form the core pedagogical experience, not meaningless memorization. Students, and nonstudents, should instead be exposed to the concepts and themes of history. Students do not need to know every name and date from America's past as though it was some sort of Sunday school recitation. Concepts form the building blocks upon which further analysis, interrogation, and understanding of the complex field of the human past can be truly learned and understood. Students taught to challenge history will more than likely come to the field on their own during their school years and

1

after and have a greater appreciation and understanding of not only our American history, but the history of others as well.

This work approaches historical literacy through the pens of America's writers of history: those men and women, prior to 1850, who sought to "set the record straight" for not just future generations, but for their own as well. This work is not a study of the entire meaning of the American writing experience. Rather, it will focus on the portion of the writing within the American repertory that begins to grow with the rise of American regional aspirations and culminates with the crescendo of nationalistic writing during the mid- to late eighteenth century. Finally, the crescendo matures with Jared Sparks by 1850.[1] This century-long development, or even creation, of a written cultural record, puts onto the printed page the aspirations, desires, fears, and most importantly, myths of the colonial and founding generations.

This work seeks to provide readers with an overview of why American history came to be written and the approaches to its style and meaning and most importantly why America's history was—and is—so valuable to Americans; whether they truly understand it is another topic. In that spirit of meaning this work is presented as a full and complete stand-alone topic, yet acknowledging the obvious connections to allied academic disciplines such as literature, psychology and others. Early American historical writing is a vast and far from settled field of study. To use the term to indicate a precision within the understanding of how the field is approached risks eliminating the complexity of the vast expanse of literature and writing that can fall under the heading of "American." Therefore, history is not just for the historian or the historically minded. The patterns of thought and scholarship represented by the figures and themes covered in this work range across many areas of literature and scholarship and will be distinguished when necessary to more fully delineate a point of comparison between writing as literature and as history. History is a part of literature just like poetry or playwriting is a part of literature, and only in specific instances do they differ. Words, crafted by historians, novelists, playwrights, essayists, in short, writers, represent the people who quite simply put pen to paper and create meaning through written language. The meaning they create oftentimes resonates far beyond their immediate audience and place in time.

While a geographical consideration envelops America's early history writing (the eastern seaboard of the North American continent, the area which comprises the present day states from Maine to Florida), so too does the theme which American writers relied on as a starting point. Taken as a whole, the theme in the beginning was the future of the scattered outposts that transitioned from settlement, to colony, to state, and to country—and especially how they compared and would compare to England and Europe.

In the early years of settlement, America only had a future; a past was nearly unthinkable, especially when settlers looked at the past of Europe. Historical writers from about 1650 to 1850, besides the geographic continuity, shared the theme of America's future as seen only dimly in the beginning. Not until American-born Europeans matured could a writer conceive of a past rooted in his or her own homeland. Writers such as Thomas Prince, Ebenezer Hazard, Jeremy Belknap, Mercy Otis Warren, and David Ramsay are examples of the historians who attempted to approach the huge, still unfolding drama of their day: the development of what ultimately became the United States. Few writers could say they made a living writing until the nineteenth century. Trying to create not just history, but a meaningful and purposeful history, came to be seen as more difficult than first anticipated.

As the wariness of the American colonial enterprise began to wane following the passage of generations in America, writers began to reflect this feeling of passing time by putting down their thoughts on the written and printed page. Yet, even promises had to have a foundation to provide a stable sense of acceptance. The foundational stories came in many varieties and were entirely similar, in many cases the same, as the historical stories associated with the creation of a political entity such as a country; even a colony or colonies thousands of miles across an ocean and removed from the center of political power by months of travel.

One important aspect of early American writing was that, more than any other aspect of colonial American life, it was where "American culture's myths of origin" were found, and this helped to establish the cohesive aspects so vital to national awareness.[2] It was not enough to write about the foundation stories—myths or otherwise—it also needed to be consumed and understood by readers, and finally repeated and taught to the new generation of Americans born in the colonies who did not necessarily see themselves as Englishmen in the same way as their parents and grandparents who came from England. The further removed each generation became from the first colonial settlers, the greater the pull and promise of American greatness put in words became. The population boom in colonial America only intensified this process by generating more and more Americans, each one further and further removed by the passage of time from England.

Discovery narratives provided some of the first examples of historical writing associated with the American mainland. In 1747, Virginia historian William Stith lamented the sad reputation of "age of discovery" types of narratives and hoped the colonies would somehow not feel the further need for that type of myth-laden founding story. Stith wrote,

> Every Country, hath it's Fables concerning it's Original, which give great Scope to light and fanciful Historians, but are usually passed over with a slight Men-

tion by the solid and judicious. The late Discovery of America, in historical and well-known Times, might, one would think, have exempted it from the common Fate of Nations. Yet ... even this new World hath been endowed with it's Fabulous Age.[3]

Stith was hopeful, yet realistic, that America would have the "solid and judicious" people writing or reading the history of the founding period without resort to the "fabulous" tales often associated with such heroic feats as discovery of new continents. Consequently, writings detailing the unique, pristine features of the vast stretch of coast of North America quickly became of interest to Englishmen and Europeans as economic and academic reasons helped to generate interest and the greater need for solid, factual information.

Historical writing was certainly not the only type of writing available in the colonies prior to the Revolution. Historical writing accounted for only a small portion of the writing produced in the 175 years between 1600 and 1775. As with other parts of Europe, genres such as poetry, prose, adventure and exploration, and religious topics, were responsible for the vast majority of published works.[4] The market for history as such was weak at best. The colonies, to anyone who gave the subject much thought, were simply too young themselves for proper history and relied on European history for their forays into the past. History as a discipline, or even a concept, didn't resonate with a public preoccupied with more pressing concerns. Reflections on a shared past seemed pointless to pursue during the early decades. What was important was the here and now, and, within the proper confines of religious reflection, the future.

Historical narratives seemed to instinctively need heroes; preferably only one, who could serve to rally the conscious aspirations of a national theme. By 1780, during the American struggle for independence, a guiding, physical, living presence was necessary to the developing national consciousness for creating a national history. Fortunately, America had such a figure. The role, presence, dignity, and character (myth or otherwise) of George Washington became paramount; by common consent the main figure of the American independence struggle became the main figure of American history.

Historians such as David Ramsay, Jared Sparks, and John Marshall, who had as their main theme the specter of George Washington after his death in 1799, were able to utilize his memory in a way which earlier historians could not. While part one of this work will provide a basic analysis of the overall theme of American historical writing, the creation of a triumphal type of historical literature based on the Washington memory will form the foundation for parts two and three, focusing on the early to mid–nineteenth century historical writing which culminated with Jared Sparks by 1850.

Introduction

......

History. The word embraces many feelings. For elementary, high school, and even college students, it is not a popular subject of study. For many adults, it often reminds them of the trepidation they experienced as students and is also reminiscent of unpleasant memories of classroom tedium and boring, obligatory visits to museums. Only for a handful of the population does history represent the unique qualities of learning that make indulging in the field so rewarding, and challenging.

Jane Austen puts into the dialogue of Miss Morland in *Northanger Abbey* the thoughts most might feel toward studying or reading history: "I read it a little as a duty, but it tells me nothing that does not either vex or weary me."[1] Even worse, Miss Morland sees the work of the historian as "laboring only for the torment of little boys and girls" who must study their history in school regardless.[2] These less than encouraging references to the historical profession and process helped to set a tone just when the historical field was beginning to coalesce as a separate discipline in America. Although fiction as written, Austen's writing influenced millions at the time, and continues to do so today.[3]

As with other areas of study, history as a discipline has expanded greatly over the past 200 years. We are no longer content with having to memorize the sovereigns of England or the presidents of the United States in order to consider ourselves learned in a particular section of history. Requirements have become more stringent and sophisticated.

As a national outgrowth of earlier writing (poetry and prose), history developed slowly yet with determination in the colonies (later states), which rebelled against England. There was not, however, a seamless line of descent from the development of an American historical writing voice in the seven-

5

teenth century and the establishment of the first chair of history at a major American university (Harvard) in 1839.

The rise of American historical writing can be traced to roughly fewer than fifty people.[4] They represented the vanguard of what became a new academic discipline in the mid-nineteenth century with Jared Sparks (the first occupant of the chair in history at Harvard University), and together they formed the boundaries wherein much of the accepted outlines of the emerging discipline developed.[5] Still heavily dependent on the Revolution as a theme for study, the historians within the boundaries between the Revolution and 1850 crafted more nuanced and focused studies than those who preceded them.[6]

Some of the earliest American historical writing in the seventeenth century had only one purpose: to promote the legitimacy of the existing power base. This type of history still exists today, but we tend to view it more as politically inspired writing. In the early seventeenth century, when survival was far from certain for early American settlers, writers often turned to themes designed to strengthen the ties of social and political connection. These writers sought to find the common bonds that above all others would fill readers with a sense of belonging and a willingness to sacrifice for a cause greater than themselves.

Despite an overall rise in writing by Americans in the eighteenth century, history as a separate element of the written record would not have developed as such a powerful component of the writer's tool chest without the foundation already existing. Taking into account historical writing prior to Jared Sparks, there was no single moment when historians (or the country overall) came to the conclusion that a department of history should be established somewhere.[7]

The yearning, the growing pains, and the anxiety of an uncertain future manifested itself on the printed page throughout the seventeenth century in American writing through poetry, narrative, plays, and songs, which sought to push the boundaries of social and political acceptability within a crumbling system of conformity dominated by colonial charters and heavenly edicts. As writers stretched and pushed through their work, society responded in kind with political aspirations which kept pace with the writing. Particularly during the seventeenth century, these aspirations were allowed to incubate due to the preoccupation of England and Europe in horrible wars, which marginalized the colonies.

The development of American historical writing to heighten a sense of American destiny in part fueled the desire of later historians to write their heroic histories of the founding generation. This represented the unique and powerful cohesion of forces catalyzed by the epic events of 1775–1783.[8] An examination of the limited popularity of historical writing beginning in the early eighteenth century and ending with the efforts of Jared Sparks by 1840 allows us to see the continuities with earlier American efforts at the printed historical word while at the same time allowing us to appreciate the uniqueness and differences that came with the advent of historical writing.

Most countries strive to frame their creation in terms which inspire and promote patriotism, and indeed, reverence. For expressing power and developing a sense of devotion in a society, this was a proven method for establishing the "establishment." In the United States, "it was the sense of patriotic duty to a national society, perhaps more than anything else that led to the remarkable outpouring of historical works during the years from 1783 to 1815."[9]

The influence of the written word as an emulsifier in the political ingredients allows us to see a much larger picture in the development of an effective national story. This story and how it was presented was itself a story which further heightens our awareness of just how Americans came to think and see themselves by the end of the Revolution. History thus helped to "foster patriotism, a national consciousness and consensus."[10]

Once the Revolution was successfully concluded in 1783, it became necessary to figure out not just how to govern an independent country; it also became necessary to figure out how we wanted to perceive ourselves and project that perception to the outside world. This latter role is where a portion of the historian's story can be told. In the United States, late eighteenth century approaches to historical writing focused on the American Revolution and the heroics involved with achieving independence.[11] The Revolution itself provided the impetus which spurred beyond the local or state level the advancement of the national historical narrative. Yet, even before the Treaty of Paris in 1783 (officially ending the American Revolution) was signed, and certainly before the Constitution was adopted in 1788, writers were contemplating and preparing histories of the events which led to American independence. The American historian was as valuable to the success of the American enterprise during the Revolution and after as any other participant in America's struggles during that period. While not easy to quantify, it is not impossible to show how the historian provided a written record of the events which brought about American independence.

The idea of studying the Revolutionary period through the perspective of the writer is not entirely new. In 1897, Moses Coit Tyler, a professor of history at Cornell, published *The Literary History of the American Revolution*. In Tyler's own words, his work was designed to provide readers with a view of the Revolution not often encountered:

> Instead of fixing over our eyes almost exclusively ... upon statements and generals, upon party leaders, upon armies and navies, upon Congress, upon parliament ... and instead of viewing all these people as the sole or principle movers and

doers of the things that made the American Revolution, we ... turn our eyes away toward certain persons hitherto much neglected, in many cases wholly forgotten—toward persons who, as mere writers, ... nourished the springs of great historic events by creating and shaping and directing public opinion.[12]

The printed, published works of historians and semi-historians provided the "ammunition" necessary to place arguments in a historical context, which, while often embellished, were not indistinguishable from fact. Whether this dealt with ancient English history or colonial American history was immaterial—"the history made by the American Revolutionaries was in part the product of the history they read."[13]

A characteristic feature of nearly all the Revolutionary era historians was not necessarily their various local prejudices—which certainly existed. A defining feature of nearly every early national period historian was their reliance on the Revolution as both a culmination and starting point. History was and is determined by who you are: not in the sense of predetermining one's station in life, but one's station in life determining what type of history one wished to consume. The Revolution was the culmination of (in the writings of the time) years of British "tyranny" over the colonies. Conversely, that event was also seen as a starting point for the new United States. The Revolution was both beginning, and end. Historians had to figure out how these two sides of the same event went together. And, once that was accomplished, they needed to establish that event as unique to the American experience to ensure a filial attachment was attained by readers in order to encourage patriotism.

The approaches taken by the competing political regional interpretations in the 1790s had a monarchist versus a non-monarchist identification. The monarchists did not truly want a king, and their criticism of the British attack on colonial freedoms prior to the Revolution tended to be more conciliatory. The dichotomy engendered by competing historical interpretations had its major flourish noticeably during the ratification of the Constitution.

Historians at the time reflected this uneasy tension between the opposing philosophies by ignoring all discussion of the debate. In fact "from 1795 to 1805, when national politics reached fever pitch, no historian accorded the Constitution more than a cursory treatment."[14] As an example, the historian Jedidiah Morse, not content with bypassing just the Constitutional debate, completely passed over the tumultuous period of the Articles of Confederation in the history he wrote and published in 1789.[15]

One easy way around the controversy was to attach the Constitution to the Revolution as though the two were directly connected. Thus the Revolutionary military victory lent itself nicely as a foundation to append to the development of the Constitution almost as though they were two totally connected, seamless events.

Beyond the mere facts—names, dates, etc.—interpreting the founding generation quickly became an arduous task, which was being accentuated by regional differences. Writers, consciously or not, began to drift into the minefield which is historical cause and effect impacting the governing and political capacities of the new nation. While most came to agree on the basic outlines of the Revolution in terms of cause and effect, it was not long before the political uses of cause and effect came to be seen after the Revolution. This fault line ran essentially between the northern and southern states. This was by no means a precise delineation; nonetheless the competing interpretations that led to the development of the party system in the 1790s were reflected initially in the approaches to historical interpretation immediately following the War.

From a practical standpoint, what connects all of the historians as well at this point (1800) was the uniformity of poor sales—a theme which will be referred to many times in this study. Each historian had mediocre sales among a devoted or at least interested group of readers. Sadly, though,

the reading public of the period lacked literary sophistication; its writers lacked self-confidence. Both were prone to accept the fashionable and the popular without discrimination, no doubt because both writers and readers were uncertain of their own critical judgments and reluctant to differ with British and European trends.[16]

Not only was the available talent for culture limited in the colonies, but an available audience for mass consumption of cultural production was lacking. Very few, if any, writers, actors, or entertainers actually made a living at their craft. Not until enough of the population came to demand and appreciate more American-inspired cultural offerings would the supply of such offerings expand.

Thomas Jefferson—Promoter of American History

In 1813, Thomas Jefferson wrote to John Adams regarding the Revolution as a turning point in the approach to history writing: "before the establishment of the American states, nothing was known to History but the Man of the old world."[17] Jefferson saw American historians as breaking with the past just as the colonists broke politically with the past. History for Jefferson was far more than a compilation of names and dates. For Jefferson, history possessed a "social utility" which could and would (if appropriately written) draw citizens closer together.[18]

Thomas Jefferson was an ardent and lifelong supporter of historical enquiry and education in general. Jefferson authored the Diffusion of Knowledge Bill in 1779, the first such legislation advocating the study of American history in schools. As an early advocate during the Revolutionary era of the utility of historical writing, Jefferson worked to provide support to early historians like Ebenezer Hazard and Jeremy Belknap, who strove to write and develop history as it happened as opposed to history as a past, already having occurred event.[19] Support by Jefferson and others like him provided lesser known individuals with influential connections in high places.

Throughout his career, Jefferson supported and promoted the efforts of historians to capture the uniqueness of the American experience. The fate of David Ramsay's *The History of South Carolina from a British Province to an Independent State* is instructional for the reception it received in America and England. Ramsay had the work printed in Trenton, New Jersey, in 1786. Poor sales in America forced Ramsay to attempt to sell the book in England instead. The English booksellers would have none of the work. They saw it as one-sided and lacking objectivity. Abigail Adams, in London with her ambassador husband John, commented in a letter written on May 27, 1786, to Isaac Smith, Sr., "Mr Ramsey's History which is written in a cool dispassionate Stile and is chiefly a detail of facts, cannot find a Bookseller here who dares openly to vend the ready printed copies which are sent him."[20]

Thomas Jefferson, in France as the American minister, was as ever keenly in tune not only with American-produced products, but with perceived slights to American dignity as well. Jefferson, upon learning of the plight of Ramsay's book (the two did not know each other), decided to run his own mail-order business from France in an effort to sell it.[21] Jefferson's anger over perceived slights to American writing was, while understandable, somewhat reactionary. After all, barely four years had passed since the Treaty of Paris, and Britain was not yet ready for American commerce, whatever the source. As John Adams, American minister to Great Britain at the same time Thomas Jefferson was in France, wrote to Mercy Otis Warren in a general observation, "Nothing American sells here."[22]

The first work which brought Jefferson immediate attention as a writer, thinker, and historian among his peers was *A Summary View of the Rights of British America*. This pamphlet proved to be Jefferson's first exposure on a national stage. He wrote the *Summary View* in 1774 for a special convention of Virginia delegates. Jefferson's direct, clear, and prosecutorial writing style combined with his extensive use of historical material found favor with his colleagues. Jefferson proved successful partly because he "was telling men what they wanted to believe [by citing historical precedent] and arguing the American cause in language immediately familiar."[23] Like many of his contemporaries who had an understanding of history, Jefferson was certainly not unfamiliar with the tumultuous times through which England had passed during the seventeenth century. Specifically, "he thought of the similarity of his own times to the days of the Puritan revolution in seventeenth-century England."[24]

Similar to other writers of the time (such as James Otis), Jefferson, in *A Summary View*, journeyed back to the Anglo-Saxon period of English history. From a land-owning theory of legal history, Jefferson argued that the colonists (based on historical precedent) should have held their land free and clear from the crown. By 1770, as the dispute with England was deepening, he felt most Americans had been misled by the King's lawyers "into thinking that all American lands really did belong to the King."[25] Jefferson felt most Americans had been lulled into complacency: "as long as administration was mild, there was no occasion for the historical reality to be discovered."[26] This was a theme which resurfaced in the Declaration of Independence regarding how people were willing to accept tyrants as long as they were mild or benevolent tyrants.

Parliament too was an element of scorn for Jefferson in England's attempt to subjugate the colonies. Through his research in English Common Law legal theory Jefferson was convinced of Parliament's abdication of their constitutional requirements.

Jefferson by no means felt constrained to American history as his model. An early admirer of David Hume's eighteenth-century work *The History of England,* Jefferson came to see the pro-monarchical approach to English history as potentially damaging to American democratic sensibilities. Jefferson was convinced of "the essential goodness of human nature and [in the] continual progress of civilization."[27] For Jefferson, a history which denied the inherent worth in humankind separate from a divinely anointed monarch was not suitable for the republic which he was working so hard to establish in the 1770s.

The rise of the American two-party system in the 1790s, of which Jefferson was a major part, caused him to refine his approach to the possibilities of written history and how that history could be utilized for political gain. Like his contemporaries, Jefferson was not only a student of history, but an applier of historical precedent. As his political career developed, his use of history to advance his political concerns expanded too, reaching a crescendo in his crusade against John Marshall and his biography of George Washington, in the early nineteenth century. From being an advocate for the unique characteristics of nationalism that historical writings can provide or promote, Jefferson by 1800 was working to develop an approach to historical writing that presented history in a manner which benefitted his political sensibilities. In many ways, "in 1800 ... the newly elected President of the United States prepared to take control of the nation's past as well as its future."[28]

By his presidency, Jefferson "began to realize that he did not want to give people simply a knowledge of history"; instead, the history provided needed to be tempered, refined, and nuanced to ensure an interpretation of events and characters promoted the qualities most espoused by Jefferson's Republicans.[29] By his entry into the presidency in 1801, Jefferson had moved to a position which saw him make "a concerted effort to influence the writing of American history throughout the rest of his life."[30]

Jefferson's first foray into the world of politically driven written history was with the British author John Wood, a few years before he was elected president. Wood had moved to the United States in 1797 and went to work on a history of the John Adams administration in 1801. The work turned into a political contest with Adams' Federalists wanting to suppress the book and Jefferson's Republicans generally in favor of publication. Jefferson personally worked to promote the work into print as a way of broadcasting his political policies. Wood was able in his history to reclaim Washington from the Federalist camp and place him firmly within Jefferson's Republican Party as Jefferson himself saw it. This was a significant feat, as both parties struggled to claim the heritage of Washington's memory. The struggle over Washington's legacy would only intensify after his death in 1799, a little over a year before Jefferson took office in March 1801, and will occupy the latter chapters of this work.

Thomas Jefferson was instrumental, at the same time he was working with Wood, in also working with John Carey of London in the early 1790s to produce an edition of Washington's writings to the Continental Congress. Carey saw a valuable market available which was not being exploited by American historians and sought to take the initiative. (Volumes were published in England and the United States, but poor sales prevented the completion of the set.)

From a strictly practical historical standpoint, as opposed to political manipulation, Carey's plan suited one of Jefferson's approaches to history by creating multiple copies of the most important historical material then available. While not expressly advocating his political causes, this approach would ensure against loss of manuscripts by providing copies which could then be held at other locations. Even though the venture with Carey was unsuccessful, Jefferson had expressed repeatedly that the best insurance against the loss of archival manuscripts was through multiplication of copies. This idea set Jefferson apart from the more worshipful approaches to historical presentation, which saw many instill a near reverential quality to original documents. In Jefferson's way of thinking, it was not the actual original manuscript that was the most important; instead, it was the content of that manuscript that mattered. Words and their meaning were more important than the paper or vellum they rested on.[31]

Jefferson knew full well the limits of relying on the writings alone of a historical figure. Writing in the *Anas* (his brief autobiography), Jefferson specifically referred to Washington's writings and the caution with which they should be approached—"we are not to suppose that everything found among Genl. Washington's papers is to be taken as gospel truth."[32] Jefferson was concerned with the way the political bias of the writer would influence the final product. Yet, Jefferson himself was engaging in just the type of political posturing through historical writing in this instance that he was accusing particularly his Federalist foe John Marshall of doing—skewing the filter of history with "the passions of the compiler" in an effort to promote and expand their cause.[33]

Jefferson continued his machinations into his second term. As will be seen in a later chapter, he and James Madison encouraged the poet Joel Barlow to undertake a *History of the United States* from a Jeffersonian Republican perspective as a counterweight to John Marshall's Federalist-leaning biography of George Washington. Jefferson strongly felt the Marshall work was designed simply to influence elections and little else by drawing on the memory of George Washington and his two terms as president. It also didn't help the Jefferson/Marshall "feud" that although they were cousins, Jefferson—for whatever reason—detested John Marshall beyond the level to which Marshall reciprocated.

In 1825, the year before his death, Jefferson also provided moral support to Jared Sparks' enterprise. This final act of Jefferson's life concerning the writing of history parallels to some extent the course of historical writing over the span of Jefferson's working life. Jefferson, through his own actions and reactions to the evolution of the writing of history during his lifetime, can represent the various strains of historical thinking played out over the years which reflected his involvement in the historical field. Jefferson's life mirrors the larger forces of historical authorship unfolding around him. His support for Sparks at the end of his life saw his support for historians go nearly across the spectrum and back during his lifetime in terms of developments and approaches to historical writing and thinking, which, as will be demonstrated in later chapters, came to a defined culmination in Jared Sparks.

Part I

......

The first part of this work (chapters one, two, and three, along with the introduction) will serve as a broad introduction to the field of American historical writing. Given the expansive nature of the topic, the overview will range collectively over 200 years of America's attempt to define itself through the historical written word. The purpose is to develop an idea through the first three chapters, which will be further refined and narrowed as this study progresses.

From the very beginning of the English colonization at their Jamestown settlement, history served a multifaceted purpose. History reminded the settlers of the Europe they left behind; it gave them a future to aspire to; it encouraged them to keep their loyalties; and, it provided a form of entertainment.

History as a separate discipline during the seventeenth and much of the eighteenth century did not exist. History was often combined with poetry, drama, or playwriting. This approach produced hybrid history and in most cases entertaining adaptations of historical events rather than a formal history narrative. This process also produced a format that was more accessible to the general reader.

The introduction and chapters one, two, and three will introduce the concepts and theories and the individuals who struggled over which concepts and theories to pursue in order to produce their histories. These writers and historians in America were often working with older European models of history to guide them, and they had difficulty prior to the Revolution finding an organic, American historical voice.

After multiple attempts, the organic voice of historical writing found an impetus through the Revolution and its successful conclusion. After the Revolution historians finally had genuine American, heroic, history. Now, the question became how to best utilize the story presented to them and how to best craft their story and to develop their craft into a discipline.

1

America as a Topic of Historical Inquiry

••••••

The written descriptions of what is today the North American continent had their beginnings as far back as 1000 CE, when the New World began to be visited and speculated about by Europeans. The Icelandic sagas in particular begin the story of Vinland, somewhere in the northern reaches of North America today, in two works—*The Saga of Eric the Red,* and *Vinland History of the Flat Island Book.* These two works clearly identify an area far into the western Atlantic Ocean from where the Danish sailors had embarked on journeys of exploration. And, based on descriptions contained in the writings, particularly of the native peoples encountered, it is generally understood that the area is somewhere in the location of present-day New England or further north along the coast into Canada.[1]

It was, however, the stories and explorations of Christopher Columbus, Amerigo Vespucci, and others, in the late fifteenth century and early sixteenth century, that ensured the European "discovery" of the Western Hemisphere would forever have a date of 1492, rather than centuries earlier.

With hindsight, it's now known that Columbus and others made some mistakes in their explanations of voyages while still being convinced of their accuracy at the time. Nonetheless, it was their exploits that set the boundary of what "America" means geographically in reality and popular myth today. From their day forward,

> the world that ... was to realize itself within the compass of the name "America" was to be a world shaped as much by the energies of the imagination as by the substance of the actual; that it was to be defined as much by the ambiguities of desire as by the structures of the empirical. The world called "America," both

North and South, would ever after be a world dominated and controlled by meanings as much as by facts; it would be a world where fantasy, fear, and fabrication would determine many of the contours of the real.[2]

Thus it was that American history had a beginning partially in myth and fantasy and would forever seemingly straddle a line between fact and fiction in historical writing and other types as well.

The line from the "ambiguities of desire" to the "contours of the real" would prove to be a long and in fact bloody journey of survival in the New World for the colonists. The journey the colonists traveled was variously punctuated by violent outbursts of longing for identification beyond that provided by England. The need in part for a unique self-understanding culminated more than two-and-a-half centuries after Columbus in the American Revolution.

Numerous writers contemporary with Columbus can be identified in preserving his story. One was a Spanish diplomat and scholar named Peter Martyr. His ambitions were clear early on with respect to Columbus' exploits; Martyr wrote to a colleague in 1494, barely two years after the first voyage, "I have begun to write a work concerning this great discovery. If I am suffered to live I shall omit nothing worthy of being recorded.... At all events I shall supply the learned world, in undertaking the history of great things, with a vast sea of new materials."[3] The opening of the Western Hemisphere indeed created a "vast sea of new materials" for writers and historians. Spain produced no lack of historians to tell the story of their conquest of South America either, men such as Bartolome de las Casas (who was extremely critical of Spanish treatment of the natives), Gonzalo Fernandez de Oviedo y Valdes, Franciso Lopez de Gomara, Bernal Diaz del Castillo, Francisco de Xerez, and de Soto, to name a few. Like las Casas, not all of these men were uniformly solicitous of the way Spain conducted itself in the New World. The new opportunities challenged centuries-old, cherished assumptions about the world and man's place in it from both a religious and practical standpoint. History after 1492 became something that began an irrevocable move toward human events cast in a human mold.

The New World thus helped to create a new history. This was a history inching toward objectivity free of falsification and fable and able to challenge readers to think. The advent of mass printing so close to Columbus' voyage also was a catalyst to a significant extent. Without the ability to broadly disseminate written material in printed form, little incentive existed to push the boundaries of historical narrative.

In the year of the Spanish Armada (1588), when Spain sought to return England to the ancient past through religion, one of the first influential books on the New World appeared in England. An Oxford professor, Thomas Hariot, published *A briefe and true report of the New found land of Virginia*. This work "for many decades ... fixed in the minds of its readers a romantic image of the New World" for the English and heralded a new vision and hope beyond the tired and stifling past.[4] For all of the faults recognized with this work today, it was seminal in keeping the prospect of the New World before the English as they entered into a century of near constant warfare, which complicated and diminished their colonization efforts. By the late sixteenth century (a full century after Columbus's discovery), the English were once again becoming aware and involved in the exploration of North America. (It was the English under Walter Raleigh's direction from England who suffered the inglorious disaster of the Roanoke Colony in the 1580s.)

Some of the First American Historians

One of the first books published by an American colonist that can be called a historical account was by Nathaniel Morton of Plymouth, Massachusetts, in 1669. The title, *New Englands Memoriall: Or, A Brief Relation of the most Memorable and Remarkable Passages of the Providence of God, manifested to the Planters of New-England in America; with special Reference to the first Colony thereof, Called New-Plimouth,* which does not roll easily off the tongue, was printed in Cambridge, Massachusetts, as an official publication paid for by the authorities.[5] Morton was a good choice for an official work such as he undertook. He was one of the last surviving of the original Pilgrims who arrived in 1620. His work is generally considered the first history because he was charged with tracking the course of the colony based on the surviving documentation and not necessarily infused or guided by the "hand of God." While primitive by our modern standards, it still bears the hallmark of a work of historical nonfiction based on primary resources.

The invocation of a higher authority is a most effective tool for a variety of endeavors. To many early American Puritan (both Plymouth and Massachusetts Bay varieties) writers, "the task of the historian was not to entertain the reader, but to discover his people's place in God's plan for the universe."[6] Because of this approach against entertainment, history, when combined with the search for the meaning of life, became "a versatile tool in the hands of the Puritans."[7] In addition to and combined with their God, these Puritan historians out of the Massachusetts Bay experience tended to dwell extensively on their relationship with Native Americans and the contrast between themselves and their exalted relationship with God and the nonexistent relationship the Indians had (from the Puritan perspective).

The Indians, after ensuring the survival of the first Pilgrims, had been recognized as (in the eyes of the Puritans) savages, ungodly creatures who were ungrateful for the "civilization" brought to them by the English. In 1675, Increase Mather, surveying the triumphs experienced by the Puritans since their arrival, was able to see the hand of God in the victories over the Indians and thus was able to ensure his fellow Puritans of God's protection and of their status as a chosen people. The Indians, according to Mather, "fought to dispossess us of the land, which the Lord our God hath given to us."[8]

Another example of a writer narrowing in on Native American populations for source material was Daniel Neal, who sought a similar story line in his *History of New England ... to ... 1700* published in 1720.[9] Neal's most ambitious project, however, was a four-volume history of the Puritans published between 1732 and 1738.[10] While certainly not as well known as Mather, Neal exemplifies the negative approach many writers and historians took to Native Americans once they (Puritans) had been saved by the Indians.

Among the wide array of writers who worked during the period preceding the Revolution were those whose interests were decidedly noncultural. In this group can be listed those individuals who sought a greater understanding of the natural world around them. The natural aspects of the New World also included American Indians. The American Indian was as much an object of scientific inquiry as the flora and fauna among which they seemed to live so effortlessly. Cadwallader Colden did much to advance the interest in, and understanding of, the upstate New York tribes. His *The History of the Five Indian Nations* (completed in 1747) sought to "convince the public in America and England of the importance of the Iroquois to the colony as a bulwark against the French and as a means of holding the West."[11] Aside from the political and strategic advantage of knowing the Indians, his work sought to portray them in a more understanding light.

The interest in the American Indian was not as simple as attempting to trace their ancestry to some mythical migration of one of the twelve tribes of Israel as some writers theorized to explain the Native Americans' presence in the New World. Instead, the serious American scientist saw the Native Americans as a part of the topography in the same sense as flora and fauna. This is not to say the eighteenth-century scientist saw some biological connection between the Native Americans and their surroundings. What they attempted to determine was how these human beings, seemingly lost in time in the New World, adapted so well to their habitat without the comforts and benefits of Western "civilization." Early scientists and travelers wrote "narratives of travel among the native peoples, with sketches of their characters and ways."[12] Some of the more notable writers included Robert Rogers, William Stork, and James Adair. These men, and others, set the stage for the explosive growth in the interest in, and output of, later nineteenth-century natural history writers.

By the beginning of the eighteenth century, other writers were not as quick to ascribe the course of events to divine intervention as the Puritans had been. William Hubbard was a historian who sought a more balanced, albeit nuanced, interpretation of Puritan ascendency. He still had the obligatory deference to God in his writing, as evidenced by the report of the General Court who agreed that Hubbard should receive remuneration for his work to accurately portray (as the Massachusetts Bay authorities saw it) the history of the colony thus far revealed in the religious meaning of the word. Hubbard had the unique problem though of not being able to put his scattered notes together coherently in manuscript form, and although he was paid a portion of the total offered him, his manuscript was not printed until 1815, at a time when the God-centric view of New England had faded considerably from favor and the God-themed history now belonged to the Revolution and the characters and events associated with that period.[13] By the time it did finally get printed, it seemed almost pointless to do so, because "Hubbard's *History* was sucked dry of factual material by Cotton Mather, Thomas Prince, and Governor Thomas Hutchinson, long before it got into print; and the work had not literary merit to give it a renewed lease on life."[14]

The strain of divine intervention in American historical writing would punctuate the writing of history for over a century until (approximately 1800) a more reasoned, human account of events would begin to appear. Even in Hubbard's case, although the theme that God favored the Puritans was evident, it still was not vociferous enough in its reliance on God to smite the Indians for the general reader's consumption. Unfortunately, "Hubbard spoke to a rising generation not yet strong enough to change the interpretation of history" away from the traditional reliance on a deity delivering their land to them through violent conquest and into the hands of the human beings who actually made the history in many different ways.[15]

One of the first writers to try to move beyond the purely supernatural explanations of historical events after Hubbard was Thomas Prince.[16] In 1703, while a student at Harvard, Prince began to collect a selection of works focusing on or pertaining to New England, rather than religious, history; "as far as history was concerned, [he] ... was more New Englander ... supporting the claims of a region rather than a religion."[17] By 1736, Prince's work *A Chronological History of New England* was published with its goal the "orderly succession of events ... as they precisely fell out in time."[18] Prince would describe his approach to history writing as presenting events as "disposed in the order of time wherein they happened, together with the rise and progress of the several towns, churches, counties, colonies, and provinces throughout this country."[19] Like many religious, Prince "felt obliged to begin his history with the creation of the world, making New England the acme of human aspiration since Adam's fall."[20]

As with many of the early eighteenth-century written histories, Prince's work saw disappointing sales. Historical scholarship (especially removed from supernatural explanation) was still too much in its infancy to develop a following. Americans, still colonists at this point, were still too unsure about their role not only within the British Empire, but with their status in the new land that still held many, many dangers. It could be reasonably argued the Americans were not yet prepared or confident enough to move beyond the more traditional, comfortable approaches to what passed for historical writing in the seventeenth century and consequently felt compelled to reject the writings that did not conform to any already preconceived notion about God's role in the founding and forming of the colonies.

The rise and practice of historical writing was not confined to the Massachusetts Bay area and northern colonies during the seventeenth century. Today, we tend to see the Pilgrims as the first colonizers of the North American continent; and this is due to many reasons, some relating to the quality of the writing produced there. But it cannot be dismissed that the earliest surviving Virginian settlements were nearly fifteen years prior to the Pilgrims. At nearly the beginning of American colonial history names such as Captain John Smith, Williams Strachy, and Alexander Witaker are found, among others, who attempted to write histories of the early years of English southern colonization up to the period just before the start of the Revolution. Captain John Smith (of Jamestown fame) was probably the best known of the early southern writers. Smith was wholly English and in fact spent the last fifteen years of his life in England. His books chronicled his exploits in Virginia and the New World, and he has come to be most strongly identified as southern. His most famous book of history was *The Generall Historie of Virginia, New-England and the Summer Isles.* Lesser known but no less important historical writers include Stephen Hopkins, Amos Adams, Nathan Fiske, Robert Pround, Morgan Edwards, and Isaac Backus. The Reverend William Stith in Virginia began in the early 1740s a *History of the First Discovery and Settlement of Virginia.* Stith, the southerner, much like his northern colleague Prince in Massachusetts, sought a less fantastic story in American history and more realism in its grounding.

Following much the same patterns as writers in the north, writers in the southern colonies sought to frame their unique experience in terms acceptable to their readers. In many ways, their contribution overall could be seen as more important than those few individual historians who managed to garner some attention and earn some money because while those who did earn acknowledgment were preparing their works at a slower pace, these lesser known writers and historians served the tenuous role of keeping the public interest in the larger theme of history alive.

A distinguishing characteristic of the southern approach to life in the eighteenth century was the way which in part the class system of England was transformed so fully (and in part on racial grounds) into the plantation system and indeed into the fabric of social life. This attitude was reflected in the writings of many of the southern historians. A large number of southern planters sent their sons to England for an education, thus further ingraining the idea of a graduated system of life which came to dominate and identify the southern lifestyle well into the eighteenth and nineteenth centuries. Some well-known writers who spent years studying in England were Daniel Dulany (father and son), Charles Carroll of Maryland, and William Henry Drayton of South Carolina.

The basis or foundation for each regional approach could not have been more different. While one (southern) sought to exploit the natural resources, the other (northern) sought to exploit the lack of governmental and religious control to establish an empire of a different kind. In the north it was a heavenly empire, in the south, it was an earthly empire, albeit firmly controlled by heaven.

While a definite difference in the histories produced existed between northern and southern attitudes, one element tended to unify them. Most seventeenth-century works, north and south, sought to accentuate their respective greatness in the context of the English Empire. These writers included Robert Beverly, John Lawson, and William Byrd, who produced works within a decade of the start of what became a momentous eighteenth century. Beverly was an exceptional writer; his style was "fresh, his comments often shrewd, and his appreciation of nature exceptional. His style had a noticeably lighter touch than most of contemporary New England historical literature, which often appears labored by contrast."[21] William Byrd II did as much for history as he did to delineate the proper role and function of the American colonial aristocrat, particularly of the southern variety. He is best remembered for *History of the Dividing Line betwixt Virginia and North Carolina.* Byrd had a very personal interest in the subject, given that he was the patriarch of a family with extensive land under their control.

Many other writers, north and south, including Edward Winslow, William Wood, William Bradford, and Edward Johnson, among others, worked to chronicle everything from Bacon's rebellion in Virginia to the rise of the representative model of government and settlement in New England. This required subtle verbal gymnastics so as not to be too Tory, or on the other hand, too much of a Whig. This became particularly acute during the last half of the seventeenth century when England was rocked by civil war, the restoration of the Stuarts, and finally the trials and tribulations attendant upon the Glorious Revolution.

Political Consequences

For writers in the eighteenth century, especially British, the most recent revolution they had to work with was the Glorious Revolution of 1688. This revolution needs to be dealt with and understood when placing one's self inside the mindset of the eighteenth century in relation to the clash of ideals the Americans had with the British. "To understand the peculiarities of the colonists' historical vision, one should recall that history in eighteenth-century England was not only subject to the vagaries of intellectual vogue but was also under heavy political pressures."[22]

Similarly, for Revolutionary era Americans too, the event which produced the most political pressure from a historical perspective was the Glorious Revolution of 1688. For many colonists in 1688, the happenings in England seemed somewhat inconsequential, given the great distance and the infrequency of travel opportunities. From a political perspective the events of 1688, although 3,000 miles away, would produce an impact 100 years later far in excess of the attention paid to the Glorious Revolution at the time. (The English Glorious Revolution of 1688 replaced the Catholic James II with his Protestant daughter and son-in-law as William and Mary.)

Writing prior to the Revolution about the relationship with England was accentuated by the intensity of the argument of constitutionalism. The idea of a progression of human understanding and maturation having somehow revealed itself in eighteenth century thought and political conditions was a concept that was easily transferred to America, where belief in a future greatness permeated much of the writing prior to the Revolution.

England's constitution was, and is, unwritten. During the debate with England in the decade preceding armed conflict in 1775 the refrain to constitutional principles was most loudly heard from a growing number of historians and writers. The sense of transgression by Parliament is vicious in some cases. It is a palpable fundamentalist approach to a concept (constitutionalism) that in some sense would seem quite nerve-rattling to officials who might be more inclined to discussion and moderation. The level of intensity produced a situation where "only in America [was there] belief that the ancient constitution had a chance of survival."[23]

In most discussions the ancient English constitution generally referred to the Anglo-Saxon conception of a social compact based on individual liberty and freedom. This was the pre–Norman (pre–1066 invasion) thinking which many Americans felt themselves the heirs to. Richard Bland, a member of the Continental Congress from Virginia and a historian much like Jefferson, wrote, "Colonists had 'as natural a Right to the Liberties and Privileges of *Englishmen*, as if they were actually resident within the Kingdom.'"[24]

The post–Norman convention that was most regularly cited as a guiding document was the Magna Carta. A vaguely understood document at the time (1770s), the Magna Carta at its base was an agreement between nobles, not among the people like America's founding was to be. And, it was generally silent on the theoretical and practical issue of upon whom English rights were conferred at birth. Still, the Magna Carta was the one ancient written text that could be singled out and which virtually every educated colonist had at least heard of.

Much of early American writing (both seventeenth and eighteenth centuries) was focused on the future. Visions of cultural and artistic greatness filled pages of writing by authors who were concerned about the somewhat juvenile state of the arts in the colonies. In many instances American writers were attempting to convince not only themselves, but Europeans, who mostly denigrated American artistic aspirations and productions by American writers and artists. The tendency to view America's future cultural greatness as inevitable by Americans was in part a natural reaction prompted by the disparaging writings of some Europeans. American writers during the colonial period were unable to counter charges of cultural (and civilized life overall) inferiority and could only hope their feeble predictions in defense of their country would come to pass. Certainly, little evidence existed in 1750 that would indicate the colonies were primed for cultural and civilized relevancy. Michael Kraus has written, "Historians were conscious of the necessity to correct English misconceptions of America, and their writing revealed a nascent pride in the evolution of a distinctive colonial society diverging from that of the homeland."[25]

The most unusual aspect of all the writing concerning future greatness is that it rarely hinted at American independence. Americans in the mid-eighteenth century were prone to view themselves as destined for great things, but yet still as part of the English Empire. The general feeling of impending greatness carried over throughout the 1760s and into decisions about war and resistance. In an effort to add legitimacy to this belief, many in the clergy sought to connect future triumph on an earthly level with future triumph on a heavenly level. Ezra Stiles in Rhode Island preached that future American cultural greatness "was both imminent and inevitable."[26] Andrew Burnaby was a traveler who reported the tendency to this belief in 1759.[27] John Adams too commented on the trend toward this belief while still a young lawyer.[28]

Perhaps Benjamin Franklin had the best analogy. Franklin borrowed an old idea from Renaissance Italy that "civilization, like the sun, moved from east to west and that the North American continent was therefore destined to become the habitat for the arts and sciences at some unspecified time in the future."[29] Still, even before Franklin, George Berkeley, the British churchman and philosopher, wrote a poem on this nearly identical concept where he speculated on migration of culture and civilization from east to west.[30]

Further examples from throughout the seventeenth century include writers who, looking to the prospect of a great future for America as a potent theme, found a successful storyline. In Connecticut, Martha Brewster published a collection of poems entitled *Poems on Diverse Subjects*. One of the poems in the collection conjures up a dream whose vision is of a world dominated by Americans in the fields of "philosophy, literature, and the arts."[31]

In Woodbridge, New Jersey, an anonymous writer in the mid-eighteenth century wrote in the *New American Magazine* and prophesized on "the emergence of an Augustan Age 'this side of the Atlantic' now that the French had been defeated and the continent was safely under the aegis of English influence."[32] In Boston, Jonathan Mayhew longed for the day when "poetry and philosophy" would place America on par with Europe.[33] There was a long and rich theme to the future of America which carried over into concepts of historical writing, as will be seen in later chapters.

Perspective

In a situation where only one perspective is provided, the overall output of a particular genre (in this case history writing) becomes suspect of authenticity. If the outcome or overall balance and perspective are already defined prior to writing, the objective history will not be found. What will be found is history designed for mass consumption which sets a tone for readers which seldom engages their intellectual abilities—it may perhaps engage them emotionally, but not intellectually. In America, this was very much the case in the roughly twenty years between 1775 and 1795. Historians and writers of that period were more important and valuable to society for their ability to strike a chord of nationalistic resonance producing an empathetic response from readers or nonreading members of the public.

Those who could not afford to buy books or who were illiterate could still get information about the topics and themes (liberty, American uniqueness, British tyranny) inspiring American independence being circulated through print. Traditional forms of disseminating information thus became even more valuable to the colonial war effort as a means to keep public interest high. In addition to public readings and sermons/lectures, many of the prevailing themes and currents of thought were crafted into musical essays which became an even simpler way to spread information. Music and song also provided a time-proven method for memorizing and storing such information. These compositions included

> the numberless verses, commonly quite inelaborate and unadorned, that were written to be sung at the hearth-stove, by the campfire, on the march, on the battle field, in all places of solemn worship,—songs for the new fatherland, for home, for liberty,—party songs, army songs, ballads, hymns of patriotic thankfulness and trust.[34]

When viewed in this manner, it becomes easy to see why writers found it difficult to earn a living from their work during the period. What writers produced was almost common property the moment it was printed.

In the colonies, the tradition had been for writers and historians to frame colonial history more as a preparation for some future greatness, not just in culture or the arts exclusively, but in the realms of government and human happiness. Colonial history was as much looking to the future as it did the past. This created a uniquely optimistic strain in the colonial dialogue between writers/historians and their readers. This strain of optimism was in a sense being called for by the European intellectuals who saw their historians as mere fact finders. The intellectuals wanted to see how the lessons of history would improve humankind rather than simply provide a litany of births and deaths; war and peace; ruler and ruled. In the colonies by contrast the story pointed to a new promise waiting somewhere in the future. Even though colonial America had yet to distinguish itself, writers felt they instinctively knew (or at least hoped) that America was destined not just for greatness, but for exceptional greatness. These writers (Thomas Prince, Samuel Smith, Hannah Adams, and others from the mid- to late eighteenth century) in turn shaped a generation of writers and emerging historians to pick up the theme with concrete examples that proved their impulses to be accurate. This faith in the future as inspired by the past—departing from the past—set the psychological stage for the historians and writers who worked following the Revolution.

Americans saw every aspect of their experience as pointing the way to the future, and not always via the past. This approach ensured American histories overall had a more objective handle on reality than their European colleagues. It helped the American historian to see larger forces at work (non-spiritual forces) in America's development. The larger viewpoint allowed for more objectivity, and less homogeneity, in the historical process. The work of the

American historian was made more complicated by this because "men argued that as Newton had discovered universal physical laws, so must there be universal laws of history, that human nature must be the same everywhere."[35] The concept of universal laws of history held much more currency in Europe than America. During the Revolution, America was operating outside the universal laws of history as they were understood to be true among European eighteenth-century thinkers by rebelling against centuries of established practice.

The work of the colonial writer and historian made the work of the post–Revolution writer and historian more difficult. While the pre–Revolution historian dealt in expectation, the post–Revolution historian dealt in realized expectations. It fell to the post–Revolution historian to finally and fully explain how and why the predictions of greatness had been met. In no field of human understanding was this more exploited than in the concept of democratic government. It would be the one element above all others that would not just distinguish Americans from Europeans, but the present and future from the past. This difference, a virtually tangible one, is precisely what European intellectuals were asking their historians to show. It would be the American historians who would prove the Scottish historian and philosopher David Hume's comment to be inaccurate—"Mankind are so much the same, in all times and places, that history informs us of nothing new or strange in this particular. Its chief use is only to discover the constant and universal principles of human nature."[36] The Americans wanted to show just how inconstant and nonuniversal was the Revolution. In fact, the Revolutionaries in many ways truly believed that they were indeed conservative—not a term associated with revolutions. Some leaders of the revolt, those more inclined to reflection rather than knee-jerk reactions, felt they were simply conserving the ancient, historical-based, liberties they were entitled to as Englishmen.

A striking aspect of later eighteenth-century and early nineteenth-century American writing was the greater uniformity which occurred by roughly 1825. Seventeenth-century writing was filled with examples by French, Spanish, African, and even American Indians. By American independence in 1776, the face of American writing was white and English. This does not mean that minorities suddenly stopped writing. What it does mean is that their perspective, their interests and concerns, essentially, their voice, was excluded in the increasingly monophonic writing of the American creation established along a thin line of inclusion based on mostly race and gender.

In some ways the New World opened a variety of opportunities for those individuals, men and women, minority and majority, who felt compelled to write. Oddly though, the newness and opportunity of the colonial experience did not touch off the flurry and exclusivity of writing associated with the Revolutionary period. The winning of independence had something to do with the approach and the need to say something; the maturity and confidence of the American public certainly compared more favorably in 1780 than 1680 or earlier. One reason for the maturity and confidence by 1780 was simply the sense of belonging to a place. Seventeenth-century Americans were still transplants; eighteenth-century Americans were indigenous (newly indigenous).[37]

2

European Models of History and the American Revolution

••••••

The mid to late eighteenth century is often referred to as the Age of Enlightenment. This shorthand way of identifying the complex overarching view of Western thought during that time has been a popular subject for many writers. Still, not much is widely known today about the concept of Enlightenment when applied to eighteenth-century philosophical exposition. As a name, it is very appealing—who would not want enlightenment? While the name has been around for well over a century, today's readers are as likely to think of Eastern religious mysticism as much as Western European philosophy when they hear the phrase enlightenment.

Setting aside the enormous question of just what precisely enlightenment meant philosophically and politically in the eighteenth century leaves the opportunity to contemplate the significance of history and enlightenment to the mind of the period. The overall view of life as perceived by those who lived and thought at the time, was how and where did history fit into the equation? In other words, what was history? How was it practiced, and why? As Trevor Colbourn has written, "To the eighteenth-century colonist, the study of history was a prestigious and a practical pursuit."[1] Just like the applied sciences sought irrefutable laws of nature for science, some historians and philosophers sought irrefutable laws of nature for humanity, and this search continued well into the nineteenth century (and even to the present). History became a way to contemplate and theorize about the basic aspects of life.

During the eighteenth century, the phrase enlightenment denoted the broad parameters associated with the general movements of "the people" to detach themselves from the traditional governmental systems of monarchy and the divine right of rulers. The two most obvious examples of this occurrence in the historical record to the modern mind are the American and French Revolutions. The American Revolution is in fact so emblematic of this detachment by the people from traditional government that Americans are still occasionally referred to as "children of the Enlightenment."

The European historians who epitomized variations of Enlightenment thought of the eighteenth century were generally men of great scholarly accomplishment. David Hume, Voltaire, William Robertson, James Boswell, and of course, Edward Gibbon all cast enormous shadows in literary and intellectual circles during their time. These historians produced more than histories, yet it was their historical writing which tended to generate the most publicity, in part because history was a topic more accessible to the general educated reader. As Gibbon noted, "History is the most popular species of writing since it can adapt itself to the highest or lowest capacity."[2]

The fame of many historians outside the field of history helped to ensure a ready market once these writers turned to history. "The eighteenth century was in fact an age of consuming interest in history [in Europe]," and this general atmosphere certainly helped boost the stature, while not always the income, of many historians.[3] Many of these historians were by training philosophers and expounded in a style that in ways mirrored their exuberant philosophy. "The most distinguished philosophers and poets of the age wrote history confident that as historians they were neither betraying their vocation nor lowering their dignity."[4]

Attempting to compare exactly the intellectual atmosphere of Europe and America in the last quarter of the eighteenth century is not an easy task. So many variables are required to add to the mix that at some point the comparison seemingly breaks down. Yet, a comparison is still valuable in that it helps to frame the opposing views on the concept of English liberty and freedom in relation to the Revolution and as they were interpreted in America in 1776 related to the perception of the 1688 Glorious Revolution in England.

In Europe during the seventeenth and eighteenth centuries, history had a distinct quality which separated it on one level from the American version. Intellectuals in Europe decried the pattern adopted by historians of the time who overwhelmingly attempted to set down in dry fashion the simple chronological accumulation of dates, places, and names.[5] Some Europeans were obsessed with attempts at universal history, which invariably began with the challenge to bring biblical chronologies into alignment with present-day realities. This did not of course work; and it could not. Many of the simple chronological historians' critics sought to "learn why it was that men were still, after so many centuries of experience, bound by the follies and errors of their predecessors."[6]

Colonial and American historians and writers realized they had a tall order to fill in convincing their colleagues in Europe. A brief comparison of the approach to historical writing in Europe and America shows that Europeans by and large were more concerned with the past to justify the present. American historians overall were more concerned with the past to justify the future. "Their [Americans'] history reading was purposeful, part of their quest for a usable past as a guide to the present and the future."[7]

Historians during the sixteenth and seventeenth centuries often served as apologists, in that they provided a version of events from the past to justify contemporary politics. While this role is all but shunned by respectable historians in our day, it was quite acceptable, even encouraged, for historians to prepare works that would identify certain characteristics which promoted vital and important civic qualities. During the colonial period, "historians came to the defense of their colonies in the face of the growing desire on the part of British minorities for more effective control of the empire."[8] Many sought to point out after the Revolution just how different the American experience was in order to delineate why the Revolution was both necessary and indeed successful. American historians had to make the Revolution revolutionary; they also needed to try to somehow appreciate the tendency to view the Revolution as merely a struggle for the reestablishment of the rights of ancient Englishmen. The Revolution was both revolutionary and conservative. American historians did not have an easy task explaining that.

The actual clash of arms in conflict is always caused by more than simple misunderstandings. But once arms are resorted to, when dialogue has failed, when supplication has proven ineffectual and no other recourse can be found, the persuasive techniques employed to secure an understanding suddenly are needed to champion the cause of arms. In terms of understanding and writing about the Revolution, John Adams perhaps stated it best in a letter to Jedidiah Morse in 1814; "A history of military operations from April 19, 1775, to the 3d of September, 1783, is not a history of the American Revolution."[9] Adams was cautioning new historians that there was more to gaining independence than the contest of arms. Most keen observers knew the actual conflict was secondary (although necessary) to establishing independence. Adams did not want this to go unnoticed, especially since he gained his reputation not on the battlefield but in the committee rooms and halls of Congress.

In the case of the American Revolution, writers employed their skills during the fighting in an effort to help establish the reasons war had occurred and why it must continue until victory. In this approach, "History lent strength and persuasion to the Revolutionaries' argument."[10]

The historians of the period allowed for the larger public to feel connected to this history in ways that were impossible without the printed word. At the same time they sought to entice other countries to follow the American example. The one element which could prove the historians correct concerning Americans remaking society would be by exporting the qualities which they showed to be so unique in the American example. "With history the Revolutionary generation of Americans sought to extend its political experience" and to fashion the debate for a free country.[11]

American writers had the difficult task of continually making and remaking the case for American independence. For the historians, words and history became their weapons much as firearms were weapons for the military. The writing of this period by Americans had "almost everywhere the combative note; its habitual method is argumentative, persuasive, appealing, rasping, retaliatory."[12] Even the higher forms of literature were employed for the cause at hand; "in this literature we must not expect to find art used for art's sake."[13] Literature was being used to wage war, and like war, the literature was not always pleasant. It reflected the tenor of the times and did not seek to refine itself. The Revolutionary period was an "epoch of revolutionary strife [and] a strife of ideas: a long warfare of political logic."[14]

The use of literature in the cause of American independence was not as unusual as it may first appear. Intangible boundaries, unlike the ones drawn on a map, ideas seemed less real because so many perspectives impacted the development of them. The role of the writer therefore was to manifest the reality of an intangible thought. Even with literacy rates at a low level in the colonies, public speakers often filled the void and provided the sound to articulate a writer's thought. One of the most prevalent examples of this was the (usually) humble clergyman. Their role, like the historians, cannot be overestimated in spreading the word about political and civil rights as they were constituted in the eighteenth century.[15]

Many clergymen felt compelled to offer their viewpoint of why the independence of America was a good, indeed ordained and thus obligatory, objective for the political problems facing the colonies prior to and during the war. As Ellis Sandoz wrote in the preface to a collection of political sermons,

> To permit the religious perspective concerning the rise of American nationhood to have representative expression is important because a steady attention to the pulpit from 1730 to 1805 unveils a distinctive rhetoric of political discourse. Preachers interpreted pragmatic events in terms of a political theology imbued with philosophical and revelatory learning.[16]

Literate colonists were active readers who took advantage of the subscription libraries available in the colonies in the decades leading up to the Revolution. There were sixty such libraries in 1776—the most famous being in Philadelphia.[17] These libraries provided an outlet for the steady stream of histories produced in England and provided valuable research material for the growing political viewpoints of many colonists. A fascinating bit of information concerning libraries in the early republic is that "in 1825 ... New York, Boston, Philadelphia, and Baltimore libraries had twenty times as many books to lend as the entire nation had owned in 1800."[18] That is a staggering statistic and only further highlights the invaluable role libraries played in American society. Although the sales of history writing lagged, interest in history was still high, and libraries allowed many to indulge their predilection without much if any investment.

As early as 1676, when John Winthrop, Jr., died in Connecticut, his library—one of the finest in New England—contained "books on religion, travel, philosophy, law, and sundry grammars and dictionaries. Half the books [were] in Latin, 71 in English, 23 in German, 17 in French, 12 in Dutch, 7 in Italian, 4 in Greek, and 1 in Spanish."[19] This was a remarkable representation of diversity in what was often thought of as a closed, Puritan mind-set in seventeenth century New England. While Winthrop's collection was an example of a very well-to-do private collection, it was often these types of collections which formed the nucleus of many semi-public and public library collections after their owners donated their holdings.

The first truly public library in Boston was begun in 1656. Not to be confused with our current notion of a public library, the idea nonetheless was there. Also, in eighteenth-century America those able and eligible to use a library were quite a small number as compared to today's clientele. Other areas of the colonies soon fell in line behind Boston and founded some approximation of a public library in the decades preceding the Revolution. Then as now, libraries ostensibly formed the background of an educated and informed citizenry. This would prove an important element in American independence. Books were engines of change, and the ideas they contained and transmitted were found in many outlets. "Besides subscription, private, and academic libraries, another important indicator of historical tastes of the eighteenth-century colonist was naturally enough, the American book trade."[20] Even though the main agitators for independence had personal libraries to draw on, they probably did not have every title they would ever need to reference, expect perhaps Thomas Jefferson—whose personal library was considered America's best private library. Therefore it was necessary for most to rely on the public or subscription library to some extent. The most important conception in these early years was the importance attached by colonial communities to a place where knowledge could be obtained easily and relatively inexpensively.

Beyond the libraries and individual writers, learned societies similar to those in Europe began to form (roughly around 1790 as a natural outgrowth of the private libraries) with various goals designed to acquire and enhance historical knowledge. Jeremy Belknap wrote to his friend and fellow historian Ebenezer Hazard and presented his "Plan of an Antiquarian Society," which ultimately became the Massachusetts Historical Society. Belknap, the author of the *History of New Hampshire*, wrote that the society which intends "to be an *active*, not a *passive*, literary body; ... to *seek* and *find*, to *preserve* and *communicate*, literary intelligence, especially in the historical way," must aggressively promote itself to the citizens and engage them as partners.[21]

This plan was not to be myopic, however. Early planners, including James Bowdoin (of Bowdoin College fame) realized that for a true historical society to have legitimacy it needed to be more than just a place to celebrate American greatness. A practice of objectivity and sensitivity needed to be established in order to set the foundation for meaningful research and respected publications. This approach, followed in other states, ensured that American literary and historical societies moved beyond the standards set in Europe, where such institutions were little more than propaganda clubs for the nationalistic minded leaders who feared above all else a society of free-thinkers willing and able to pursue aspects of "truth" beyond an official version. Also, these societies had one other profound distinguishing characteristic: they sought to diffuse knowledge. They sought not only to collect manuscripts and preserve them; they wanted the public to know what they had and to join in the thrill of discovery. This concept represented in its own way a revolution as meaningful as the armed conflict version did in the 1770s.

By 1825, Jared Sparks observed how valuable historical societies could be to the preservation and dissemination of America's heritage. Much like a library sought to provide access to the world of thought, the historical society too was held to function in much the same way. This would ensure that America's unique story would be always available for research and reflection. One way to ensure this resource was available would be to publish the information held by each unique society. This would also help their preservation by providing copies of certain documents as a guard against loss or destruction—much as Jefferson had recommended.

Some institutions had indeed already started to follow this advice. The Massachusetts Historical Society, the New York Historical Society, the Historical Society of Pennsylvania, and the New Hampshire Historical Society had all started to publish limited editions of a select portion of their collection by the early nineteenth century.[22] As Sparks wrote, historical societies "should therefore 'search out every printed volume, pamphlet, and document relating to the history of America'" and provide them to the public.[23] Additionally, Sparks felt to a great extent that the federal government had a responsibility to ensure this occurred.[24]

3

American Writing in the Age of American Independence

......

Americans wanted a national story by 1789; something to bind together the various states which were having trouble politically and economically. The national component of their approach was something new in the development of historical writing as well. A national perspective was contemplated by the new generation forged in war where everything was put through the perspective of national development, whereas prior to the Revolution the concept would have been less developed.

Considering a more national focus overall, there were still writers who worked only on state histories. Writers such as Jeremy Belknap (whose professor at Harvard was the eighteenth-century historian Thomas Prince) wrote about New Hampshire; Robert Proud wrote about Pennsylvania and the Quakers; George Minot (in a Federalist tradition) about Massachusetts; Benjamin Trumbull, as discussed, about Connecticut; David Ramsay wrote about South Carolina; John Burk about Virginia; and Hugh Williamson about North Carolina.[1] Alexander Hewat, originally from Scotland, wrote on the history of South Carolina and Georgia in two volumes that were published in 1779 in London, not America.[2] Vermont too had its author in Samuel Williams.

Many historians felt compelled to promote their colonial heritage on the individual colony level. Regardless of sales potential, many "state historians would jealously guard [their] colonial heritage and maintain the individuality which it implied in their contest against the historical oblivion to which the rising national chronicles threatened to condemn their stories."[3] Many colonial writers who wrote state history focused on a single colony and "wrote in order

36

that posterity might not forget how the early perils had been met and overcome."[4] One example of this type of work came in 1764 from Samuel Smith, in his history of New Jersey. Smith sought to direct "his book to readers in New Jersey to unite them in the knowledge of their past."[5] Smith also sought to enlighten his readers in the political consequences of their success as a colony and of the ramification of British policy. The high point of state histories was reached just before the Revolution; "by the time the Revolution broke upon the American continent, each colony had recorded its own history as an independent unit of the British Empire."[6]

Most historians at the time wrote histories based on one colony or region. One writer who sought to broaden the field to view the colonies as a whole was William Douglass. In the late 1740s, Douglass published *Summary, Historical and Political ... of the British Settlements in North America.* Douglass will always be remembered for two items surrounding his work: first, his somewhat famous attack on research with primary sources: "This is a laborious affair, being obliged to consult manuscript records"; Douglass "sneered at New England historians, whom he considered 'beyond all excuse, intolerably erroneous.'"[7] Secondly, Douglass had the distinction of having his work mentioned in one of the seminal works of the eighteenth century which is still widely discussed today, Adam Smith's *The Wealth of Nations.*

By the mid-eighteenth century and through to the Revolution, the writers sought more vigorously to demarcate the colonies into their unique sphere until in fact the colonies were no more. The mental attempt of a century earlier to separate yet combine the colonies and England ceased to exist by 1783. Now the quest became to promote, vindicate, and in fact validate the existence of the United States. Even throughout the war years, when politicians and military leaders were despondent over the course of events, historians such as Ebenezer Hazard were already planning works to extol the history and development of an independent country.

It was entirely necessary to advance historical writing for this feeling of removal to remain in the forefront of the American imagination. This theme in writing, even if not purchased on a mass scale through book sales, was necessary in the independence effort to keep just enough Americans interested in the Revolution to partake actively in the material struggle to make it successful.

American Publishing

One aspect which fed into the difficulties of writing and publishing in the seventeenth, eighteenth, and nineteenth centuries was the entire nature of the business of publishing. This was due in part to the legal concerns surrounding copyright. It was not until the early nineteenth century that a writer could make a reasonable living from his or her craft and have sufficient legal protection to do so. Washington Irving in the nineteenth century was the first American writer to make a living at his craft, and his historical works were only part of his overall output. It was not until Jared Sparks in the 1840s that a historian could be said to have made a living from the writing of history in America.

Aside from the task of writing or reproducing manuscripts for publication, authors faced a complex task of seeing a manuscript through to print without an advisory infrastructure readily in place. With little standardization and even less encouragement, the conflicting and complicated terrain posed quite a formidable challenge. With all the difficulties inherent in the field of historical writing, America did not lack writers who sought to expound on the nature and quality of the American experience. Hannah Adams was just one example of someone who would confront this barrier only to find the struggle to be nearly too much in her efforts confronting Jedidiah Morse in the early nineteenth century.

Partly because Europe had a much longer history of literary achievement (and because European historians also had careers beyond history which made them well known), the arrival of the historians in the marketplace was more financially successful there than when transferred to America. The colonies produced few writers of European quality and a large readership was not available in sufficient numbers to consume the works produced for sale. Part of the challenge simply had to do with public perception. Was America a land where printed material should be produced? As has been observed, "citizens of the young republic understood the printedness of documents as being charged with a significance that set them apart from manuscript production and oral performance."[8] This reticence on the part of Americans to accept themselves as producers of print culture was also somewhat symptomatic of the writer's view in the period up to about 1800. Since the earliest period in the seventeenth century, authors spent time forecasting in their collective writings that America would arrive on the world cultural scene through the printed word at some future date. Each generation however thought that the period of greatness had not yet arrived—at least until after the Revolution.

During the eighteenth century, the pamphlet reigned supreme as the medium of choice to transmit information quickly, economically, and effectively. Pamphlets were the blogs of the eighteenth century. Colonial policy generated some of the most spirited and in-depth discussions about government and English imperial policy that ever existed. The writing and production of pamphlets "became a distinct profession with its own techniques and forms, the pamphlet was the dominant vehicle of propaganda and debate."[9]

The beginnings of the rancor in pamphlets can be traced to the flowering of American writings after 1700, when the future of America held some ill-defined notion of American greatness at all levels and aspects of society. The spark of ignition which fused these disparate perspectives of colonial policy via the pamphlet occurred with James Otis and the Writs case (to be discussed later) and those who closely followed him.

An example of a pamphlet writer was Otis' contemporary Oxenbridge Thacher. In late summer 1764, Thacher published *The Sentiments of a British American*. Thacher's thesis was that Britain "has overstepped the line of justice toward [the] colonies."[10] In particular, Thacher listed five primary areas of concern for colonists regarding the new British positions relating to the colonies. The five areas were (1) taxation, (2) the extension of courts of Admiralty, (3) the expanded authority of ships' commanders over Americans, (4) new powers of government officers without colony recourse to usual checks on power, (5) and if these types of acts can be imposed on Americans, will inhabitants of England be next?[11]

Thacher's argument hinges on the damage Britain was doing to itself economically. The American colonies were the best market for British goods in the world, and for Parliament to impose such measures to threaten their ancient rights was lunacy. Britain would be jeopardizing their largest source of revenue in terms of markets. Thacher saw the twin poles of the argument with Britain—money (taxation), and political rights (ancient entitlements as Englishmen). These two topics, taxation and political rights, were a matter of intense debate, which occupied the minds of some of the greatest thinkers in both the colonies and England for over fifty years during the eighteenth century—and indeed ever since colonial settlement began in Jamestown.

Prior to the Revolution, the colonists were exposed to a steady diet of histories from England and Europe that sought to show the historical antecedents of parliamentary power in the British constitutional system. It is no surprise that the colonists formally rebelled against the King, not Parliament.

Similar to the pamphlet, the magazine was a related type of publication, which had a more difficult time starting out. In 1741, Andrew Bradford and Benjamin Franklin, both Philadelphia printers and writers, started magazines. They featured among other things topics of historical interest but neither lasted more than six months. Still, by 1750, "newspapers, magazines, and almanacs began to reflect a rising interest in history."[12] This interest was borne along by, among others, Nathaniel Ames and Samuel Nevill. Their work helped to continue to foster the idea of building a virtuous citizenry designed to participate in civic affairs.[13] For a nation contemplating a violent break from a nonparticipatory (on the individual level) type of government this role of indoctrination was vital. Franklin, Bradford, and others like them helped to ensure a modicum of attention was paid to a very important topic.

Americans had a difficult time overall viewing themselves as "cultured" in the same sense that Europeans saw themselves as cultured. Many obstacles existed to developing a refined American essence. One example was the country's business focus. By 1800 the mercantile development within the young United States, "busily engaged in gathering land and wealth, stifled literature."[14] The political system too was seen as detrimental to the creation of American culture. John Quincy Adams and Joel Barlow (who will be discussed in depth in chapter five), among others, "doubted whether a society built on equality could yield genius; did not democracy produce mediocrity, a dead-level flatness of art?"[15] Combined with this was the whole notion that America in 1825 just was simply too young. The country did not yet have a proper history—aside from the Revolutionary War—or enough of an educated class to appreciate the arts. Beyond the timid reaction to their perceived cultural irrelevance lay the meaning of authority and the printed word.[16] It has been commented upon that while publishing their work was a major goal of American writers, the chances of actually earning a living from one's work were quite slim. The printed word for aspiring writers was not a wholly satisfying venture. The notion that one's ideas could be bound and sold to profit the author was not a fully engrained concept in America in either the seventeenth or eighteenth century—and into the nineteenth.

America also did not have the intrigue and human drama associated with epic moments in European history of which most everyone was familiar.[17] America did not yet have the "soap opera" effect of gripping human emotion played out against the backdrop of centuries of history dominated by competing royal families and punctuated by the dismal status of the peasant.[18] This attitude can in part be attributable to the homogenous nature of American history writing and the apprehension historians had in challenging any of the preconceived notions about America's founding from the early seventeenth century to the Revolution.

Two other concepts of the print culture beyond the financial model are cited by Leon Jackson in an article for *Early American Literature*. These two concepts were important to the continuing attempts by writers, especially historians, to further their craft in the eighteenth century. One concept dealt with the idea of civic engagement through print culture, while the other dealt with the authority of the writer to expound on a particular topic.[19] These two concepts are significant relating to the approach that defines the style and perceived consequences that many historians sought. Beyond making a living, most historians sought to establish the American experience as an exceptional event with divine overtones. This collective consciousness in historical writing obviously limited objective research and allowed for a subjective quality to seep into American historical writing, especially prior to 1800.

This was probably not the worst development that could have occurred. After the Revolution particularly, the unified concept of historical consistency was more necessary to bring about the concept of a whole nation with one history and one culture. This was an extension of the notion that the victors write the history, and it no doubt served its purpose. In its own way, the stress of objective writing would have certainly created fissures in the cohesive social, civic, and political fabric which was so necessary after the Revolution.

By 1825, the need for national acceptance (the "buy-in" necessary in a time of war by the population to promote and continue the conflict) was no longer necessary as it had been in 1775. With victory and independence a settled fact, the United States entered a period of reflective historical writing designed to affirm only the most uncontested aspects of the American experience—*uncontested* meaning to reflect those qualities that would put the founding generation and their exploits in the most favorable light and ensure their lives evidenced the qualities of citizenship which promoted a virtuous lifestyle. This is not to say that the virtuous lifestyle had not already been debated in its specifics. The rise of the two-party political system in the 1790s attested to the early start of the public discussion over just what a virtuous republican citizen was to be.

Writers accepted that the dual approach to government was designed to ensure the promotion and long-term validation of the values which Americans felt were necessary out of the experience of 1776. By promoting values (liberty, American uniqueness, opposition to British tyranny), writers sought to establish themselves as the source of record concerning the sentiments necessary for modern (contemporary early nineteenth century) republican citizens.

Those writers who sought a more objective understanding of the events associated with the war and did not conform to the emerging historical consensus on the meaning of the Revolution were often marginalized (many were seen as not patriotic enough) due to their work—if they could even find a publisher to make their work available to the public.[20] One writer in particular, George Chalmers, was a loyalist from Scotland who practiced law in Maryland for a number of years before returning to England at the outbreak of hostilities. His history was heavily focused on attempting to prove the legal arguments of the colonists were inaccurate and that the English actually had the better of the legal debate over the Revolution.[21] This approach, regardless of its merits, was certainly doomed.

James Otis and Samuel Adams

The power of history through the written word to move public opinion on a large scale toward resistance to England began in earnest with the lawyer James Otis. His work on the Writs case in 1761 "vastly increased the public sensitiveness respecting official encroachment" upon the constitutional rights of colonists.[22]

Not only did Otis argue the Writs case against British encroachment of colonial rights, he wrote about it in a series of pamphlets which were extremely influential in stating the colonial position. In 1764, ten years before Jefferson's *Summary View*, Otis published *The Rights of the British Colonies Asserted and Proved*. Otis energized a new generation through his writing by asking colonists to look to the past rather than the future as most American writers did. Otis sought to guide American colonists by their past to a known future having already once existed and now to be understood and recreated through history. Among the most prominent of his readers was John Adams. Otis also had a profound impact on his sister, Mercy, who a generation later would become a well-respected historian and writer in her own right and whose contributions will be explored in chapter five.

Reliance on historical study was first recorded in opposition to British policy in 1761, when James Otis investigated the history of common law to argue his famous Writs of Assistance case. Writs were a type of search warrant used extensively against smugglers during the 1750s, which so incensed many colonies as being an excessive reach of parliamentary power. Otis built his case from hundreds of years of precedent that Parliament could not enact laws contrary to England's ancient constitutional system. Otis searched back into the mists of time to uncover Anglo-Saxon laws and customs which predated the founding of modern England. Unfortunately, Otis lost his case. His research, however, was not rendered useless, as he did set a powerful precedent in place of relying on history to justify contemporary political events. With historical precedent on one hand, and religious sermons supporting the legal interpretation of history from a perceived moral perspective, two independent lines of thought started to converge in the 1760s, which ultimately led to the Revolution and Jefferson's Declaration with its amalgam of history, law, and religion. The Declaration was the ultimate example of a piece of historical narrative in service to contemporary political needs.

In addition to James Otis, another Massachusetts man who used history to advance his political cause was Samuel Adams. However, as compared to Otis, or even his cousin John, Samuel Adams was purely a political operative for whom history was inherently subjective—"History to [Samuel] Adams was mainly a manner of expressing a political argument."[23] Adams' use of history "indicates something of the historical sensitivity of his colonial audience."[24] Fact or truth resided in the extent to which he could utilize a particular story in his highly charged attempts at overthrowing the existing political structure. Unlike James Otis, who lost his argument over the Writs, Samuel was not inclined to lose anything. History became what he said it was and in his hands it had the ability to lead others to see and favor the conclusions he sought.

Samuel's cousin John by contrast had a much more objective and nuanced view of history. John Adams "studied history more from a sense of critical curiosity than from a desire for substantiation of colonial claims."[25] John saw history as a means, not the end, of the rapidly developing conflict with England. John's use of history was much more objective than his caustic cousin Samuel's use. John Adams "found history, law, and philosophy relevant to an examination of colonial rights," but he never saw them as incendiary in and of themselves.[26]

In his study and research over the Stamp Act crisis in 1765, John Adams found parallels in the annals of the first English settlers to America. Adams saw that "his colonial ancestors came not for religious reasons alone, but out of a 'love of universal liberty.'"[27] Adams saw comparisons in the turmoil brewing in 1765 to the turbulent seventeenth century, when England was convulsed with political agitation in nearly every decade, beginning with the death of Queen Elizabeth in 1603 and not ending until at least 1688. To Adams, the 1765 Stamp Act was in some respects a continuation of nearly a century and a half of political upheaval over the concept and meaning of liberty. Adams saw the imperative in studying history—"Americans," he felt, "were under a historical obligation to protest invasions of their rights and to resist any resurrection of canon and feudal tyranny."[28]

Part II

......

With independence won, America entered a new and dangerous realm of self-government. Difficult decisions led to less than respectful debates between states and their preeminent citizens.

The constant theme in American history writing, and nearly all American writing prior to the Revolution, was that the colonies were destined for greatness. With independence achieved, this prophecy seemingly had come to pass.

The defining period of American history had arrived. What type of history would the new country have? Who would be the intended audience? How would the stories be written? These and many other questions challenged writers, politicians, academics, the press, and everyday citizens. Moving forward was not a settled path.

As with all new countries though, a generous amount of deference was necessarily due to mythic elements of the American founding. This would be provided in abundance by writers of all types who struggled to "out-patriot" one another in an attempt to establish themselves. Yet, it was also a time where writers were also asking questions about what occurred and more importantly, why.

Through multiple representative vignettes, historians in general will be shown to have focused their efforts around the story of the American Revolution and how that story should and would be interpreted and presented. The historians presented in the next several chapters, while all well known during their lives and more or less successful, represent the challenges and accomplishments of all writers during the Age of Independence less well known during their time and certainly today.

4

Writing About the Founding

......

Writing during the Revolution itself did not have a strong appeal. "During the imperial crisis few scholars could find the calm and the time for research and writing or the opportunity for the intellectual exchange essential to serious historical work."[1] Writing to avowedly stake a position with one side or the other could leave a writer open to recrimination should his or her side lose; it was too difficult to determine who would win.[2] Ebenezer Hazard, "who had in mind great historical projects" wrote: "The War and the numerous avocations consequent upon it, have thrown every man's mind into such an unsettled and confused state that but few can think steadily upon any subject."[3] By 1800 though, the war was long over and doubts about who would win were a moot point and the accepted outlines were agreed upon; "all American historians agreed that the Revolution was justified, that the colonies were forced into it, and that they fought not just for political independence, but for the rights of man."[4]

Deviating from the accepted storyline of the Revolution could be perilous. Writing so close to the events of the Revolution could be fraught with problems; "with independence a settled issue, Americans were in no mood to tolerate views alternative to the standard Patriotic interpretation of the Revolution."[5] This concern was generated in part by a desire not to criticize leaders of the war when many of those leaders held important roles in the government. More importantly though, the concern over violating some hallowed concept by challenging the perceived interpretation of events could serve to remove the writer from the community of citizens of the new United States—essentially ostracized, emotionally if not physically. Pressure to conform to accepted standards of interpretation ensured a fairly uniform concept of the founding generation's efforts was established. This certainly did not please everyone. Writers with a political bias or writers who were disposed to be contrarian were put in unenviable situations.[6]

For any country's creation to be successful, it needs at least two, probably more, events or combination thereof to occur: (1) it needs to succeed in its goal of independence—however they define it; (2) it needs to establish itself through the written record for its own immediate benefit, but also for the benefit of posterity. "Victors write the history" is a cliché that, like most clichés, has some foundation in truth.[7] The victorious must establish and legitimize their presence in a way which draws upon the emotional components most likely to achieve the maximum sense of destiny among the populous. As Arthur Shaffer quotes Richard Hofstader, "Men who have achieved any civic existence at all must, to sustain it, have some kind of history though it may be history that is partly mythological or simply untrue."[8] Victory must also be written to seem as though it were preordained. If writers can achieve this, they have ensured for themselves a place in the founding period's literary canon.[9] Part of the irony of the history of American historical writing was that virtually every writer attempted to frame his or her historical writing in terms of the inevitability of the American victory—yet these historians did not achieve canonical status. Literally none are remembered much less studied today. As compared to Europe, the United States has always had a somewhat strained relationship with its authors.

Loyalist Writers

Many writers loyal to King George III exemplified this hesitation too by not trying to pick the winner before the war was over when they wrote of their adventures near the end of the war. Loyalists "wrote histories of their own colony detailing the complex political maneuvering with them."[10] Loyalists, much like a historian who got the story wrong in determining which side was winning, felt their stories were "explicable only in terms of the internal history of their own particular colony."[11] Through this process, loyalists or historians (or any writer who picked the losing side) could make the best claim possible for "rehabilitating" their social standing and character.

Writers such as Thomas Hutchinson, William Smith, and Thomas Jones all sought to defend their actions in defense of the crown with works published, in the case of Hutchinson and Smith, posthumously. Thomas Hutchinson provides a unique example in the story of history writing and just how promising the genre was. His *History of the Colony and Province of Massachusetts Bay* suffered an unfortunate fate during the Stamp Act crisis in the mid–1760s. As governor of the colony, and thus by extension directly connected to the crown, Hutchinson took the brunt of the anger from colonists upset over the imposition of the Stamp Act. Although volume one had been safely issued in

1764, the pre-published manuscript of the second volume was destroyed by a rioting mob in 1765—along with many unique and valuable primary resources that Hutchinson had been collecting his entire life. Due to his diligence, Hutchinson was nonetheless able to publish the second volume in 1767. Remarkably, Hutchinson, who abandoned the colonies for England in 1774, completed his *History of Massachusetts* from his new home and maintained a significant level of objectivity despite all that happened to him. The volume, however, was not even published until 1828. Hutchinson was a gifted man whose work was quite respectable, especially given the way in which he was treated by the American mobs. An American by birth, he was involved in the civic affairs of the colony of Massachusetts from an early age. A moderate, he sought to facilitate between his kinsmen and the British in the years before open rebellion. His loss to emigration "had an adverse effect on the intellectual life of the young republic for a whole generation."[12]

William Smith's *The History of New York* was considered highly respectable even long after independence was gained. Smith was an outspoken loyalist who fled to England only to return to Canada in 1786, where he served as chief justice until his death. During the Revolution and certainly until his death in 1793, Smith's work was considered as strictly the work of a loyalist. Thomas Jones was the victim of a less than enthusiastic reception for his work and as a result fled to England, where he continued to write diatribes against the former colonists. Unfortunately, with the exception of Hutchinson, too many of these histories were filled with venom and were never widely accepted by their readers. Overall though, "Americans gave harsh treatment to foreign and loyalist versions of the Revolution and eventually seized control of their own history."[13]

In many of these early national histories, the colonists are depicted by the historians as good Englishmen who had no choice but to defend their liberties. They portray the cause as the cause of freedom and liberty not just for themselves but for all of mankind. This is not anything new to anyone who has read these now obscure works; or to those who have read the modern day equivalent. Modern historians of the Revolutionary period have a tall order to fill—trying to find something new to say about a topic whose story has changed very little since its basic outline was first laid down over 200 years ago. The simple storyline is that "the Revolution was an event to be defended and glorified and the men who participated in it were heroes."[14] This continuity in part has ensured that a stable, defined, and coherent reflection of the Revolutionary period was passed from generation to generation. From the beginning, as Noah Webster stated, the nationalist historian's job was to "encourage 'habits of obedience' and submission to the new government"; and this was achieved in large measure through a homogenized historical timeline. This was not only for the purposes of promoting nationalism, but also because Americans, like most others, want simple and easy-to-digest history.[15] As with any subject, when variables of multiple perspectives enter the discussion, the tolerance level drops accordingly.

Evaluating the Revolution

The Revolution itself, after independence was achieved, became the focus, or core, of most of the history written after that event.[16] Within the first several decades after the end of the war, "the men and women attracted to writing the history of the Revolution were united by a common bond: a psychological and intellectual commitment to the Revolution."[17] Independence achieved, Americans needed a cohesive, understandable, and heroic story of their founding.

For the American Revolution, the critical period of elaboration on the meaning and success of the venture occurred between roughly 1780 until about 1815, just after the War of 1812.[18] By the end of the War of 1812, the first generation of historians of the Revolution had said nearly all that they could think to say and how to say it.

In its own right, the War of 1812 itself presented new challenges to factor into the repertory of American historical writing up to that time. Rather than expounding exclusively on the uniqueness of the Revolution and how it had ushered in a new age in the political dynamic of eighteenth-century nations, the War of 1812 generation of historical writers was presented with a much different set of propositions by attempting to determine a meaning to that seemingly senseless struggle, particularly since the adversary—England—was the same one from 1776; only the reasoning was different. The new age of history begun through the Revolutionary victory was clearly being challenged in 1812. Had the outcome in 1812 of the fighting been different, American historians would have had to reevaluate the uniqueness of 1776.

Ego

Colonial historians and writers at times were hypersensitive to the notion that colonial America lacked cultural components that many European intellectuals saw as vital for national development and continuity. Just as the pre–Revolutionary historians sought to dispel this perception, so did post–Revolutionary historians attempt to establish the same quality in their work concerning American cultural development. What set the post–Revolutionary historians apart from their predecessors was that the former had an independent nation to work with. This provided inspiration but also created demands that did not exist for earlier writers. Post-independence writers had to deal with the fact that the colonies were now a country, something their pre-independence writer ancestors could only imagine. Colonial America proved too fragmentary a patchwork to be bound together through the written word for many decades.

Yet, for all of these writers, both pre- and post–Revolutionary, the written word was supreme, in relation to art and their own perception of their calling in life. Regardless of what happened on the battlefield, the printed page provided the setting, the canvas for writers to create their written art. For these historians and writers, the written word proved a daily companion by which they were able to share their aspirations for their country with their readers. Historian David Ramsay and his colleagues saw "historical writing as a weapon in the struggle to create a national society and culture" that was as powerful as any weapon mustered on the battlefield. The trick for historians (they had bills to pay and families to provide for) was to find the right mixture of fact, story, and nationalism to appeal to enough readers to make a decent living.

Without the centuries of cultural, political, economic, and religious development that European countries had experienced, Americans sought to infuse the Revolution—the actual event itself—with all the qualities and aspirations they longed for. Americans, historians, writers, and their readers—even those illiterate—sought to encapsulate within the six years of armed conflict not just the nascent or incipient qualities of civilization, but they sought to compress all of the stages of national development into the passage of just six short years. This was their objective; "the primary goal of the Revolutionary generation of historians was to establish a national past."[19]

It was as though a process which took centuries under normal conditions in Europe needed to be condensed into a radically short period of time. All the elements of national greatness—mythical and non-mythical—were conceived, germinated, and delivered within less a period of time than a high-quality bottle of wine takes to mature. This reliance on hyper-maturity is with us to this day. America, if anything, is a nation defined by its impatience.

Many American founders understood this too. Those who chose not to destroy their correspondence oftentimes sought to rewrite official versions. Washington himself is known to have employed copyists to rework thousands of pieces of correspondence, creating doubt today as to what exactly is an "original" Washington manuscript.[20]

An Overview of Some of the Writers

A successful (relatively) writer with a national story was David Ramsay. His success with his overall narrative history of the Revolution was an inspiration to other writers approaching the same subject. Ramsay's work on the Revolution and the winning of independence, "which for some years after the termination of the late arduous conflict with Britain, existed only in name," helped to ensure greater acceptance from an audience ready for the type of work which sought to show America as a single, united nation.[21] Among the names Ramsay inspired which are no longer recognized today belong Jedidiah Morse (father of Samuel F. B. Morse) and Richard Snowden. Another writer to take on the historical challenge was Noah Webster, better known today for his dictionary.[22]

An episode—somewhat unusual among historians—bordering on internecine warfare erupted between Jedidiah Morse and Hannah Adams in the first decade of the nineteenth century. Morse had spent the decades following the Revolution embroiled in theological disputations with fellow academics at Yale and Harvard. He operated on a very slight field that tolerated little in the way of backsliding on doctrinal issues that he pursued. He was mainly an old-school Calvinist who saw the liberal evolution of religion in New England as a serious cause for concern. Morse was well known and respected even by his enemies. In addition to his religious efforts, Morse also wrote history and geography and as a result, more than anyone in his generation, due to his diversification, was a successful author.

Hannah Adams was as much of an opposite of Morse as was possible. Aside from the obvious difference of gender, Adams was a shy, withdrawn woman who had few prospects in life. She never married and was constantly in need of money. Although she had a famous last name, she was not one of *the* Adamses—despite being a distant cousin. Hannah Adams however had the brilliance of mind that characterized other more famous New Englanders who shared her last name. As a result Hannah Adams relied on her mind to make her living and by 1800 had produced a history of New England in her own right. Her study portrayed as liberal a story of New England as Morse's portrayed a conservative one. This brought her into direct competition with Morse by 1805, when both decided to publish abridgements of their works.

Hannah Adams clearly had the most to lose. She was impoverished, little known (even with her famous last name), and totally out of her league with the urbane and well-known and admired Morse. Finally, she was a woman.[23] This last point may have been the most odious detriment against her ability in what was at the time a male-dominated field. Charles Brockden Brown, noted Philadelphia novelist, writer, and editor, famously reviewed Adams' study in his magazine (when few would consider reviewing a work by a woman) and encouraged her to continue her efforts.

Brown found Hannah Adams to have one of the most broadly conceived histories of America then in existence. Brown criticized male historians for being too narrow or myopic in their approach to the topic of the American story. These writers were somehow trying to compete not just with contemporaries in Europe, but with each other in trying to "out-history" the next writer. Hannah Adams on the other hand, produced "a narrative more comprehensive than any we have ever seen."[24] Furthermore, Adams' work encompassed the entire period of the Revolution, not just the six years of open warfare—this was a complaint her distant cousin John Adams was to make in 1813, i.e., Americans were too fixated on the clash of arms and left the real issues unstudied.

Emboldened by Brown and some of his like-minded friends, Hannah Adams directly confronted Morse and persuaded him to allow her to publish her abridgement first to give her a head start in the market for which they both were competing. In the court of public opinion, Adams had the upper hand though. Her semipublic feud with Morse became known when word started to spread about Morse's greed and lack of compassion. As Leon Jackson has written, "What bothered the liberals more was the overweening greed and concomitant lack of charity Morse had shown in his dealing with Adams."[25] Adams herself compared Morse's wealth and status with her own station. Jackson quotes Adams as writing that Morse was "in the yearly receipt of from $1,500 to $2,000 from his other books, besides his ample salary as a clergyman" as opposed to herself, "a helpless woman, dependent on the scanty products of my pen for sustenance."[26]

Furthermore, in a large sense, Adams was working against two writers. Jedidiah Morse had received the materials of Benjamin Trumbull of Connecticut. Trumbull was a minister who, like nearly every other writer, sought to "promote a national feeling" through his work.[27] Trumbull felt the factions of the Revolution and of gaining independence were beginning to tear at the American spirit. His work was one of the few which acknowledged a less than unanimous feeling among Americans toward the patriot cause. As a minister, Trumbull felt compelled to heal through his work; to create a monument to the divine aid which he felt guided the colonies to independence.[28] Yet, the task proved too much, and in 1810 he turned his work over to Morse to complete or incorporate into the latter's work.

Although the sales of historical works were disappointing in America for American authors and European authors, the ideas generated in Europe were known to a small but dedicated group of American scholars and writers who filled pages of books and journals with their musings. Charles Brockden Brown was one example of the type of thinker and historian who sought a more reasoned explanation of American history with his version of American excep-

tionalness in his writings around 1800. In writing a review of Hannah Adams'
A Summary History of New England for his magazine *The Monthly Magazine
and American Review,* Brown took the liberty to extol on the virtues of history
as he saw them:

> The history of our native country justly merits the highest place in our regard; if
> not on account of the magnitude and singularity of its revolutions, yet for the
> unbounded influence of these revolutions on the happiness of us and our poster-
> ity. It constitutes an instructive and inestimable spectacle, because it relates, in
> some sort, to ourselves; because we are fully qualified to understand it; because
> its lessons are of indispensable use in teaching us our duty, as citizens of a free
> state, as guardians of our own liberty and happiness, and of those of that part of
> mankind who are placed within the sphere of our activity, and are best entitled
> to our affection and beneficence.[29]

The significant aspect of Brown's statement is that "we are fully qualified to
understand it." History, made by human beings for human beings was a radical,
remarkable statement. Americans, in their own capacity, could understand and
learn from history. No divine intervention was necessary; this was our story
in the fullest humanistic sense.

Throughout the first quarter of the nineteenth century, there were other
writers who sought to portray the rise of the United States. Men such as Abiel
Holmes, Benjamin Trumbull, Timothy Pitkin, and Charles Brockden Brown
and women such as Hannah Adams and Mercy Otis Warren sought to give
voice through the printed page to the aspirations and goals of the founding
generation. While none of these writers rise to the status of household names
today, during their lifetimes they did reach a certain amount of notoriety. That
notoriety aside, their work today is of value to us as a means of tracking the
course of historical thought and writing of the early decades of the nineteenth
century. Most of these historians are totally lost to history and are known
today only because of their more famous descendants or known to those who
study and research American writing as a profession. During their own lifetimes, these now obscure writers made little impact with their literary output.
In fact, much of their work was disdained precisely because it lacked redeeming
literary merit. In regard to historical competency, these obscure writers more
often than not simply copied from the earlier works of more established writers. It was during the dearth of historical production that a new generation of
writers was beginning to plan their works to in part address the lack of literary
merit and the lack of historical rigor. These new writers, men such as Jared
Sparks, George Bancroft, and William Hickling Prescott, would breathe new
life into the field and indeed establish the field as a separate academic discipline
in the nineteenth century.

Ebenezer Hazard

Ebenezer Hazard was born in Philadelphia in 1744, the same year as Jeremy Belknap in Boston. He graduated from the College of New Jersey in Princeton in 1762, the same year that Belknap graduated from Harvard. Hazard's classmate while at Princeton was the future New Jersey senator and Supreme Court Justice William Paterson. Professionally, Hazard rose through the postal service during the Revolution and became the postmaster general under the Articles of Confederation. As recorded in the journals of the Continental Congress, Hazard was first appointed to a postal position on July 29, 1775. It was recorded that "Mr. Hazard is appointed Deputy Postmaster for New York."[30] Hazard would continue his work as a postal employee for over a decade and conduct his study and writing in his spare time.

Throughout most of his life, Hazard was involved from a professional or a vocational standpoint with the business of books. As early as 1765, when he was twenty years old, Hazard became "the junior partner in the firm of Noll and Hazard, Booksellers."[31] Bookselling was still a marginal business in 1765; however, "Boston in the 1770s had fifty bookstores, Philadelphia probably thirty or more, and peddlers hawked almanacs, chapbooks, broadsides, and standard books through every city street and backwoods hamlet."[32] The employment of the itinerant bookseller was a popular way to not only sell books but also to allow for those outside of the metropolitan areas (which was most of the population) to keep some contact with the centers of the country. The earliest bookshop in the colonies, opened by Hezekiah Usher in Boston, began business around 1642.[33]

Hazard began his career as a historian by gathering together documentary evidence of laws in effect in each colony for publication. As Hazard proceeded with the project he was shocked to learn how much information was either nonexistent or prone to destruction. His overriding goal thus became preservation; "he sought to clarify the idea of preserving against all threats of man and nature the basic, fundamental records on which the story of his forebears and his generation would certainly rest."[34] As Fred Shelley quotes Hazard in a letter to Trumbull:

> I wish to be the means of saving from oblivion many important papers which without something like this collection will infallibly be lost.... [Some papers] are intimately connected with the liberties of the people; others will furnish some future historian with valuable materials. The time will doubtless come when early periods of American history will be eagerly inquired into, and it is the duty of every generation to hand to its successor the necessary means of acquiring such knowledge, in order to prevent their groping in the dark, and perplexing themselves in the labyrinths of error.[35]

It should be remembered that Hazard was proposing this task just prior to the start of actual armed conflict with Britain. By 1775, Hazard had written to many of the leading men of learning in the colonies asking for their views and possible participation in his endeavor. Hazard received the following reply from Thomas Jefferson:

> It is an undertaking of great utility to the continent in general, as it will not only contribute to the information of all those concerned in the administration of government, but will furnish to any historical genius which may happen to arise those materials which he would otherwise acquire with great difficulty and perhaps not acquire at all.[36]

Hazard was concerned that the production of the American historical story was being left to those who simply were "writers" by vocation and had little or no concern with the unique American experience and worse, those who did not care about the topic to which they applied their trade. Hazard was advocating the creation of a collection he termed American State Papers.[37] This collection, even after Hazard acquired the assistance of many of the leading men of the time, sadly failed to be produced. The outbreak of the war with Great Britain effectively put an end to a project which was, while worthy and necessary, discretionary in the end. What is however almost more important was the idea Hazard had. His proposal was radical for the time—apparently he did not immediately anticipate war—in that it approached history from a *documentary* and resource standpoint, as opposed to human narrative obtained through interviews.

In many ways, Hazard was something of a prototype of Jared Sparks, who started to write around 1820, several decades after Hazard. Hazard had grand visions for compiling America's history in the form of collections of evidential documents. Among some of his plans were the "American Chronology" (which he did not produce) and the preparation of a study of American geography.[38] He even contemplated an early version of the "Dictionary of American Biography"—which Jeremy Belknap compiled instead of Hazard several decades later and before Sparks did so too in the nineteenth century.[39] The idea for a Dictionary of American Biography was something nearly every generation of historians felt the need to put their hand to.

Not to be dissuaded, by 1778 and in the midst of war, Hazard was contemplating a general history of America based on archival resources. This, even though the Revolution had not yet been won and in fact the overall course of the war effort at that time was less than encouraging. He knew many members of the Continental Congress through his work as a post office official and he eagerly tried to encourage them to sanction and contribute to his work. His plan was to "visit every state and [ask] Congress for a recommendation to the governors to grant him free access to the records of their respective states and permission to copy pertinent records."[40] A congressional committee found much to like about Hazard's plan and heartily recommended to their colleagues that as much assistance be rendered to Hazard as could be spared. As recorded in the journals of the Continental Congress for July 20, 1778, Hazard received "encouragement ... to collect materials for a history, and [Congress recommended] to the several states to aid and assist him."[41]

What was so fascinating about this whole enterprise was that Congress actually encouraged Hazard to work to document not just colonial American history, but the history of the development of the conflict with Great Britain before it was even won and in fact when it looked like it would not be. Congress recognized the importance of such an undertaking for the future to understand what transpired during the perilous difficulties with Great Britain. It was the opinion of Congress "that the undertaking was laudable, and deserved public patronage and encouragement, as being productive of public utility."[42]

Hazard spent the terrible winter of 1779–1780 at the home of the Reverend William Gordon in Jamaica Bay outside of Boston talking about history. The Reverend Gordon was not just interested in Hazard's project; he himself contemplated his own study to be called the *Establishment of the Independence of the United States.*[43] George Washington, holed up in Morristown, New Jersey, that winter, must not have been informed of the confidence Hazard and Gordon had in ultimate American victory as he—as far as anyone can tell—spent the winter brooding over the prospects of American victory.[44]

Results

Hazard spent the 1780s working at his postal position and spending countless hours in research and writing. Throughout the decade he gradually lost the moral support of Congress he once enjoyed, not through any change of heart of local or state officials, but rather through the political difficulties of the times. By 1789, when the new government under the Constitution was formed, Hazard had completely lost favor with newly elected officials. President Washington skipped over Hazard to name his friend and comrade Samuel Osgood as the first Postmaster General of the United States. Hazard was completely and unceremoniously dismissed and discarded from the position he held under the Continental Congress by the administration and government he served so faithfully, and with so much enthusiasm, for over a decade. Hazard abandoned nearly all his historical projects and returned disillusioned to Philadelphia and became a businessman.

Later Career

Hazard was a worrisome type of writer. He constantly fretted over whether his drafts would meet with some destructive calamity before publication and render his research useless. In the days before electronic backups, cloud computing, and file-sharing, Hazard closely guarded his evolving manuscript. Happy to bring his American history work to completion, Hazard watched as the first volume was distributed in April 1792.[45] The work began with Columbus and ran to the present period of Hazard's time.

Unfortunately for Hazard, sales were dismal. As any author, he suffered from feelings of doubt and rejection—"my encouragement to proceed is but small."[46] Yet, Hazard did persevere. The second volume of the work, however, did suffer the fate he most feared, destruction of his manuscript in a fire at the printer's shop in 1793. Due to his diligent record-keeping, though, brought on by the worry of just such an accident, Hazard was able to recreate the lost volume, and it appeared for sale in late spring of 1794.[47] The poor sales of the second, coupled with the great energies expended in research and writing on top of his dismissal by Washington a few years prior, caused Hazard to forego a third volume, however.

Hazard represents something of a turning point (or perhaps a starting point) in the writing of history. Rather than simply compose a narrative through observation or interviewing, Hazard proposed that historical writing be grounded in the documentary evidence such as it might exist. Hazard "was the first American to attempt to preserve the documentary heritage of the nation."[48] Hazard was one who in many ways laid the groundwork from which other historians throughout the nineteenth century benefitted. Setting the standard for later historians, "He [Hazard] formulated policies and set editorial standards of excellence and scope" that laid the foundation upon which others built.[49]

Hazard's work inspired many during his life and for years after his death. He was an inspiration to a generation of writers and researchers who sought to approach history from the demanding perspective of documentary evidence.[50] Hazard died in 1817, having never completed his third volume of his American history, let alone the four volumes originally planned.

Abiel Holmes

Another example of a once famous and now forgotten historian is Abiel Holmes. Abiel Holmes was the father and grandfather of two of the most famous men in Boston who shared the name Oliver. Oliver Wendell Holmes,

Sr., was a prolific and respected poet, author, and physician from the mid-nineteenth century until his death in 1892. His son, and the grandson of Abiel, was Oliver Wendell Holmes, Jr., one of the most profound jurists America has produced. Both Olivers, Sr. and Jr., carried on the literary tradition started by Abiel Holmes.

Abiel's *American Annals* were quite popular and often copied throughout the nineteenth century, and his "two volumes were looked to for guidance for many years."[51] Abiel Holmes relished his role in Boston's literary circles as a scholar and thinker who helped to spread the history his ancestors were so involved in. Abiel's work was designed to try to unify the overall story of the American colonies; according to Abiel, "no attempt has been made to give even the outline of its [America's] entire history."[52] Neither Oliver Wendell, Sr. nor Jr., inherited Abiel's lackluster writing style; his son and grandson "were in this respect more gifted."[53] Both of Abiel's famous descendants moved well beyond him in literary ability. The works left by Oliver Wendell, Sr. and Jr., are still read, studied, and enjoyed by readers today, unlike Abiel's.

5

Three Giants of Historical Writing in America in 1800

● ● ● ● ● ●

Between the years 1790 and 1810, three historians dominated the scene for the writing of history and historical-themed poetry and prose in a way that foreshadowed the rise of the professional historian by the mid-nineteenth century. Mercy Otis Warren, Joel Barlow, and Charles Brockden Brown were each in their own way unique enough to warrant individual biographies; indeed, each has been the subject of stand-alone biographies in recent years. Each one approached history and the purpose of history from a perspective that the others would have found problematic. Still, they represent the general outlines—not a nexus—in the still evolving corpus of American historical writing.

Mercy Otis Warren was a New England patrician who nonetheless wrote in a manner which did not always square with her background. Yet, she was no flaming liberal by today's standards. Still, she was able to draw the ire of her friend and fellow New England traditionalist John Adams. A sister of James Otis (of the Writs of Assistance Case fame), Mercy was a shrewd observer and writer who saw events in more than just a regional setting.

Joel Barlow was educated at Yale in a strict Federalist manner infused with the typical amount of religion which that institution was famous for in the late eighteenth century. However, upon graduation and through a period of mature reflection, he entered into an agreement with Thomas Jefferson (tantamount to a pact with the Devil as far as some of his Yale classmates were concerned) to produce an anti–Federalist inspired history of the early United States under Jefferson's guidance.

Charles Brockden Brown was perhaps the most intelligent of the three historians surveyed in this chapter. His approach to history was bold. He was not someone who sought to utilize history to make anyone feel good about themselves. To Brown, history was about motives, and people, with all their good and bad faults. In many ways, Brown approached a question most would rather have left alone—what exactly is good, and what is bad?

Mercy Otis Warren

The portrait of Mercy Otis Warren by John Singleton Copley is a study in contrasts. Her face identifies a woman of high moral character; with strong, large eyes, a powerful nose, and a slightly rounded chin evoking a woman of charm, grace, and accomplishment. Above all however, is Warren's determination; her strength and physical carriage portend a woman not easily swayed and one who likely did not suffer fools easily.

By contrast, her gown is breathtaking in its style and luxury. The silk seems almost ready to pour off the canvas. The lace is of a most delicate quality, while her hands are exquisitely slender and refined. Naturally, some of the profound sense of immediacy of the portrait can be attributed to the artist John Singleton Copley. Yet, even Copley needed raw material to work with. Mercy Otis Warren clearly provided that.

Mercy Otis Warren was born in 1728 and came to be recognized as "the most formidable female intellectual in eighteenth-century America."[1] She was a poet, playwright, essayist, and historian. Her *History of the Rise, Progress and Termination of the American Revolution* proved her magnum opus. In it she sought to "fuse her personal and public convictions"; she sought "to unite her ethical, political, and philosophical concerns."[2]

In keeping with many of her male counterparts, Warren sought "to form minds, fix principles, and cultivate virtue" in her writing.[3] Warren, much like Hazard, Ramsay, or Belknap, sought to instruct, to teach, and to persuade through her writing. She eventually saw history as the primary vehicle in which to combine and deliver these instructional qualities to her readers. It has been discussed before that writers, particularly historians, saw the history of the American struggle during the colonial period and eventually through to independence as exhibiting the qualities of providential interaction in the affairs of man. This interaction of God and man ensured an unassailable foundation from which historians like Warren could construct their histories. History therefore was a tool to mold, to shape; it was a device which almost could extrude a virtuous American. The lessons of history, the meaning of history, are so compactly utilized in Warren, Joel Barlow, and others, that the American historian was by 1800 setting a new path for historical writing. Vanished was the elemental power of history to teach; rather, what emerged in historical

writing by 1800 in America was instructional, which can be discerned or separated from teaching.

Warren's writing was in many ways structured and prompted by her close
association to both John and Abigail Adams. In fact, Warren's efforts generated
some of the most poignant commentary on the historical process from the
famous couple. During the struggle for independence, Abigail Adams, sensing
the momentous times through which she and her friend were living, wrote,
"Many very memorable events which ought to be handed down to posterity
will be buried in oblivion merely for want of a proper hand to record them."[4]
Whether Abigail knew of Mercy's desire to write history at this point is not
known; Mercy however probably saw the comment as encouragement either
way. John Adams, who was not thrilled with the perceived bias in Warren's
writing, was blunter: history, he wrote, is "not the Province of Ladies."[5] John
Adams was, much like Jefferson concerning John Marshall's work, very sensitive to Warren's supposed partisan uses of history. Adams felt that Warren was
too Jeffersonian in her interpretation for a good Federalist. Adams wrote,
"Your History has been written to the taste of the nineteenth century, and
accommodated to gratify the passions, prejudices, and feelings of the party
who are now predominant."[6]

As with other historians who attempted to work during the war years, Warren saw the difficulty in determining the outcome of the conflict. Lester Cohen
writes concerning Warren (and it is applicable to other writers of the time)
"that no one could predict how the struggle would turn out."[7] While this feeling was consistent with other writers, at the same time it also identifies Warren
as far more pessimistic than some of her colleagues. Warren was, though, very
much like her New England friends John and Abigail Adams through the
moralistic approach to the Revolution and of political considerations relative
to the tyranny and corruption Warren saw in the British administration of the
colonies. "At the heart of that commitment was [a] complex of motives....
Writing history was less a means of edification than a mode of exhortation."[8]
Much like that of John Marshall and others, Warren's work was believed to
have been infused with political demagoguery. Unlike Marshall however, Warren herself feared this possibility and consequently probably delayed publication of her major work to await a more stable time—such as when Jefferson
was president.

Joel Barlow

As will be discussed in detail in chapter nine, a secondary saga accompanied
the work John Marshall undertook in 1802 and involved his cousin President

Thomas Jefferson. As has already been described, Jefferson had a profound interest in, and impact upon, the writing of history in this country. It has also been mentioned that Jefferson was immensely sensitive to criticism and profoundly partisan. Those two aspects, one admirable, one not so admirable, combined and fused together over the news of Marshall's work.

Jefferson was completely convinced that Marshall and Bushrod Washington were up to no good with their biography of George Washington. When Barlow was a diplomat in Europe in 1802, Jefferson contacted him with a sense of urgency, as Jefferson wanted to find an antidote for Marshall's *Life of Washington*—at that point just in the initial phase. He claimed he *knew* Marshall's biography would be a political indictment of his Republican party. As late as 1815, nearly ten years after its completion, in a letter to John Adams he referred to Marshall's biography as nothing more than a "party diatribe."[9]

Prior to the election of 1804, Jefferson and James Madison sought to employ Joel Barlow to write a counterweight history of the 1790s—the period which Marshall concentrates on extensively in his Washington biography. Jefferson and Madison wanted Barlow to produce an appropriate history of the United States from their perspective. Both Jefferson and Madison saw Marshall's work as a hopelessly partisan general history first, and a biography second. To them, Washington's life was simply a convenient setting for the Federalist, monarchical viewpoint.

Barlow was not a bad choice to write a counterpoint history. He had "converted to Jeffersonian republicanism in 1792, [and] Barlow devoted his considerable talents to promoting and improving constitutional government."[10] By 1805 he was a well-known poet, essayist, and playwright; his list of vocations was quite long too. He operated on both sides of the Atlantic. Throughout the first decade of the nineteenth century, Barlow served in diplomatic missions in Europe, and was well known there for his advocacy of republican democratic principles. Although he returned to the United States in 1805, he still maintained his contacts overseas. These contacts proved helpful. Barlow made his contemplated history and planning known to several correspondents. This in a way ensured a sort of pressure remained on Barlow to proceed with the project.

After his return to the United States in 1805, Barlow was not yet in a position to move forward with the study for Jefferson. Marshall was nearing completion of his work, and little if any evidence of political benefit accruing to the Federalists could be found. Unmoved, Jefferson continued to agitate for Barlow—who by 1808 had publically committed himself to the project.[11] At this point Jefferson was preparing to leave office and retire from politics. What his motivation was at such a late date can only be guessed at. Whatever the motivation, Jefferson met with Barlow at Monticello in September, 1808, to plan further strategy.

Barlow began to assemble material from a variety of sources, not just Jefferson. He corresponded with Mercy Otis Warren, whose own history appeared in 1805. By 1810, nearly twenty years after first conceiving the idea of a history, he started to design the layout of the work. Barlow looked to dividing his work into three parts, "the colonial period, the revolutionary period, and the first 20 years of the Federal Constitution."[12] Although his plans were taking shape and he was corresponding on materials, Barlow, through his letters, did not seem to have the drive by 1810 to engage in the level of study and writing necessary for completion of his project. It is as if he recognized the late date to prepare a political counterweight to Marshall's *Life*. The need just wasn't there anymore. This responsibility can rest partly with Jefferson's wild partisan views and his vehement dislike of his cousin John Marshall.

Near the end, prior to 1811, Barlow embarked on a series of essays meant to act as something of a "warm up" exercise to the production of the larger history. The four essays formed more of a political treatise than history. Barlow traced through some minor historical reflection the rise of the American state. Barlow's American was exceptional; not in an unverified or unquestionable way, but exceptional nonetheless.

Barlow the Thinker

Barlow "was never a settled individual, either in his intellectual life or in his career."[13] His questioning of American morals was as much a personal questioning of his own views, while at the same time questioning the "cultural and social problems of America."[14] This doubt was arrived at in part due to Barlow's deep religious conviction.[15] His transformation in the 1780s from conservative to liberal, from organized religion to Deism, seems only to have heightened his appeal to someone like Jefferson, although Barlow had solid Republican credentials by the time he met Jefferson, this following his conversion to Republicanism at Yale years before.

This conversion at such a known Federalist bastion as Yale is partly what drove Jefferson to approach Barlow about a Republican-themed history in the first place. Barlow himself had contemplated such a work but never acted upon it. Barlow had lived the transformation that Jefferson saw and desired writ large in the United States. Before he met Jefferson, "Barlow underwent a complete change of philosophy within two years. He concluded that a radical and immediate reorganization of Western societies was necessary."[16] This is the type of thinking and experience (political conversion to his side) Jefferson was looking for. In 1811, when Barlow left on a diplomatic mission to France, with the project still not completed, Jefferson wrote, "What is to become of our past revolutionary history? Of the antidotes of truth to the misrepresentation of Marshall?"[17] Barlow's peripatetic wanderings however put him clearly in line with the currents of expressive American thought. The overriding challenge faced by American writers was the absence of cultural greatness in the arts and social sphere. This topic obsessed Americans from the seventeenth century onward, as has been shown. Barlow's numerous careers and literary undertakings all attest to the restless nature of his psyche and can substitute for the general overall feeling within the new United States for recognition and for an embrace of the American way by other world powers.

Barlow, as did many of his contemporaries, wanted not just recognition of American independence, but also an acknowledgment of the unique place the American Revolution played in world history. Barlow wanted to see an imitation of the American independence fight as a validation for what he and others felt was a millennial experience that occurred between America and Great Britain. In some mystical sense, America's promise was the promise of mankind, the awakening through enlightenment principles of the deliverance of human liberty and freedom to the throngs corralled in the despair of monarchy.

Leaving aside the huge philosophical problems posed by this reasoning and concentrating instead on the historical impetus to this theory, it is easy to see why idealistic, intelligent, and committed individuals took up the challenge of historical writing and editing. They saw themselves as political ministers who sought to spread the word about political freedom and liberty as they saw it in the United States. Through this process the patterns of American exceptionalness were borne to the fore of America's reading public. The historians and writers put into print the often tangled concepts Americans felt moving forward after the Revolution.

This was partly why Barlow delayed in the publication of his *The Vision of Columbus* poem. In one sense, like his countrymen, Barlow was not sure of his own personal vision regarding America. The angst over an uncertain war led to an uncertain near-term future. Rather than clarifying America's future as many hoped, the war made it more opaque. Much like historians writing during or immediately after the Revolution, Barlow, as a poet, was busy at work on his epic poem *The Vision of Columbus*. As the name implies, Barlow saw Columbus as the ultimate progenitor of the colonial American country which became the United States. This work extolled the American colonies as a new nation unlike any seen before. Although not published until 1787, the poem was finished in draft form by 1779. American exceptionalness was on full view. The fact that he had the work finished before the end of the war indicates his tremendous optimism in the American effort. Much like historians not wanting to publish during the war until they knew who would win, Barlow kept his poem unpublished until nearly five years after the Treaty of Paris. Barlow's Columbus character reflects this in the *Vision* and comes across as a less than convincing figure. "This forced amalgam of traditional religious imagery and Enlightenment epistemology exposes the internal tension of the poem *and the period*" [italics added].[18]

John Daly Burk

Barlow would be one in a long line of authors Jefferson would approach (sometimes simultaneously) over nearly twenty-five years with the idea of countering the Marshall biography before his death in 1826. In fact, Barlow was first approached by Jefferson to write a history of the United States as early as 1791—ten years before Marshall even started his history. This early attempt would have put Jefferson in the unquestioned position of fostering the "official" history of the new United States.

John Daly Burk was recruited by Jefferson around 1800 to use his writing skills to produce a history of which Jefferson could be proud. Burk, a fairly well-known Irish dramatist and later failed American dramatist, immigrated to the United States in 1796. He was forced to leave Ireland due to his radical associations and actions while a student at Trinity College. Burk was a quick-tempered man who had a keen sensitivity to perceived injustice, whether to himself or nations. As such he went to the one place he thought he would find direction; "like many eighteenth-century European liberals, he regarded the United States as a fulfillment of the high hopes he held for his native Ireland."[19] Burk became friendly with Aaron Burr and entered some of the most radical circles of the Republican Party.

Burk was arrested under the Alien and Sedition Acts for claiming President John Adams had altered correspondence during the XYZ affair to further a war stance. Upon release on bail, he fled to Virginia rather than face deportation. In hiding under an assumed name, he quickly became a hero to powerful Republicans in the state, including Thomas Jefferson. Burk was a natural choice after his release and escape to Virginia for a partisan like Jefferson to approach with his goal of finding a mouthpiece to promote his version of American history. Burk, already a radical in his native Ireland and sought by the authorities there, readily took up Jefferson's proposal. Jefferson even allowed Burk access to his precious library at Monticello in preparation of what became the *History of Virginia* published in 1804 and 1805. These works were published at the same time that Jefferson's enemy John Marshall was beginning to publish his *Life of Washington*, which threw Jefferson into such a fit. Burk sadly let his fiery, rebellious temper get the best of him, and he was killed in a duel in 1808, leaving his anti–Marshall work unfinished. In Jefferson's seemingly never-ending attempts to find other writers (another of whom was killed too in a duel), he found his options increasingly limited by the available talent before abandoning the search and concentrating on his efforts with Barlow.

Unfortunately for Jefferson, Barlow, who had solid credentials as a partisan, nationalist, and writer, and was probably the most capable of the men employed by Jefferson, could not put together the work before his death in 1812, three years after Jefferson left office. Not to be dissuaded, Jefferson eventually attempted to write his own autobiography and history in 1817. His work, titled *Anas*, was not published during his lifetime and did little to address the errors he saw in Marshall's work.

The fear Jefferson felt and generated in the early 1800s over Marshall's *Life* were largely unfounded. By 1810, the Federalist Party had died a slow, natural death; the country was well entrenched in Jeffersonian political philosophy, and James Madison, Jefferson's chosen successor, was into his second year as president. Yet, Jefferson still wanted his version of history written.

Finally in 1823, three years before his own death, Jefferson sought to enlist Supreme Court associate justice William Johnson. Johnson was appointed to the Court by Jefferson in 1804 and was considered a stalwart Republican by Jefferson. Johnson stated he was interested in the history project after being approached by Jefferson but never even got started and probably actually had little or no desire to undertake the project. Jefferson's whole sorry twenty-year episode of trying to counter Marshall's history shows Jefferson in an unflattering light. Starting in 1804, and lasting until his death in 1826, he seethed over the existence of Marshall's history.

Charles Brockden Brown

Among the historians who wrote within the first twenty-five years of the founding of the federal government in 1789, Philadelphia native Charles Brockden Brown stands out for his bold approach not just to the historical process, but to how that process was applied to the still new American story. In terms more specifically probing rather than trying to enhance or build upon a notion of American exceptionalness, Brown focused more on the elements of humankind which tended to be applicable to all people, not just Americans; and thereby tell a tale which anyone could comprehend and relate to.[20] Brown therefore wrote for all peoples, not just Americans. Yet, this tale that Brown sought was nonetheless an American tale with peculiarly American overtones. Most importantly, Brown was an antidote to the traditional approach of historians to place the founding of the United States within some framework of providential design.

> The fact is that history after history of colonial America and the early Republic anchored its representation of America's past in the assumption that [America] was responsible for manifesting God's divine providence.[21]

Brown was born in 1771 in Philadelphia to a Quaker family. He had extensive training in the classics and was well acquainted with the major Greek and Roman writers. It was a mixture of influences from his Quaker faith—which for him was less faith and more individualism—and some of the more intensely intellectual studies which set Brown on the path to history.

Brown saw history as human and kept his distance from interpretations which sought meaning outside of the human realm. He "wrote history in a mode that was, for its time, a secular and innovative departure from the existing cultural mythos."[22] Brown attempted to move beyond the model of history that had dominated Western Europe since the Middle Ages when historians tended to "privilege theological and allegorical explanations of the past that justified progress to the present."[23] Brown moved his history out of the realm of chronicler and into the realm which brought history and philosophy much closer together—in a way he saw as more conducive to "truth." Winners in life may get to write the history, but they don't necessarily write the truth. And for Brown, truth must begin with a question.

Virtually every writer and historian prior to Brown sought to ground his or her work in the understanding that the United States was the result of larger-than-life forces that propelled the American movement into a mission culminating in independence. That stage achieved, the next step would be "converting" the globe to American ideals. Much like Caleb Wayne, publisher of John Marshall's *Life of Washington,* Brown saw history as universal, something that happened to all people. Wayne at one point wrote to Marshall when the latter was getting too nationalistic in his draft manuscript, "An author ought not to write as an American, but assume an independent ground."[24]

Early colonial writers of the sixteenth century sought comfort and positive reinforcement for their suffering and ordeals during the first phases of settlement by drawing what parallels or conclusions they could from the Bible. These writers sought to justify their adventures, the expenditure of huge amounts of money, and the appalling loss of life (both English and Native American) through reliance on their interpretation of God's plan of progress, in which they sought to impose the writings of men who lived over a millennium and a half prior to their own time on current circumstances. As discussed earlier, prior to Brown, "Colonial and early republican historiography clearly embraced a providential paradigm for understanding the past, a set of ideas about America's founding and special purpose that would shape historical accounts for generations to come."[25]

Nonetheless, this inspiration clearly had its benefits, as it put the temporal struggles the early colonists faced into a project of much larger proportion than just what they represented through their efforts. "Biblical history, the history of the Reformation, and the unfolding story of New England were seen for generations of historians as complementary texts about redemption and progress, divine or otherwise."[26]

Brown was truly at the vanguard of historians at the turn of the nineteenth century when considering the breadth and scope of his survey and thinking. Rather than history nationalized and moralized, Brown was among the first to *think* about history. That is, what did it mean to have a history; how did history determine one's life—indeed, should it determine one's life? These were questions that from a historian were quite new and when compared to other historical writings, quite distressing. Brown in effect was asking his fellow historians, and in fact all Americans, what they actually saw when they looked at the history of America. Certainly, he suggested, there must be more than a sanitized, monochromatic view and approach utilized in every instance to ensure a uniform ending to the story. By "endorsing a historical narrative that attempted to convey a secular ... point of view and to discount an overtly providential or partisan interpretation of historical events, Brown arguably supports a liberal or unorthodox view of the past."[27] Brown's arrival at this intersection was not an overnight event. Instead it was a process that occurred throughout his formative years and can be glimpsed periodically through references in his writings, most specifically in his novels.

His Work

Charles Brockden Brown is known today—admittedly by a small group of literary scholars and devotees—as a novelist whose groundbreaking works at the turn of the nineteenth century set the stage for later, more well-known writers such as Nathaniel Hawthorne and Herman Melville.[28] It is in this role that Brown emerges as a seminal figure in the literary combination of historical writing and fiction writing. Brown's career and work straddled both genres, and at times his work is a seamless blend of both writing perspectives. His further influence on the craft or artistry of historical writing can be seen later in the nineteenth century with the success of such literary historians as George Bancroft or William Hickling Prescott.

As an experiment in style and concept, Brown often used historical events as a way to frame his novels and to provide a backdrop before which to frame his action. The historical events chosen, as already discussed, dealt not with the heroics of founding a new country; Brown sought human stories devoid of providential speculation and manifestations of causation. "The nature of Brown's power eludes exact definition, but its property is to compel the reader's attention irresistibly not only to the exciting narrative but also to the gravity of whatever ... problem is implicit in it."[29] Those problems invariably had a genesis in historical events impacting the human interaction among families, residences, or even racial and ethnic interaction. Examples of themes include "freer divorce laws, political rights for women, deistic religion, a more humane treatment of criminals, [and] amelioration of the lot of the peasant class."[30] These were topics which shed a light on areas of the American experience that most would rather have not thought too strenuously about at the time. Yet, his works sold well and he was something of a celebrity in Philadelphia.[31]

This status allowed Brown in part to capture a reliable audience for his rapid output. Over the course of three years, from 1798 to 1801, he wrote and published six novels. After 1801, until his untimely death in 1810 from tuberculosis, Brown wrote for magazines and pamphlets.

Periodical Publications

In his magazine and pamphlets Brown wrestled with concepts of history. For Brown, writing about American history from one perspective was far too simplistic. Perhaps the mono-perspective approach was patriotic, but it lacked the grueling complexity that for him characterized the human story in a larger sense. America was a micro-story of the larger world. And, having just gained independence, the United States was not a topic for in-depth objective inquiry by Brown or any other historian—too many questions would spoil the party for a majority of Americans.

By the turn of the nineteenth century, magazines had begun to play a crucial role in the continuing development of American national literature, especially history writing. To encourage the writing of more American-produced works, "literary clubs (such as New York's Friendly Club and Boston's Anthology Club) announced contests, magazines sponsored native authors, critics puffed native works, newspapers demanded greater production from domestic talent."[32]

Brown's magazine was the *Monthly Magazine and American Review,* a short-lived publication at the turn of the nineteenth century. In this magazine,

Brown explored some central elements of historical writing in America. He reviewed writers such as Benjamin Trumbull, Abiel Holmes, William Robertson, and Hannah Adams, all writers referred to earlier in this work.[33] In these reviews Brown tried to come to terms with the power of history to perform the functions of pulling society together around a common, unifying theme. Brown is not so much defining his approach to history as he is refining it by highlighting examples of varying styles. Furthermore, Brown "displayed an acute interest in the nature and effect of its composition."[34] In these pages Brown began to strengthen his concept of historical writing as pertaining to the American story. Brown "valued a more secular approach to history writing" and "he endorsed its more skeptical dimensions."[35] In other words, as he explored in his novels, Americans were not a chosen people called by God. One need only to look at some of the atrocities committed by Americans to know there was nothing inherently supernatural (if by supernatural we mean a positive life-affirming quality) in their activities. That approach made for good, comforting stories, but for bad history. In many respects, Americans were no different in their actions from the Europeans the early colonists fled from. Those early colonists were here to make money, and any difficulties and hardships they experienced were not unique to the American story. All peoples experience hardships, and Americans were no different. Therefore, Americans were not exceptional or heroic, rather, they were human beings like everybody else trying to make their way as they saw fit.

Bold Ideas

While Brown surveyed the work of American, English and European writers, the only American woman that he treated was Hannah Adams. Her work, *A Summary History of New England,* was well praised by Brown as one of the more sober accounts prepared by an American of either gender. Brown encouraged "Adams to continue with her work and [included]—apparently for the first time—an extract of her narrative" in his magazine.[36] This was related in part to the episode discussed in chapter four involving Hannah Adams and Jedidiah Morse.

Brown restructured his publication around 1805 and rechristened it the *Literary Magazine and American Register.* It had essentially the same mission but focused more on the literary aspects of writing, with a particular focus on historical writing in both fiction and nonfiction form. Brown was evolving more into a critic of literature focusing on the American story. His nemesis was the writer who wrote tired, worn-out prose or narrative that simply refashioned uplifting, moralizing stories, which Brown saw as useless. He wanted writers to say *why* Americans were exceptional, not just write that they were. Brown, and he felt his readers, needed to be shown or be told why Americans were unique. Brown was not the type of writer or critic who Jefferson would have enjoyed because Jefferson wanted writers to engage in petty politics and upstaging with sources—whether those sources were used objectively or not. Charles Brockden Brown was not at all about petty topics.

Brown's writing, theorizing, and overall approach was accepted by a small percentage of the population of Philadelphia, much less so outside the city. Brown's approach tended to appeal to the intellectual avant-garde who sought more meaning, more dimensional acuity in their interaction with the literary world of early nineteenth-century America. Brown was far ahead of his time in that historiography as a whole didn't reach the level Brown had until well into the twentieth century. By some accounts, various writers still haven't evolved to Brown's level of objectivity in relation to how we view our past.

So why talk about Brown? The simple answer is that he deserves an airing. Why? Brown represents the earliest spark of imaginative use of narrative historical writing (nonfiction but developing into fiction) which brought aspects of the story of America beyond the traditional digests of the "great men." While many scoff at the notion of history from the perspective of "the people," it is a much more nuanced (and therefore complicated) story to articulate and consume. This not only impacts sales, it impacts people's sense of self-satisfaction. Most people like a clean, neat story packaged in a pleasant container of a not too large size, which makes life much easier to understand, and live. Charles Brockden Brown rejected that view.

In contrast to Charles Brockden Brown, the previously discussed Joel Barlow, who was writing at the same time but entirely independent of Brown, represents one of the last attempts at the heroic model of history undertaken when many of the founders were still alive. Brown, on the other hand, represented a more forward focusing, analytical historical perspective. Brown was not privy to the counsel of surviving founders the way Barlow was. Brown stayed clear of politics and thereby kept history cleaner and more objective. To Barlow, history was a tool; for Brown history was a discipline.

6

Other Genres of
Writing About History

......

Novels

During the early republic period (1790–1820) the world of American writing was transforming in the same manner as the nation was. New styles and patterns of writing were being fused with older, more established standards. Transformative American writers such as Henry Wadsworth Longfellow, Walt Whitman, Edgar Allen Poe, and Nathaniel Hawthorn, among many others, were born and raised during this heady period when there were still veterans of the Revolutionary War alive who could tell not just their stories of that period, but their aspirations and hopes for the new country. These high ideals extend back to the earliest seventeenth-century writers who prophesied the greatness of America at some future time. Those who lived through the Revolution saw themselves as the generation that brought about the fulfillment of the high ideals set by their ancestors. And now, in their turn, they told those stories to a new generation. A new generation of writers, in all types of genres, brought about an emergence of "an American profession of letters, and with it a dim recognition of the function of literature as art rather than utility."[1]

As a novelist, Charles Brockden Brown has been credited with creating some of the first Gothic-style novels written by an American. This style of writing was to become quite popular through about the mid–1840s. While Brown represents this subgenre within the overall genre of the novel, other writers were experimenting with another style or approach within the setting of the novel. The historical novel, a work of fiction based on actual events, while an established form today, was only beginning to receive notice in the

United States by the end of the eighteenth century. It wasn't in part until the colonies were independent and with their own national government that writers felt enough material existed for the plausible preparation of narrative historical fiction about that topic. Yet, the historical novel would prove extremely versatile in adapting to the needs of American writers; "no other literary form, so far as the majority of readers are concerned, has more acceptably expressed the nation's origins, its development, its ideals, and its meaning."[2] Very much like their colleagues who wrote history, novelists were slow to develop without a national identity; "what we have is a genre emerging within a culture precisely as that culture attempts to define itself."[3]

In the southern colonies, which were to be greatly impacted by Sir Walter Scott's works in the 1820s, themes tended to revolve around the settlement patterns associated with the gentry lifestyle. Plantations, slavery, a rigidly patriarchal family life, class distinctions, and an individualistic ethos not entirely in line with reality were common themes found in southern fiction. Topics included

> the arrival of the first white settlers in Virginia, the Carolinas, and Maryland; the Smith-Pocahontas romance; the Virginia Massacre of 1622; life in Jamestown under Governor Berkeley at the time of Bacon's Rebellion; events at the capital of Williamsburg; [and] the Yemassee wars in Carolina.[4]

Examples of the most popular, the John Smith and Pocahontas story, appeared as early as 1802. John Davis, an Englishman, wrote *The First Settlers of Virginia, an Historical Novel.* Another treatment of the theme appeared in 1814, when a style favored by Charles Brockden Brown, the Gothic tale, was employed in the anonymously published *The History of the Female American, or the Adventures of Unca Winkfield.*[5] Bacon's rebellion proved too irresistible as a topic, especially after the Revolutionary War. The magic year 1776 is reflected in the year of Bacon's own "revolution," 1676, and in the theme of the revolt against the excessive taxation and arbitrary rule of Virginia governor William Berkeley. Until the events of 1776, the 1676 uprising proved to have little interest as a theme or story. Two early examples were William A. Caruthers' *The Cavaliers of Virginia, or the Recluse of Jamestown* in 1834; and *Hansford,* by St. George Tucker, in 1857.[6] Tucker was the grandson of the famed jurist and College of William and Mary law professor of the same name. In South Carolina, William Gilmore Simms continued the theme of Indian conflict with the Europeans in his 1835 novel *The Yemassee.* Simms sets the story in 1715 and incorporates "legends told [him] by his grandmother" and has the Indians assisted in their campaign against the white men by the Spaniards.[7] Overall, novelists treated the Native American theme no more objectively than any other writer. The feelings exhibited towards the Native Americans were fairly stable—negativity.

In New England, the focus turned more toward the Puritan experience and the overall impact of the religious founding of the region.[8] Contrasted to the southern colonies, with their emphasis on the gallantry and romanticism of days gone by, New England sought an explanation for the religious concentration of settlement. The one theme constant in all colonial fiction, north or south, was the interface of native populations and arriving settlers. One female author, Harriet V. Cheney, in 1824 published *A Peep at the Pilgrims in Sixteen Hundred Thirty-Six*. Not only was the theme of native against settler mined for material; in the opposite direction, fiction allowed for the imaginative romantic connection between the two peoples. Of course, this happened in real life too; but fiction allowed for a fuller play of motives and desires.

> By the eighteen twenties, when the first of these novels appeared, red men in that region were no longer a menace. As a result, there developed a sentimental attitude toward them. Young women novelists speculated on what kind of husband an Indian would make.[9]

The middle colonies produced something of a hybrid of the other two sections. Given the greater mixture of the cultures in the middle areas of North America, this is not surprising. Washington Irving is one of the prime examples of the type of writer who created the stories out of half-truth and half-fiction — much like the region wherein he lived. A classic example of his work combining fact and fiction is arguably the most famous horror story by an American: "The Headless Horseman." This story has a basis in fact from an incident in rural northern New Jersey during the Revolution, and has a mingling of fiction in that Irving reset and transposed the tale he heard about to rural New York. Not only did Irving possibly get the inspiration for the story from New Jersey, he also possibly got the main character's name, Ichabod Crane, from the Presbyterian Church graveyard in Morristown.

As with the two other regions of the United States, the issue of the American Indian was never far from a writer's consciousness. Rivaling Irving in popularity and combining the native tradition into his writing was James Fenimore Cooper. Cooper and Irving are probably the two most remembered writers from the period before 1850 whose work mixed themes of historical fact and prose fiction, and with some exceptions, are still avidly read today — certainly more than any historian of the period is.

Only one known writer took as his fictional topic the one American whom Americans could not seem to get enough of in works of nonfiction historical narrative: George Washington. James McHenry published *The Wilderness, or Braddock's Times* in 1823. In this work, McHenry humanizes America's hero through his activities during the French and Indian Wars.

Young Washington is represented as finding in the settler's ward (really Mary Philipse) a person whose attractions and tastes, thanks to her tutelage by an Indian prophet, he declares "'better than any met with in society.'" He sues most eloquently for this elegant lady's favor, presents her with a copy of Shenstone as a token of his affection, and, in the guise of an Indian chief, saves her from the villainous Frenchman at Fort Le Boeuf, only to learn that she has been previously betrothed to a young man of the wilderness. He thereupon resolves, high-minded gentleman that he is, to devote himself to his country.[10]

Even in fiction, Washington must be "high-minded" and committed to his country. Interestingly, McHenry has Washington don a native disguise as though the moral rectitude of the natives and of Washington himself were one and the same. The mystical impact of the Indian prophet also lends itself to Washington mythology in the sense that he (Washington) was somehow in communication with higher powers. By 1835, the time that Jared Sparks was publishing his *Writings of Washington,* the mystical connection with Washington and the supernatural founding of the United States was reaching fever pitch. Catharine M. Sedgwick wrote that at the mere mention of his name "a sentiment resembling the awe of the pious Israelite when he approached the ark of the Lord" was palpable among those present.[11]

Memoir

In addition to the histories and novels being written about the Revolutionary experiences of Americans, another popular subset of the written historical genre was the memoir. Plenty of writers undertook this format, and as such they fall within the scope of this work. Yet, their approach was not necessarily in line with the evolution of American historiography which led in part to the creation of the first chair of history at Harvard in 1839. This particular style (memoir) allowed for more of the unknown individuals, the common soldier among others, to leave his mark via the written word in the format of a historical narrative of his adventures. Perhaps the most famous of these soldiers was Joseph Plumb Martin, whose *A Narrative of Some of the Adventures, Dangers and Sufferings of a Revolutionary Soldier, Interspersed with Anecdotes of Incidents That Occurred Within His Own Observation* was originally published in 1830, anonymously. Martin's account was largely forgotten until it was resurrected by Dr. Francis Ronalds, superintendent of Morristown National Historical Park, who brought the first edition in the Morristown collection to the attention of George F. Scheer.[12] Scheer edited the volume and published it as *Private Yankee Doodle*; it has not been out of print since the 1950s in its resurrected form.

While the Martin story is fairly commonplace among most of the memoirists, one of the most unusual has got to be the case of Israel Potter. His story entailed not only a memoir, but also a short novel by one of America's greatest writers, Herman Melville. The story is important because unlike other writers, novelists or historians, Melville chose to focus on a true unknown. Rather than build a story around the heroics of the great leaders, Melville chose to turn his tale around the virtually invisible exploits of a common soldier, a man who was a prisoner, a beggar for fifty years, and ignored by his country. In some measure, Melville invokes Potter as a cover for his own disenchantment over his reception into America's literary world. For Melville, "the hero of the *Life and Remarkable Adventures* [of Israel Potter] was a common man of limited perception and depthless virtue, whose fidelity to his cause led him into misadventures and oblivion. Such a guileless, innocent victim was an irresistible subject for satire."[13]

Potter's tale was first told by Henry Trumbull of Providence, Rhode Island, in a work published on January 30, 1824, under the title of *The Life and Remarkable Adventures of Israel R. Potter.* Potter was indeed a real individual who experienced more than his share of misfortune in life. In some ways, reading it brings to mind the circumstances of which Voltaire writes about in *Candide.* While *Candide* was fiction, *The Life ... of Israel Potter* was not, mostly. After experiencing personal humiliation and unfortunate outcomes to life's challenges, Potter suffers the indignity of anonymity and pauperism in England for over fifty years, having been effectively stranded there as a prisoner during and after the Revolution. Making his way back to his native Rhode Island, he finds he is utterly forgotten and ignored aside from Henry Trumbull who puts his story into print. Yet, all the while during "captivity" Potter felt his country must surely be waiting for him to return.

Henry Trumbull was far from a serious literary man. Much like Mason Weems, Trumbull was well qualified to take a compelling tale and twist it into something virtually unrecognizable from its original. The "bizarre and incredible book is so much of a piece with Trumbull's other writings, so neatly fits the pattern of tall tale and shopworn melodrama, that an attempt to discover in it the truth of Israel Potter's life would seem a futile proposition."[14]

Trumbull was not, however, without his generous side. Ever attuned to the chance to make money, he saw in Potter an opportunity to fashion a yarn about an obscure New Englander. Not just obscure either, but totally unremarkable, completely unknown, someone who had seemingly never had an ounce of good luck in his life. Potter, to Trumbull, was as common as grass. Yet, this could not necessarily be his stated selling point. Therefore, Trumbull took yet another episode of hard luck in Potter's life and fashioned it into the preface of the memoir to explain his purpose in writing.

His motive for doing so, [writing about Potter] which he states in a preface to the memoir, was to assist Potter in obtaining a pension from the United States government for his service in the Continental army. Potter's application for a pension had already been rejected on the ground that he had been absent from the country when the pension law was passed in 1818, but a petition to Congress for a special exception was still pending at the time of the publication of the *Life and Remarkable Adventures*.[15]

Whether the inaccuracies were invented by Trumbull to heighten the sales potential, or whether Potter's memory was confused, or whether they both worked to pad the narrative to help Potter's pension case is really unknown. Given the potential for real money to be made from an exciting story, and with a history of these types of memoirs selling, it seems reasonable to conclude that both men had pecuniary interests in telling the best possible tale for public consumption. Sadly, for later-day historians of the Revolutionary era interested in researching the experiences of the common soldier, when "the narrative enters upon the period of the Revolution, when the seminal events of Potter's life transpire, it deviates from the truth at almost every turn."[16]

Potter was actually a captive taken from the American ship *Washington* in late 1775 and transported to England as a prisoner with other seamen. Sadly, this is where the story really enters fantasy—with one exception. For whatever reason, Potter (or Trumbull) fabricated an entirely new episode of his early time in England. This fantastic tale signified that by this point in the memoir "Potter's credibility has eroded to the exact point of absurdity where Herman Melville chose to abandon the memoir for his own wild inventions."[17] In other words, Potter and Trumbull's fiction was not suitable for a professional novelist like Melville.

Still, Potter did in fact somehow make his way to France and met with Franklin as his memoir claims. And he does seem to have served as some sort of courier (between England and France), perhaps for Franklin, getting stranded in England before he could make a third trip to Paris from England. But, was Potter a true spy, or more of a mule? Was he aware of his role, actively pursuing intrigue and espionage? And, if so, whom was he communicating with in England presumably for Franklin?

The Israel Potter episode reveals just how far nationalism, patriotism, history, and money can all be put to the ethical and factual test. The disingenuous approach employed by Trumbull (assuming Trumbull was the more guilty party) would barely be tolerated by a tabloid today. The singular aspect of altering the events of the Revolution seem strange, given that there were plenty of survivors still alive in the early 1820s when Trumbull and Potter published their work. Still, "for all the blame that once could have been assigned to the careless authorship of Henry Trumbull, we can now see that Israel Potter himself was responsible for most of the inconsistencies, errors, and inventions in the *Life and Remarkable Adventures*. For Potter, the lies were a matter of survival."[18] So much of the Potter story is today infected with untruth that really nothing beyond the bare outlines of the story is accepted as genuine—and there is debate about that too. What does however make the whole episode so compelling for its inclusion into this story of American historical writing is the fact that history can be so easily twisted and distorted without anyone seeming to challenge it. As was the case with Mason Weems, the public appetite for a good story about a virtuous man unjustly beaten down by fate but never giving up his American pride proved a successful combination—for everyone but Potter. After his petition failed, "Potter was escorted from the limits of the town of Providence to the adjacent town of Cranston, where he had been born unwanted and half-named" nearly seventy-five years earlier.[19] He is believed to have died in 1826. It is this canard, this duplicitous irony, which drew Melville to the story twenty-five years later.

Melville's Twist

By the time Melville repackaged the story into a novel, it is fair to say there were no living veterans of the Revolution who could "fact check" by memory. Melville had nothing to be concerned with regarding trying to obtain a pension for service rendered like Potter had to. For Melville the artist, he sought to take the story, warts and all, and twist the tale to read as a historical novel, while at the same time criticizing the American public for their gullibility. Melville sought to write a wicked work of irony masquerading as a historical novel, which no one would be able to pin down one way or the other.

Melville begins his story of Potter by describing the country from whence the fictional Potter came—the Berkshire region of Massachusetts, which was home to Melville at the time he wrote the work. For Melville, Potter is as pure and stable as the land he sprang from:

> To this day the best wood choppers, come from those solitary mountain towns; a tall, athletic, and hardy race, unerring with the axe as the Indian with the tomahawk; at stone rolling, patient as Sisyphus, powerful as Sampson.[20]

In this opening paragraph Melville hits virtually every quality necessary in the mythical Revolutionary War hero. Potter is as precise with his utility tool as the Native American—a symbol of courage and ability. Potter, like the land he comes from, is athletic and hardy, qualities necessary in a soldier, especially one fighting against tyranny and struggling to create a new nation. Naturally, a soldier in the Revolution needed patience; the war lasted eight years, so Melville gives Potter the patience of Sisyphus. Strength too was necessary to defeat Britain; hence Potter is compared with Sampson. The land Melville paints of Potter's birth is pure America, New England to be precise. Of course, it is also fiction, for Potter was from Rhode Island.

Melville was having fun with the story of Potter produced by Henry Trumbull thirty years prior. More importantly though, Melville was having fun with Americans and what he saw as their seeming gullibility to believe or desire to believe the most sentimentalized or romantic aspects of their past, and in particular their founding. Their whole perception of themselves seemed bound up in the way they viewed the founding of their country, and Melville was keen on mocking that sham historical viewpoint. Melville was someone who in many ways had a bone to pick with American readers and chose to pick it by insulting their ignorance, by appealing to their patriotism. The forced patriotism which Melville found he of course thought shallow and historically uninformed. The entire work is one long, extended meditation on satire; and of course it is as much fiction as Trumbull's account written thirty years before.

Essentially, Melville's short story represents the uses, misuses, and abuses of American history. Melville's brilliant work encapsulates all of the emotional awareness which history, especially patriotic history, can generate and how that energy can be manipulated through a reading public that is seeking validation for themselves by linking with the past. *Israel Potter* could easily be the one work students today should read and discuss to learn virtually everything they need to know about history and how people consume history and choose to understand history.

7

George Washington— Retirement and Death

•••••

After his death, Washington's life itself provided guidance or reflection on the course of American national history. After nearly 150 years of imagining a history for America (roughly 1650–1800), historians suddenly *had* history. History meant having something in the past, not current, not alive. Washington was certainly dead in 1800, and he certainly provided a centripetal focus around which to structure American history. After ten years of existence as a republic under the Constitution, the United States in 1800 could finally start to establish itself through history.

Washington's life episodes were tied or linked to the developmental episodes of the colonial experience. As such, Washington was, and still is, an extremely fruitful and bountiful subject for study. To the historical profession, Washington is the gift that keeps on giving. He is in historical terms an Everyman. Whatever virtue, lesson, model or moral a writer seeks to impart or portray, they can usually find the quality they desire in some episode of Washington's life, whether it really happened or not.

The most recent "blockbuster" biography to appear about Washington is by Ron Chernow. It is a massive book (apparently the longest single volume about Washington ever published) befitting its subject.[1] In a review of the work in a September 2010 review for *The New Yorker* magazine, Jill Lepore ranges far afield in describing how the various incarnations of Washington's biographers over the years have all had trouble defining exactly who he was. In a caption under a graphic depicting Washington in multiple guises, Lepore writes that "every biographer of George Washington has remarked on his inscrutability; every generation has tried to figure him out."[2] In fact, the truth of the matter is more likely that instead of figuring out who George Washington was, each generation was rather trying to figure who they were by trying to see their collective reflection in Washington. And they instinctively turned to the one figure who, chameleon-like, changes and adapts to the needs of every generation. "Washington's contemporaries saw in him what they wanted to see," just like future generations.[3] And this was not just the result of changing patterns throughout history. Washington himself, ever obsessed with his image, ensured that even during his lifetime no one knew who he was, including perhaps even Washington himself.

Referring to the various collected editions of Washington's writings since Jared Sparks published his in 1835, Lepore writes:

> Sparks eventually published eleven volumes of Washington's writings, together with a one-volume biography. In 1893, Worthington C. Ford published the last installment of a fourteen-volume set. An edition of thirty-nine volumes was completed in 1940. Of the University of Virginia Press's magnificent "Papers of George Washington," begun in 1968, sixty-two volumes have been published so far. But, for all those papers, Washington rarely revealed himself on the page.[4]

Lepore's point of course is that with such a reticent and guarded individual as Washington, can we ever really know him? Perhaps the question is rather do we need to know him? Is it not enough that we have him to fashion into whatever our generation or any other generation needs him to be?

Since Washington has given so much and most of that has occurred after his death, a brief reminder of his final years is in order. After his death, the tale of his life became the standard upon which to structure American history. Whether through his personal life history approached in biography or through the life history of the American nation through biography, the central figure, unquestioningly, above all others, was and is George Washington.

The death of George Washington in December of 1799 set off a wave of reflection across the country upon the meaning of his life and death. By 1800, both his life and recent death had become so intertwined with the new United States in many minds as to be almost indistinguishable from one another. It was nearly impossible to talk about the man without invoking the country, and vice versa. His character and mannerisms became what the country collectively aspired to in varying degrees of seriousness. The specter of Washington, the idealized version of his civic attitude, held sway over the developing country. Reminiscent of classical figures out of Plutarch, Washington became a lawgiver, a conqueror, a peacemaker—any title that could promote the new country and establish a virtuous citizenry could and would be placed on Washington in an effort to inspire his countrymen.

This practice for all intents and purposes served to anoint Washington in life and especially in death. He became the leader in a way that is hard to imagine in twenty-first–century America. Reality, myth, truth, or falsity mattered little in the creation of accolades of his life. Whatever accolade was chosen, it had to have a dual purpose: not only to highlight the contributions of George Washington and express the veneration which the country had for him, but also the accolades needed to promote some aspect of civic virtue thereby linking the life of Washington to the life of the country. George Washington in death became what he could not—not for lack of trying—in life, deified.[5] The process of linking the founding of the country with divine intervention was sealed in a way only Washington's prominence could ensure.

Retirement

In a postscript to a letter to Jeremiah Wadsworth on March 6, 1797, Washington wrote that "on the 8th I expect to commence my journey for Mt. Vernon."[6] With little fanfare, the former president had decided to quickly vacate the President's House in Philadelphia. His anticipation of still being pulled into public events was low; Washington later wrote to his nephew Bushrod that "I little thought when I retired ... that any event would happen, *in my day,* that could bring me again on the Public theatre."[7]

Washington and his family left Philadelphia on March 9, 1797, one day behind schedule and less than a week after John Adams was sworn in as president. Washington and his wife Martha made the social rounds to bid farewell and happily turned the government over to the new president. Without apparent pause for concern, the Washingtons left the urban hustle in Philadelphia for the tranquil and familiar pace of life at Mount Vernon. The first transfer of power peacefully in the new republic went off without a hitch.

Upon returning, Washington quickly resumed his place in the Potomac River plantation society. His status as a leader within the society was only magnified by his status as *the* Founding Father. Washington took all this adulation in stride. He had been for decades consciously and continuously cultivating his character. He recognized his status as a private citizen though and famously sought neither status nor riches from his position, although he acquired both. As Washington saw it, being a private citizen in a free country was all that was needed. Even that other George, King George III of Great Britain, was impressed by Washington's voluntary relinquishing of power.

The larger Washington family too found the change rewarding. Washington's step-granddaughter wrote to a friend that "since I left Philadelphia everything has appeared to be a dream ... [and] if it is a dream I hope never to awaken from it."[8] It is hard to argue with the beauty of the Mount Vernon estate and how it could evoke a dreamlike quality. With the Potomac River nearby, rolling hills, forests, and farmland stretching to the horizon, Mount Vernon seemed to offer everything needed or wanted for living a good life.

Plantations were miniature, self-contained islands. Virtually everything necessary for living was available or could be made available. Food, shelter, clothing, recreation; all the amenities one could wish for, one could have. Their concept however was sometimes at odds with the attitude toward life which some plantation residents maintained. Plantations allowed those who ruled them to live without the problems associated with city dwelling. Cities were, and are, monuments to compromise. Anywhere that large numbers of people come together to live, the necessity to accommodate the predilections of others is required to maintain a harmonious environment. None of these worries existed on a plantation—if you ran the place. Thomas Jefferson is well known as someone who strongly disliked city life in part because it required him to compromise his cherished attitudes toward life in a way he was not required to do at Monticello. The same approach was in part at work in Washington. Plantations were insular by nature, while many who lived on them (excluding those enslaved) were not insular. Rather, many kept very active social calendars which included a variety of amusements designed for the elite class.

The prospect of living within a tight community of landed gentry and sharing the benefits of the insular slave-driven economy was enticing to many. Although it would have been difficult to penetrate this community as an outsider, Washington and his family were guaranteed to move with ease in this social circle. Even without his lengthy and distinguished service to the country, Washington's pedigree and advantageous marriage would have guaranteed his continued participation in the most elite levels of the planter society in tidewater Virginia.

Keeping Track

The familiar routine of social interaction with his neighbors was a continual source of enjoyment. Washington enjoyed people and he liked to be with them, on his terms. He had his intimates, but he also had his relationships that were based more on acquaintances as a farmer/planter than on social equality with other plantation owners. He was well known in the community as someone who conducted his own business and maintained a day-to-day participation in the running of the estate. Washington knew what was being done at Mount Vernon, and he knew who was doing it.

Although the keeping of account books was an ongoing process, one example from January of 1799 shows how much Washington knew about Mount

Vernon. Washington occasionally signed the account of livestock on the Mount Vernon estate himself instead of his manager signing for him. It was called an account "of stock belonging to the Estate of Mt. Vernon."[9] The estate was broken down into seven administrative units such as Mansion house, River farm, and Muddy hole. The first entry for 1799 shows 449 animals were tallied for the seven units.[10]

In the farm ledger for 1797–1799, the most often listed types of workers were carpenters, gardeners, bricklayers, coopers, spinners, sewers, and knitters. Although intermittent entries are by his managers, Washington himself regularly signed in approval of work accomplished in a similar manner as for the livestock accounts. The entries concerning personnel were weekly compilations of production, income, and expenses.

These account books are part of the record of the once financially powerful Mount Vernon estate. They record the vast enterprises which made up the Mount Vernon estate and thus the wealth it afforded Washington and his family.

While it is difficult to attempt to translate factors of wealth across centuries, it can be safely understood that Washington was a very wealthy man when he retired in 1797. Years of moderately successful land speculation, diversification of commodities at his farms, and various other investments enabled Washington and his family to enjoy a lifestyle only a very few could emulate. "The first president was also likely the richest in relative terms, perhaps the only commander in chief of his day who would have made the Forbes 400 Richest in America."[11] By Washington's own calculation, his lands and investments totaled $530,000, an enormous sum for pre–1800 America.[12]

Yet, even his great wealth did not ensure Washington complete idleness in retirement. The mansion itself needed constant work. Washington wrote that Mount Vernon was "exceedingly out of repairs"; "I am already surrounded by joiners, masons, painters, etc., etc."; and "I have scarely a room to put a friend into or to set in myself without the music of hammers, or the odoriferous smell of paint."[13] Combined with the never ending overall management of the estate, Washington's retirement at times seemed anything but relaxing.

Death

The scene at Mount Vernon on December 14, 1799, is something written so widely about it needs repeating only in outline. Just to review the basics: George Washington went for a ride to survey his plantation on December 12. As he was leaving early in the morning the weather did not portend severity, and he did not prepare for the nonetheless everpresent chance of inclement weather. Washington was out for several hours, and in fact the weather did take a turn for the worse. He was subjected to howling winds, freezing temperatures, and rain, sleet, and snow without proper clothing. For someone who made his reputation partly by surviving the terrible winters during the Revolution, the fact he contracted his fatal illness from this exposure to terrible winter conditions on which he based his reputation is somewhat ironic. (Of course during those earlier Revolutionary periods, Washington was comfortably cared for. As an example, during the worst winter of the war, 1779–1780, in Morristown, New Jersey, Washington, along with Martha, was warmly ensconced in the Ford mansion.)

Returning from his farm tour in the mid-afternoon on the 12th, Washington immediately had dinner without changing his cold, wet, clothes, despite multiple requests for him to do so—he was hungry. Despite a hot meal, he quickly began to feel sick, specifically with chills and a scratchy throat. "You know I never take anything for a cold. Let it go as it came."[14] Thus did Washington respond to a suggestion that he treat the beginnings of a supposed cold which first appeared in the afternoon of December 12, 1799.

After dinner, and after spending a short time in his study, he went to his bed chamber early and went to bed. The next day, December 13, Washington wrote, "Morning snowing and abt. 3 inches deep. Wind at No. Et., and Mer. At 30. Contg. Snowing till 10 O'Clock, and abt. 4 it became perfectly clear."[15] Due to the weather early in the day he did not venture out except for a short time late in the day. By late afternoon he was feeling ill, and by bedtime he was complaining of a sore throat. Sleeping comfortably for a few hours he woke up not long after midnight and told Martha he was feeling worse, particularly his throat. During that cold, dark night Washington suddenly felt himself sinking further into illness amidst a suddenly growing resignation that the end was near. Martha, following Washington's wishes, did not send for Dr. Craick until the next morning, the 14th. Word quickly spread throughout the Mount Vernon estate that the great man was seriously ill.

The Sequence

The surviving versions of Washington's last days are not necessarily consistent as to the exact sequence of events, although, they do agree that he did indeed die on the evening of December 14, 1799.[16]

In most accounts, Washington is seen as having delayed sending for help during the night of the 13th or the very early morning of the 14th due to concern for Martha or members of his household staff. The night being too severe, Washington did not wish to risk anyone else's health. This delay, while admirable concerning the health of others, may have proved too cautious on the part of Washington in the long run.

Although the sources differ slightly as mentioned, it is clear that Washington was subjected to frequent bleedings and intestinal purges during the day of the 14th, after the doctor arrived, in an attempt to remedy his condition.[17] Various poultices were applied to Washington's throat and chest without result. His body was blistered also at various points in an attempt to draw out the infection.

Washington consistently declined attempts to provide drug sedatives to ease his discomfort and help him sleep. As the Founder revered above all others, it was left to him to perform the last supreme act of his life; he needed a fearless death. The accounts that have been published concerning Washington's death show a heroic Washington resigned to his fate and are generally seen as factual. Whether these stories are in fact an accurate description or the attempt at early hagiography, is unknown.

George Washington died at approximately 10:00 p.m. on the frosty night of December 14, 1799. It is known that Washington requested not to be buried until after three days.[18] The fear of premature—or live—burial was quite real in a day when medicine did not always correctly diagnose death.

In their account of Washington's death published in the *Times of Alexandria* on December 19, 1799, Drs. Craik and Dick wrote that when they arrived at Mount Vernon they found Washington to be suffering from an "inflammatory affection of the upper part of the windpipe."[19] By the late nineteenth century, "modern" interpretations of what caused Washington's demise began to appear. Over a half dozen attempts to identify the exact cause appeared before 1950.[20]

In 1997, Dr. White Wallenborn, of the University of Virginia School of Medicine, wrote a paper providing the latest modern interpretation of Washington's last illness and death. In it, Dr. Wallenborn discusses his reasons for indicating that Washington suffered from acute epiglottitis.[21]

Commemoration Begins

Word spread quickly throughout the country that the most important Founder had died. Biographies and lesser monographs appeared immediately after his death—in fact, Mason Weems had actually started his "biography" before Washington passed. These early works were quite popular, particularly those that tended to accentuate the myths of virtuous living, like Mason Weems' book. These myths provided simple lessons on moral rectitude designed to inspire his countrymen, even, and especially, the children. His life thus became something of a morality play. Lying, cheating, friendship, patriotism, among others, became lessons from Washington's life that were now brought out and used to educate his fellow citizens in how to be good members of society.

Washington's public life became the model for national unity, virtue, and character, while "biographers always celebrated Washington as the ideal republican leader."[22] His private life was wholly unimportant compared to the benefits to be gleaned from studying his contributions to his country. To encourage the development of a virtuous citizenry, Washington had to reflect the "symbol of two centuries of national history."[23] With his death a process of remembrance began that has continued virtually unabated for over 200 years.

In the first decade of the twenty-first century, books about George Washington continue to be written in large number. A new education center and museum opened at his Mount Vernon estate (a historic house museum since 1853) at the cost of tens of millions of dollars—all private donations. For a nation badly shaken by the attacks on September 11, 2001, and their aftermath, Washington is still seemingly instinctively looked to for inspiration.

Civic virtue and ideals tending toward patriotism were concepts that the Washington ideal was best suited for. Even today the small book of chivalric aphorisms which Washington compiled (he copied them, he did not originate them) is available nearly everywhere. In fact, the integration of this ideal has been so complete after 200 years that in some ways any restructuring of that ideal is akin to apostasy.

The Country Mourns

In the December 20, 1799, edition of the *Centinel of Liberty, or George-Town and Washington Advisor,* a detailed account of the funeral of George Washington at Mount Vernon was presented. The report began:

> On Wednesday last, the mortal part of Washington the Great—the Father Of his Country, and the Friend of man, was consigned to the tomb, with solemn honors and funeral pomp.[24]

The scene setting is fraught with multi-layered meanings of George Washington and immortality. While the scene described was carried out within days of Washington's death, commemorative events would occur throughout the United States over the next several months, each one designed to mourn, reflect, and challenge Americans to fulfill their obligations as citizens and virtuous members of the new republic.

Many of these events did not occur until, or after, February 22, 1800, Washington's birthday, due partly to the significance of the day, and to the national day of mourning that was called by congress and sponsored by Congressman John Marshall. Marshall factors greatly in the story of Washington's remembrance through the printed word and will be considered in chapter nine.[25]

In his biography of George Washington, the Hudson Valley writer Washington Irving wrote that "a deep sorrow spread over the nation on hearing that Washington was no more."[26] And, it was not just in America that George Washington was mourned. Lord Bridport, in command of over sixty British naval vessels, ordered his ships to lower their flags to half-mast.[27] Even Napoleon ordered "black crepe [to] be suspended from all standards and flags throughout the public service for ten days."[28] The remembrance of George Washington occurred in ways which served a variety of purposes, which were destined to last to our own day.

The Will

Thomas Jefferson's tombstone lists the accomplishments for which he most wanted to be remembered. Likewise Washington's will can attest to a similar feeling: "I George Washington of Mount Vernon—a citizen of the United States—and lately President of the same."[29] Washington identifies himself as a citizen; a former president; someone who had great power over other men but gave it up. It was perhaps his greatest lesson to posterity. Power is transitory; one does not have lifetime power in a government of the people.

Much has been written about Washington freeing his slaves through his will. He actually freed them only contingent upon Martha's death, and then only the slaves which were his before their marriage. Therefore, those who were enslaved on December 14, 1799, were still enslaved on December 15, 1799, the day after Washington's death (with the exception of his manservant, William Lee). Yet, the act of placing such a statement in his will indeed set him apart from other Founders. He also called for his heirs to financially care for those ultimately freed who needed assistance, which his heirs did until 1839 when the last freed slave died.[30] This act of caring for his freed slaves for forty years was quite unusual as well.

Washington was particularly generous to educational interests, perhaps reflecting his regret that he had never acquired a formal education. Even during his life Washington generously gave money and his good name to educational causes. One such institution, Washington College in Chestertown, Maryland, is alone among eponymous Washington institutions of higher learning in that the college founder actually received Washington's permission to use his name. To this day, the school rightly treasures that story of using Washington's name.

Washington did not leave his fortune to one individual, which was the custom in the planter society. His nephew, Bushrod Washington, a newly appointed associate justice on the United States Supreme Court, did however receive the largest part of his uncle's estate, including the most recognizable possession in Washington's financial empire: the mansion house—Mount Vernon. As relates to history, Bushrod received all of his uncle's papers. This bequest would ensure that Bushrod, willingly or not, would be a part of Washington's legacy for the rest of his life—although he would ultimately end up totally overshadowed by his uncle's reputation. Bushrod was considered a worthy inheritor of the Washington legacy. Although not of the physical presence of his uncle, Bushrod more than made up for that with his intellectual presence—ironically something his uncle George always felt uneasy about concerning his own lack of formal intellectual attainments.

Part III

......

Washington, always conscious of his role, worked in his later years to revise many of his own writings to more accurately reflect scenes and episodes that perhaps were not clearly stated at the time of original creation. With Washington's death in 1799, America could look to the new century and a new history unencumbered by the most famous and contradictory figure associated with the Revolution.

For historians, the outlook was now what to make of the Washington persona—rather than the actual man—in their work. Many biographies appeared during the early nineteenth century, the most notorious of which was by Mason Locke Weems. On the other side of Weems was the work by the Chief Justice of the United States Supreme Court, John Marshall.

Here again though, history would be called into play for its role in political calculations. Thomas Jefferson would wage a low-grade war against his cousin John Marshall's biography and go to his grave never having countered the work, though not for a lack of trying. Finally, it was left to Jared Sparks to accomplish two things in the realm of American historical writing: (1) Sparks published by far the largest set of original source materials up to that point on an American historical figure: George Washington; (2) Sparks was appointed to the first chair of history at an American college: Harvard.

8

Ramsay and Weems: Biographers

••••••

The remainder of this work will focus on the efforts of a few representative writers who sought to present Washington in a new light, and with him the American historical experience, through writing. American historical writing in the immediate decades after Washington's death (1800–1820) would have looked quite different had Washington survived another ten years. Writers and historians could not approach Washington in the same manner if he were alive as they did after his death. Mason Weems would probably never have concocted the story of chopping down the cherry tree if Washington had still been alive.

As important as Washington's life was to the founding and establishment of the United States, his death proved to be a seminal event for the defining of the American story through print. It thus became necessary to come to terms with his life's work. His death saw the creation of nearly a separate industry devoted to attempting to place his life in historical perspective and its meaning into context. Those two desires—historical perspective and contextual meaning—are with us to this day.

Similarly, the need for validation from the past for contemporary viewpoints is no doubt stronger today than 200 years ago. In 1800, the debate over what America was, or was to be, had really just started and could really only begin in earnest once George Washington had passed. His figure, his contribution, his meaning, could not be writ across the entire American experience while he was still alive. In many ways his death at a relatively young age (sixty-seven) allowed the country to finally enter into a debate and learning process about itself.

Immediately after his death, the first such projects began to take form and will be considered in this chapter. John Marshall, Mason Weems, and David

93

Ramsay each wrote biographies within the first ten years of Washington's death. Within the first forty years, a virtual forest of works had been produced, each one claiming to expound the "real" Washington (very much like the nearly endless stream still being produced today).

With Washington's death, the work of the biographers began in earnest. Too severe and opaque to contemplate while alive, Washington, after his death, allowed historians to adapt his life to the scenes of national greatness, which many earlier historians had already attempted without the Washington figure so available as it was now in death. With the ability to write about Washington in the past tense, historians could focus his various qualities to the needs of not just history and nationalism, but to citizenship concepts as well.

One of the most famous of the early period of George Washington biographers was Parson Mason Weems.[1] Weems' work today might be likened to an unauthorized biography at best. Rather than being a "tell all" type of work, it is a life of Washington turned into a sermon for civic virtue. Filled with myth, hearsay, and flat-out lies, Weems' work—while entertaining—is not taken seriously today. Yet, initially it sold phenomenally well and is still in print as of 2014.

Mason Weems

For the first truly financially successful "biographer" of Washington, Mason Weems was much less than the romantic, civic-minded figure he made Washington out to be. Weems spent the entire Revolution in England, although he was born and raised in Maryland. Upon returning to the United States he attached himself to Matthew Carey, the Philadelphia publisher who first collected Washington's writings into bound volumes for sale. Weems also sought during the period every chance he could get to connect with Washington personally, or at least Mount Vernon. Weems "understood Washington's iconic power ... and his work as a bookseller gave him ideas about how to turn the great man's fame into money."[2]

Weems utilized to great effect his own status as an ordained Anglican minister. Weems "used Washington's piety as a means of appealing to patriotism and public duty."[3] It was this mixing of Washington and religion that fueled later attempts to connect Washington with some sense of Christian revelation and destiny, particularly in relation to the Revolution. Writing about historians of the colonial seventeenth century, Samuel Eliot Morison makes an observation which is applicable to Weems and many of his type in the nineteenth century:

In seventeenth-century New England she [Clio, the muse of history] wore the preacher's gown. The main object of our primitive historians was to prove that God, in spite of occasional severe chastening, had a very special interest in New England as a holy experiment in Christian living.[4]

It was left to Abigail Adams, a woman whom few could overwhelm with embellishment, religious or otherwise, to comment that "To no one Man in America belongs the Epithet of *Saviour*."[5] Abigail Adams was not impressed with attempts to deify Washington as a secular political saint.[6]

Weems' *Life* was the most popular publishing venture he undertook himself. What exactly Weems was after—beyond money—still remains something of a mystery. Weems was a master at cultivating public sympathy and feelings. His work contains seemingly endless morality tale vignettes designed to appeal to a foundational belief in right and wrong. Truth or validity regarding Washington's life, though, was simply ignored by him in building his vignettes around Washington. Money can certainly be seen as a prime motivation, but why a book then about Washington? Someone like Washington, who so consciously lived his life in a manner to be perceived as beyond reproach—how could that person, be seen as a fit subject for a biography? His life was so staged, so almost un-genuine even for himself to write; he never did attempt an autobiography. Yet, Weems managed to put enough skin on the subject of Washington's life to make himself famous as a writer, and moderately well off through sales of his biography. Weems came to be seen as such an expert on Washington and so identified with him that John Marshall's publisher Caleb Wayne later employed Weems to help sell Marshall's biography of Washington. What all that says about the American public in the early 1800s is no easy task to sort out. In many ways, Americans come across as rather simplistic bumpkins, unable to grasp the fuller meanings of Washington's life without the assistance of storytelling. It is curiously reminiscent of the use of stained glass windows and carved motifs of medieval cathedrals; it's just that Weems crafted his imagery with words, not glass or stone. Henry Cabot Lodge, in his own biography of Washington decades after Weems, wrote that to the "average" American who purchased Weems' book, "its heavy and tawdry style, its staring morals, and its real patriotism all seemed eminently befitting the national hero, and thus Weems created the Washington of popular fancy."[7] It may be natural that someone who was held so high for so long in life would become something of a caricature in death.

As a former Bible salesman and a natural pitchman, Weems is easily transformed into an equivalent of a modern televangelist.[8] His crusade, though, was via the printed word, and that word used as its example the shining life of George Washington, however much he had to fabricate it.

Weems' creation then went beyond the mere fable he wrote. He identified a coalescing idea among Americans, comprised of patriotism, religion, and myth-making. Weems created a Washington superhero that was incapable of being questioned because Weems provided the ingredients but did not specify quantities. This ensured that readers could individually select the amount of patriotism, religion, or fiction, and still have a story compelling to them. In this manner, Weems' Washington could never be without his admirers. And, because of the money that could be virtually guaranteed by writing about Washington with Weemsian overtones, "Weems's imitators produced an increasingly outrageous array of myth, legend, and outright fraud in the name of recovering Washington's humanity."[9]

Mason Weems took upon himself the task of writing the moral life of George Washington (and by extension of the country) by attributing to his life qualities respecting hard work, production, and virtuous living. Like other biographers, Weems saw Washington as a "symbol of national unity"; an "embodiment of the national character," and as an "emblem of American greatness."[10] Weems' instructional biography was meant to guide young Americans starting out in life. "By conceiving of Washington as an industrious businessman Weems spoke for the new rising generation of middling entrepreneurs and others eager to get ahead."[11] Conversely, Weems, as a good churchman, looked back to a period in American colonial history where perceived Biblical qualities of honesty, truth, hard work, and discipline determined one's character.

Weems' work nonetheless did correspond with the general trend in literature at the beginning of the nineteenth century. "Literature was supposed to be morally instructional," and many writers responded in large measure to accommodate this belief.[12] Without a long history of heroes and heroines to point to, American writers, those concerned about the fate of the new Republic, sought to craft lessons into their work. Whether nonfiction, or increasingly fiction, more writers sought to utilize their work to convey a message of morality and citizenship and to connect the two as one.

There is no evidence that Washington's nephew Bushrod Washington had anything to do with Weems or others like him. The approach Bushrod favored was decidedly more bookish, more learned; much like Bushrod himself. The American people however, would ultimately deem otherwise. Even during his lifetime, "Serious scholars held Weems in low esteem."[13] Gordon Wood, in his recently published tome in the Oxford History of the United States series, was a bit blunter: "The maudlin moralizing efforts of Parson Mason Weems to humanize George Washington for ordinary people were a vulgar perversion of the ennobling art of history-writing."[14]

Washington and Memory

Naturally, try as we might, we will never fully recover the humanity of Washington. In part, this is the way Washington wanted it. His approach to his character was methodical. He planned every episode as though it were theater, with himself as director and star. When writers fawn over Washington's bearing and public demeanor, it is actually a carefully plotted and choreographed presentation of Washington's own design to which later writers were referring. In many cases, Washington's life requires a theater critic rather than a biographer to understand it. Washington was essentially two men: "a private, carefully hidden Washington, whom no one except Martha ever really met, and a public, meticulously cultivated Washington, on display for popular consumption."[15] His letters are filled with his agonizing debates over his reputation and how a particular event might impact his carefully crafted image.

Washington's image to the American people was more important anyway. His actual life was secondary, especially immediately following his death.[16] Essentially then, it is impossible to know the "real" George Washington. But that really is not important. The important aspect was, and is, what he represents to anyone and everyone who chooses to claim him for their specific cause. Against the odds, Washington actually has become a king. A monarch is someone who embodies the hopes and aspirations of a population in a variety of circumstances. A monarch provides a steady course of continuity through generations, and although Washington has been dead over 210 years he is "resurrected" to play his new role as the times demand.

Many Americans lament that school children do not know who Washington was, or that his picture is not in every classroom like a religious figure. What most of the adults don't recognize about the entire arrangement is that Washington did not know himself, so why do we expect students to know him? Adults who claim to know Washington of course only know their version of events, events designed to make them feel superior and confident in their own station in life. And hence, Washington provides that comfort, that reassuring authority that is necessary to haughtily profess one's superiority to the world. That is what being a monarch enables one to do. That is what Washington enables us to do.

The continuing reliance on Washington begs the question of why? What is it about Washington, or more importantly what he represents, that we still need? In an age which loudly proclaims the virtue and triumph of democracy and the failure of monarchy, why is it that the United States in the twenty-first century still needs to worship Washington and what he represents? Henry Adams seemed to ask this very question in his 1880 novel *Democracy*. Adams, one of the shrewdest observers of the American scene from a family of shrewd observers, puts an understanding of the Washington mythos into the mouth of the character of Senator Ratcliffe (the name itself a shrewd observance of the rodent-like qualities of politicians that Adams observed) when the senator states

> In those days [Senator Ratcliffe's youth] General Washington was a sort of American Jehovah. But the West is a poor school for Reverence. Since coming to Congress I have learned to find what a narrow base his reputation rests on. A fair military officer, who made many blunders, and who never had more men than would make a full army-corps under his command, he got an enormous reputation in Europe because he did not make himself king, as though he ever had a chance of doing it. A respectable, painstaking President, he was treated by the Opposition with an amount of deference that would have made government easy to a baby, but it worried him to death. His official papers are fairly done, and contain good average sense such as a hundred thousand men in the United States would now write. I suspect that half of his attachment to this spot [Mount Vernon] rose from his consciousness of inferior powers and his dread of responsibility.[17]

Adams was not blinded by the standard treatment of Washington mainly because of his deep family history with the Revolutionary period and of their continued service to the United States. His great-grandmother, Abigail, had written herself about Washington's undeserved deification. The Washington family by contrast in 1880 had all but disappeared.

David Ramsay

Rembrandt Peale's portrait of David Ramsay shows a man of bearing, seated in front of well-stocked bookshelves facing the viewer without a hint of flinching. His stylish clothing shows buckling at the buttons on the vest around an expanding waistline. He is not wearing a wig, exposing his thinning hair. His wide eyes are inviting and sympathetic. He seems a perfect dinner guest.

Ramsay is particularly important to this study because of his biography of George Washington, published 1807. Yet, before he tackled the subject of George Washington in written form, David Ramsay had already made a name for himself. As an academically trained physician, he found little in the practice of medicine that attracted him. Rather, he soon began to explore the foundations of the American story through the printed word. During the Revolution he was taken prisoner by the British in South Carolina; released, he was elected to the Continental Congress. He actively promoted a stronger central government and worked diligently in favor of the new Constitution by 1788 to see to its ratification in South Carolina. As a historian, Ramsay "took command of the past for the Federalists who, with the ratification of the Constitution, gained control of the present."[18]

David Ramsay was one of the most prolific of the first generation of Revolutionary and post–Revolutionary American historians. Ramsay's first work was the *History of the American Revolution,* published in 1789, the first full year of existence for the United States under the Constitution. Like other early historians of the Revolution, Ramsay relied heavily on British sources, particularly Edmund Burke, who compiled the *Annual Register,* which contained a great deal of information on the Revolutionary War.[19] For the time period, Ramsay was probably "the most active historian in his day in the United States."[20]

David Ramsay was born April 2, 1749. While the youngest of his siblings, Ramsay lacked nothing in comparison with his accomplished older brothers. His early brilliance led to acceptance at the College of New Jersey, from where he was graduated in 1765. Among his classmates at the college in the early 1760s were several future leaders of the United States, including James Madison, William Paterson, and Oliver Ellsworth, to name a few. After graduation Ramsay taught school in Maryland and on Virginia's Eastern Shore. He entered medical school in Philadelphia in 1770 and graduated in 1773. A year later he moved to Charleston, South Carolina, where he would spend the rest of his life.

With the onset of the Revolution, Ramsay became involved with the war effort. He became a surgeon to a local militia and simultaneously was elected to the state assembly. He served on various committees throughout the war and met with the tangible consequences of that service in 1780. That year, the British captured Charleston and exiled Ramsay and others to St. Augustine, Florida. He was released a year later and returned to South Carolina to resume his political and civic activities. Ramsay found himself elected to the Continental Congress in 1782 and served for one year. During this time he toggled back and forth between the state assembly and the Continental Congress. More importantly though, it was during these years in the early and mid–1780s that Ramsay began to write and study history seriously.

Ramsay's big break initially came in 1782, when as a member of the Continental Congress he had access to the official papers of the United States. He also had ready access to members of the Congress and through them some of the best connections in the country. These contacts served Ramsay well in his research.

It was also during this time, with his medical degree safely relegated to a secondary position as a career, that Ramsay began to espouse for the more muscular central government that would provide the oversight he saw as necessary for a great nation to prosper. He was well known among the highest circles of American leadership and often played crucial roles in important debates. His writing signaled a departure from the types of historical narratives that predominated prior to the Revolution. His work "illustrated the change that independence wrought in American historical writing."[21]

Ramsay's *History of the American Revolution* marked a turning point in the development of an avowedly nationalistic historical study. Therefore "Ramsay's study must ... be regarded as the major event in the development of a distinctly national historical consciousness."[22] As the first and most prominent, Ramsay sought to use his works to secure a fully united, cohesive, American approach to the past. Ramsay himself wrote that he sought to promote a "homogenous people" out of the varied experiences of the colonial experience.[23]

Ramsay's reliance on interviews with famous figures from the era also set his work apart slightly from others of the period who relied exclusively on written records. This method was by no means unheard of, yet it was unique for the history of the Revolutionary War. His combination of original sources, secondary sources, and interviews put Ramsay at the forefront of the written history profession as it existed in his lifetime.

As a romantic, Ramsay had high hopes at the successful conclusion of the Revolution and the promises this held for the people of the United States. These high ideals not being met in Ramsay's mind, he began to feel abandoned by the lofty pronouncements espoused during the war years by many of the leaders. That was why news of the Constitutional Convention meant so much to him. He thought Americans had been given a second chance.[24] "During the war we thought the termination of that [event] would end all our troubles. It is now ended three years & our public situation [is] as bad as ever."[25]

As a member of Congress, Ramsay had access to records and members as aids in furthering his research. Throughout the early 1780s Ramsay's circle of connections increased as he broadened his efforts. His work was moving along steadily by the mid–1780s. Ramsay saw the debate of 1787 in connection to the Constitutional Convention as the last best hope for his country.[26] In the end, Ramsay's strong defense of the Constitution at the state ratifying convention was considered to have cost him a seat in the new Congress. His constituents felt him to have been too northern in his viewpoint—not sufficiently southern. Ramsay's political career—never his main interest—was essentially over by 1795.

Like other historians of the period, Ramsay failed to make a living from his writing. He made a name, but not a living. He often lamented this fate not only from a financial perspective, but from the perspective of American writing overall. Ramsay saw the future of the young country as bound with its cultural, artistic, and intellectual pursuits. He took his role and work quite seriously. He corresponded with and knew many of his contemporary writers, and they formed a virtual mutual-aid society that provided encouragement and an opportunity to share their experiences in the writing and publishing world.

Historian

Ramsay's *The History of the American Revolution* was published in 1789—the first year of operation for the United States under the Constitution, which was drafted two years earlier in 1787. The year of publication portended good sales for Ramsay. With the United States celebrating its new cohesive government, the publication of a history of the event which ensured the celebratory moment in 1789 could occur. Moreover, Ramsay saw his work in the same light as most of his contemporaries; he "saw historical writing as a vehicle for fostering nationhood, an instrument for promoting the kind of unity, even homogeneity desired by most nationalists."[27]

Similar then to his contemporaries, Ramsay saw history as a tool rather than a process of objective enquiry. Ramsay's tool of history sought unity, connection, and political bonding to ensure national survival. For Ramsay, "historical writing was not so much an end in itself as it was a means to cultivate the political and moral consciousness of the present and future generations."[28]

Ramsay fit into a long line of writers in all genres who since the early seventeenth century had struggled to compare the New World favorably with the Old. This comparison moved beyond the physical similarities and dissimilarities into the topic of culture—an area about which American writers were particularly sensitive. By 1789, with a successful Revolution and a new constitutional government in power, Americans saw a general overall cultural cohesion that could not be found in Europe and indeed allowed Americans to claim superiority in one aspect of their larger culture: their political system. And for Ramsay, who actually postponed publication of his work until he knew the fate of the draft 1787 Constitution, unity, particularly state unity, was paramount.[29] In many ways, "Ramsay was as sensitive as any intellectual of his era to the kinds of divisions, real and potential, that tended to separate Americans and undermine the unity he sought."[30]

Ramsay's America had a long lineal descent founded upon English ideals, law, and government. Ramsay sought to link Americans across the decades back to the early seventeenth century in an effort to provide a seamless story. This was very much in keeping with his overall approach to the future of the United States, where he saw faction and party strife as the biggest enemy of a unified nation. If Ramsay could show through his history the long-term connections that have existed since the founding of the colonies, he felt he could set the historical stage for the future. "He feared that disunity would rend the fabric of the new nation" and that "it would become prey to the great European powers, even if it did not destroy itself from within."[31] (It is somewhat ironic that Ramsay lived for decades in South Carolina, the first state to secede from the Union seventy years after the publication of his work, which he hoped would pass down through generations as a testament to a unified country. In a sense, the battle lines which erupted in 1860 during the United States Civil War were in part laid down in a very cursory way during the last decade of the eighteenth century when Ramsay was writing. No one alive at the time seriously thought the nation would rip itself apart. Yet episodes like Shay's rebellion, the Whiskey rebellion, and the half-hearted attempts to separate New England from the rest of the country offered a chilling premonition for what could happen should the "experiment" in self-government prove less than successful—and Ramsay was terrified of that prospect.)

Ramsay's Thoughts on History

It is difficult to say that Ramsay's work contains philosophy. He adapted selections from other writers (what we would call plagiarism), which instantly calls into standing his reputation in the field of history today. Aside from that, Ramsay's greatest focus as a writer would have been on his interest in the unification of the states into a country. While not in and of itself deep thinking, Ramsay sought to present his readers with a total package combining government and citizenship; "history had only one major use, as Ramsay saw it, and that was the lessons it could provide for contemporaries."[32] His America was homogenous, much like the approach taken by his fellow historians. This is one reason why Ramsay was as energized over the prospect of the new Constitution in 1787 as described above.

Taken in its totality, Ramsay's work varies very little from his contemporaries concerning motive, result, and execution. His approach was not completely objective; rather, "his complete view of the American past was one long 'lesson' that the record displayed."[33] As with all victors who write history, the vanquished always drove their foes to battle. In Ramsay's view, and every other writer of the period, "England drove the Americans to revolt and forced them to set up an independent nation in which they could retain their earlier political and social equality."[34]

Ramsay's Legacy

Like any early historian or writer, Ramsay has come in for his share of criticism by later scholars. In Ramsay's case, his scholarly crime was plagiarism. The charge of plagiarism against Ramsay stemmed from the intersection of two works, the British *Annual Register* and William Gordon's *History of the Rise, Progress and Establishment of the Independence of the United States*.[35] "The

Annual Register was a yearly summary of events, published in London and largely edited by Edmund Burke."[36] It featured significant contributions by Gordon. Yet, Gordon is known to have utilized Ramsay's early work in his work, and Ramsay could be seen simply repaying the compliment, as it were, by generously utilizing Gordon's work.[37]

While certainly not accepted today as methods worthy of emulating by aspiring historians, Ramsay's other career as a physician likewise probably offers little to emulate by today's aspiring physicians. "If his historical work appears too simple for the standards of scholarship today, he did furnish interpretation, a point of view, that met the needs of his readers."[38]

The most important lesson that can be drawn from trying to understand a person from the past through the wisdom of the present is that it was indeed the past. Things were done differently, whether in history, medicine, or law. This is not to suggest that some type of relativism predominates in explaining and studying the past. To simply dismiss any profession's ancestors is the height of hubris. In short, we need to get over ourselves. Two hundred years from now our descendants will likely dismiss us in much the same way as we dismiss the past, relative to what we today see as incompetence.

The most curious charge of plagiarism concerning this study though would revolve around the topic of Ramsay's "use" of John Marshall's biography of Washington. While appropriating other writers' work was nothing new (in fact it was rampant), Ramsay's use of Marshall's work was adding complexity to an already existing complex situation.[39] Marshall himself was criticized for lifting the work of other writers, who themselves had possibly been accused of the same practice. Therefore, it is conceivable that by the time Ramsay's *Washington* appeared, portions of the work had been copied three or more times. A contemporary reviewer wrote of Ramsay's *Washington:* "With regard to Dr. Ramsay's book, it is plainly an abridgement of Mr. Marshall's, written, we presume, upon the supposition that a moderate octavo is more likely to be read than five massy quartos [which Marshall produced]."[40]

While simply copying the work of another is today rightly rejected as grossly inept and unprofessional (and in certain cases involves legal consequences), it did have a slightly less negative quality attached to it well into the nineteenth century. Ramsay's "habit of copying his sources literally was largely a custom of the era in which he lived." While not a totally absolving reason for lifting another's work, even in historical context, Ramsay and his contemporaries still deserve enormous credit and praise for advancing the concept of history as a written art form and for laying the groundwork for the development of the discipline of history into the field of study we recognize today.

Ramsay, however, still maintains a place apart from his contemporaries because he refrained from a too overly simplistic approach to history as understood in his time. This in and of itself is an incipient view to the modern standard of historical writing, whether scholarly or popular. Not only was Ramsay not too simple or superficial regarding American exceptionalness, he did strive—in the manner of acceptable standards in the eighteenth century—for a value-neutral interpretation or presentation of history that nonetheless sought to bring his countrymen together. This has made him one of the very few—if not the only—historical writer who is still recognized today—however reluctantly.

9

Bushrod Washington and
John Marshall Write
The Life of George Washington

••••••

John Marshall

John Marshall was born on September 24, 1755, near Germantown, Virginia, on the then western frontier in what became Fauquier County. His father, Thomas, was a member of the Virginia House of Burgesses, the advisory council to the Royal governor. Through his mother, Mary, Marshall was connected with the powerful Randolph family, which included Thomas Jefferson.

Marshall had a fairly typical childhood for a member of the Virginia gentry in colonial times. He was privately tutored at the Westmoreland County Academy, where he was a classmate of future president James Monroe. Marshall was also prepared for the semi-aristocratic lifestyle he was expected to lead, given his fortunate birth into a powerful family. There was little in his childhood which would indicate his future career path. Tradition seemed to have fated Marshall for a life in Virginia's planter/gentry society.

When armed hostilities in the American Revolution began in 1775, Marshall was twenty years old. Appropriately with his tradition-bound upbringing, he was chosen as a lieutenant in the Culpepper Minute Men and saw action at the battle of Great Bridge.[1] During the war, he fought at Brandywine, Germantown, and Stony Point. Marshall also spent the winter of 1777–1778 at Valley Forge. He attained the rank of captain before leaving the army in 1780 to study law with the learned jurist and law professor George Wythe at Williamsburg.

John Marshall must surely have had one of the shortest legal educations on record. For just three months he studied to prepare for the bar. This did not go unnoticed. Without referring to Marshall by name, one student wrote that "those who finish this study [law] in a few months, either have a strong natural parts or else they know little about it."[2] Throughout his life, Marshall's legal acumen would be questioned by those with greater education or preparation. Nonetheless, Marshall was admitted to the bar in Fauquier County and moved to Richmond in 1783 to improve his professional prospects. Indeed, Marshall's business prospered considerably with cases dealing with the debt owed to British creditors by Virginians from the war years. These types of disputes would form the basis of the case work of the first decade of the United States Supreme Court during the 1790s.

In 1796, one of these legal actions, *Ware v. Hylton*, was argued before the Supreme Court with Marshall advocating for the defendant Daniel Hylton and Alexander Hamilton advocating for the plaintiff John Ware. This case would be the first and only case Marshall argued before the Court over which he would preside as Chief Justice a few years hence. Unfortunately, Marshall lost his case but apparently did not diminish his prospects for future employment on the Court. President Adams appointed Marshall Chief Justice in 1801.

Perhaps Marshall's greatest quality was his stability and devotion to the new nation. Throughout the late 1790s, Marshall was called to positions (ambassador, congressman, secretary of state) within the federal government. His advantageous birth also helped to ensure his name was never far from consideration for special assignments. Even earlier, while in Richmond tending to his practice, Marshall served in the Virginia state government and was a member of the Virginia ratification convention in 1788 debating the federal constitution. Here, he worked with James Madison, Bushrod Washington, and others to advocate for passage of the new federal constitution. His first federal appointment from President Adams was to the post of diplomat in the delegation to France in an effort to ease tensions with America's Revolutionary War ally.

More than anything else, this mission brought Marshall to the attention of the country. The XYZ Affair, as it came to be known, did nothing to lower the already high tensions existing with France and in part contributed to President Adams' reelection failure in 1800. The XYZ Affair involved three French ministers who sought to bribe the American delegation (Marshall, Charles Cotesworth Pinckney, and Elbridge Gerry) before entering into negotiations with them. America at this time was in a quasi-war with Republican France, and President Adams had sought diplomatic channels to reduce the tensions between the two former allies. While the negotiations failed as a result of the attempted bribery (Marshall's refusal to participate made him a hero in the United States), the quasi-war fortunately never moved beyond the posturing stage.

Upon his return to the United States, Marshall ran for Congress at the urging of former President George Washington. Washington also urged his nephew Bushrod to run at the same time. Terrified at the prospect of being a politician, Bushrod nonetheless did his duty. In the midst of the congressional race, to Bushrod's great surprise and relief, his old law teacher James Wilson, associate justice of the United States Supreme Court, died. President Adams nominated Bushrod to replace Wilson, and Bushrod accepted without hesitation. This allowed him to withdraw with dignity from the congressional race and to pursue the career he desired.

Marshall, however, did win his race and spent six months (December 1799–May 1800) in the House of Representatives—where his most memorable contribution was promoting the idea of recognizing President Washington at the national level on February 22, 1800, the first birthday after the former president's December 1799 death.

In May of 1800, President Adams appointed Marshall Secretary of State, and in January 1801 Adams appointed him Chief Justice of the Supreme Court. Marshall spent the next thirty-four years charting the course which made the Court a force in American life.

The list of Marshall's achievements on the Court are the subject of countless books and articles, and the study of his role shows no sign of diminishing—in fact, it seems to be on the upswing. One aspect of his years on the Court, though, which is often overlooked, is his role as a biographer and literary man. In this role he worked very closely with his good friend Bushrod Washington for nearly thirty years, and this aspect of Marshall's career will now be considered.

An Idea

When George Washington died in 1799, his papers were inherited by his nephew Bushrod Washington. Already an associate justice of the Supreme Court (although newly appointed), Bushrod was a respected figure in his own right and someone with an ever expanding workload. Even if he preferred the quiet life, his famous last name ensured him constant attention. Partly for this reason, he turned to his close friend John Marshall when the idea of a biography occurred to him. In the months immediately following Washington's death, Bushrod did entertain working with Tobias Lear (a secretary of Washington's) on preparing an edited version of his uncle's writings—although nothing came of this.

While some evidence exists to suggest that Martha Washington requested that John Marshall write a biography of her husband, most standard evidence points to Bushrod Washington as the originator of the plan.[3] Whatever the sequence of events that precipitated the creation of the *Life of George Washington,* Martha no doubt would have had an opinion one way or the other, although because nearly all of her correspondence was destroyed, her views are unknown. However, it is hard to imagine her being against the project.

Regardless of the stature and prominence of Marshall, the real impetus for a biography of Washington came from those Washington family members closest to him. His nephew Bushrod was most connected with the notion of a biography of Washington and of the need for one to be compiled sooner rather than later. In general, the public too can be seen as having a say in the final decision of starting the biography by exerting pressure. The desire on the part of the public to read about Washington through his correspondence was certainly strong, and this feeling did not go unnoticed. However, it was Bushrod and Martha who controlled access to Washington's writings. Also, Bushrod and Martha were desirous of seeing a more balanced treatment of Washington appear as an "official" written portrait of the man. They no doubt knew it was only a matter of time before any manner of written exposition of Washington's life appeared for sale, and they wanted to get their version out in as timely a manner as possible.

In many respects, Bushrod was seen as the natural candidate for the job of biographer. His intellectual bent and scholarly demeanor were well suited for the task. Yet Bushrod was already heavily invested in editing the Virginia State Court reports for publication. Additionally, Bushrod was not as well exposed to the world of rough and tumble politics, which he knew his uncle's life had come to represent. No matter how objective he or the eventual author would be, partisans and critics would certainly pillory the final product. With that in mind, both Bushrod and Marshall knew who would ultimately have to undertake the task.

Marshall was not a bad choice to approach for the project. Important in his own right, he had been a friend of President Washington's. He served during the Revolution and spent the hard winter at Valley Forge in 1777–1778. Marshall himself, twenty-three years younger than Washington, was nonetheless very familiar with the man and his activities. While not known in the professional sense as a writer, he was someone accustomed to crafting narratives for public consumption.

Similar to other historians who preceded him, Marshall sought to convey not just the essence of Washington or the historical facts; he struggled for a grander theme of placing Washington's life squarely in the forefront of civic responsibility. Marshall and his fellow Washington biographers "treated the individual life in terms of the virtues represented that were suitable in the author's conception to a republic."[4] Still, Marshall was a genuinely laudatory follower of Washington's.[5] In fact, Marshall's father, Thomas, was a friend and colleague of Washington, and John was no doubt familiar with many stories about that relationship.

John Marshall, Author

As the Chief Justice of the United States, John Marshall was someone looked upon with the ability to produce a dignified and accurate biography of the first president. Indeed, Marshall was tasked to produce a work of "Great and Permanent Importance."[6] Marshall himself was reluctant to start the project partly due to the amount of time he knew would be necessary. Besides being Chief Justice, Marshall was married to a semi-invalid wife who required attention from him. Marshall also had business interests requiring his time and effort. Squeezing the job of author into his busy life was not something he decided on a whim. In the end however, Marshall did consent to writing the biography, and by early 1802 plans were well developed for the project. He was partly swayed by the initial financial outlook of the venture. The prosperity of the project was premised on "tens of thousands of prosperous Federalists who could be depended upon to purchase at a generous price a definitive biography of George Washington."[7]

Money

Part of the story surrounding Marshall and the biography is the fact that he needed money. Marshall was a land speculator beyond the means of his salary as Chief Justice and what family money he had. One of the reasons he conceded to undertake the biography was simply the financial prospect of a large payoff from the completed work. In 1802, Marshall was in debt for over $30,000, and he needed extra income to pay down the costs of his land speculation. Marshall and Bushrod however, wildly estimated that they could each earn $75,000 with a proposed five-volume set. This was based on 30,000 subscribers of five volumes each at $1 per volume.[8] Unfortunately, "Marshall and Bushrod made extravagant estimates of the prospective sales of the biography and of the money they would receive."[9] Their estimates were based on not just George Washington's popularity, but on the prosperity of those who most identified with Washington politically.

Marshall and Bushrod settled on the Philadelphia publisher Caleb P. Wayne to bring the manuscript prepared by Marshall to the reading public as a finished product. Wayne was a Federalist and editor of the *Gazette of the United States,* a Federalist newspaper. During the negotiation process with Wayne, Marshall began working on the first two volumes. The negotiation was protracted in part due to the overly optimistic views of Marshall and Bushrod. Wayne attempted to temper their enthusiasm by pointing out that 2,000 was the highest number of subscribers ever for an American publication and 30,000, as anticipated sales, was sheer lunacy—even if it was about the great Washington.[10] Furthermore, the highest amount ever paid for a copyright was $100,000; the $150,000 asked by Bushrod and Marshall was again totally unrealistic.[11] (In Marshall's calculations he forgot to factor in the share of the profits for the publisher. The new calculations, based on the expected total of $150,000 had to not only be split between Bushrod and Marshall, but also with Caleb P. Wayne, their publisher.) As an experienced publisher, Wayne should have been more insistent on just how unrealistic this calculation was. His efforts to dampen Marshall's enthusiasm were not overly effective.[12]

Getting Started

The final contract was signed on September 22, 1802, between Bushrod Washington and C. P. Wayne. Oddly, Marshall's name does not appear in the contract.[13] This was partly because Marshall sought to conceal his authorship from his cousin, President Thomas Jefferson. Marshall rightly feared Jefferson would see the biography in a partisan light. In fact, when Jefferson found out about the work he was concerned that it would influence the 1804 election.[14] Thus began Jefferson's futile journey discussed in chapter five, which lasted until his death in 1826, to find a historian who would write a counter-argument history to Marshall's work. There is no solid evidence that Marshall or Bushrod had any desire to try and influence the election however. Bushrod and Marshall were indeed Federalists, and Jefferson a Democrat-Republican; more to the point though, Jefferson by 1802 was hypersensitive to criticism and any perceived partisan attacks—even if he had to convince others that perceived partisan attacks were real when they were not.[15] Jefferson's attempt to thwart sales succeeded in significantly lowering profits. In this effort, Jefferson was more successful than in finding someone to write a counter–Marshall history. Yet ironically, Jefferson was among the first subscribers.[16]

Marshall began by seeking firsthand accounts of Washington through those who knew him best and those who worked alongside of him during his career. Marshall sent "letters to [Washington's] friends from Revolutionary War days and of the postwar period asking them for additional information about specific events and for their general reminiscences of Washington."[17]

Problems began immediately. Marshall, as Chief Justice, found he had virtually no time to devote to the project and began to fall hopelessly behind schedule. In the fall of 1803, a year after the contract was signed, Wayne was complaining to Bushrod about the delays. Worse though was the fact that of the 4,000 subscribers in the first year, many had begun to ask for a refund of their money.[18] Even when Marshall finally finished the first volume, it was so far over the original page estimate that Wayne nearly fell over. The extra costs involved with publishing such a tome would destroy his business.[19] Marshall sadly would come to realize that his lengthy tomes were financially overwhelming for Wayne. His physical estimates to write the projected biography—"4 or 5 volumes in octavos of from 4 to 500 pages each"—were just as unrealistic as his financial estimates.[20] The size and length of each volume would be a continual problem point with their publisher as the project advanced.

By November 1803, of the wildly enthusiastic estimate of 30,000 subscribers envisioned by Bushrod and Marshall, barely 4,000 could be tabulated. In early 1804, Marshall submitted the first volume to Wayne for publication. To add to Wayne's discontent over the progress of the project, Marshall requested that his name not appear on the title page. Wayne was dismayed after learning this. Marshall's authorship was a supposed selling point, and certainly every one of those 4,000 subscribers knew who authored the biography anyway. Now, to suddenly have an anonymous work appear would further stymie sales. The whole desire to keep Marshall's name a secret had become nothing more than an open secret. Selling subscriptions before publication was the traditional way to market books, and the anonymous approach to authorship insisted upon by Marshall would prove quite detrimental to sales, and Wayne knew that. Wayne wrote on December 31, 1803, to Marshall concerning his name on the title page that he wished "to have your name in the title, as I feel a confidence that it would enhance the value of the work in the public estimation."[21] Marshall ultimately consented to allow Wayne and Bushrod to make the final decision—however, under no circumstance would Marshall's title of Chief Justice be used; after "mature consideration and conviction of its propriety" he was willing to allow his name only; not under any circumstance however will "my title in the judiciary of the United States" be used—on this he would not alter his stance.[22] Marshall, somewhat tone deaf overall to Wayne's business concerns, could only write how he had decided to solidify and streamline his approach to the process of editing his work in preparation for publication. The less than smooth start of the project proved an accurate premonition to the project overall.

Marshall had assistance in selling his books door-to-door as was the method at the time through two professionals: Mason Weems (famous in his own right as an author as discussed in chapter eight) and John Ormrod. Ormrod was employed by Wayne to sell subscriptions to Marshall's *Life* in the north in presumably friendly, Federalist territory. Weems was engaged to sell subscriptions in the south, presumably in non–Federalist and less friendly territory. Of the two subscription salesmen, Weems undoubtedly was the most colorful and the best suited for working in "enemy" lands. Weems' curious mixture of religious revival salesmanship and nationalism on-the-go brought him into contact with much of southern America. Most of this America was not of the type that Bushrod and Marshall had in mind when they talked about all the Federalists who would buy Marshall's *Life of Washington*. Weems' America as opposed to the Federalist America that Bushrod and Marshall had in mind was truly rural. He had already come to know these Americans as an itinerant salesman of his own obtuse biography of Washington. Weems was so natural in this job because "he was a natural orator, a born entertainer, and expert violinist; and these gifts he turned to good account in his book-selling activities."[23] In essence, Weems sold more than books. He sold himself as a minstrel whose talents were quite broad and extraordinary. There is no way to really know how many copies were sold due to Weems' efforts, but it is fair to say, given the overall sales total, that it was not many.

His influence moreover was not just with his clients. Weems early on in the process of selling subscriptions to Marshall's *Life* was aware of the attitude which was growing and would be detrimental to sales—that the work was perhaps seen as too political in motivation and wanting in substance. Weems wrote to the publisher Wayne imploring him to "drop now and then a cautionary hint to John Marshall, Esq." and encourage him to think more about his writing.[24] In addition to asking Wayne to have Marshall defend his work, Weems suggested to the publisher that Marshall should also consider adding qualities to color his work that he (Marshall) simply could not fathom—material like Weems used.[25]

Weems furthered his complaint to Wayne by suggesting that Marshall needed to say something (which he was loath to do because his involvement was "secret") to counter the negative impressions generated by Jefferson and others gaining credence about the purpose of the book. The charges were taking their toll on sales—"Jefferson's attacks on the yet unwritten work caused most of the Republican postmasters to refuse to accept subscriptions."[26]

After the publication of the first volume, which Marshall spent the entire length of discussing colonial American history rather than George Washington, he was anxious to get to work on the second volume and actually bring his work up to the period of Washington's early life.[27] However, Marshall was keenly aware that the first volume was not without its faults. Not only were just a handful of mentions made of Washington while Marshall spent the entire volume reviewing colonial American history, but the work was filled with mistakes. Marshall wrote, "I have also to sustain increased mortification on account of the careless manner in which the work has been executed."[28] Upon reviewing the published first volume, already sent to subscribers, Marshall wrote that he was "mortified beyond measure to find that it [had] been so carelessly written."[29] As William Jackson, a book reviewer in 1804, wrote, "whoever expects to see in a work thus rapidly written every sentence highly polished ... may not have their expectations answered, but it [volume I] has, nevertheless, conspicuous merit."[30]

When Marshall himself read the published version he was shocked at how crude some of his writing was; how unfortunate his choice of certain words and phrases. Marshall asked that Wayne understand that he could not possibly have the further volumes ready punctually as requested due to a lack of help and due to the fact that "experience has sufficiently admonished me of the indiscretion of sending another almost unexamined volume to the press."[31] He asked Wayne to forward any reasonable criticisms of volume one so that he may evaluate its veracity and possibly correct any mistakes or misconceptions in the already published volume. Marshall hoped that those criticisms "either friendly or hostile to the work may be useful if communicated to me," as he may have overlooked certain items in his own review.[32] Marshall consented to follow Wayne's advice regarding punctuation, as he regretted his "inability to correct when I see [grammar]" used in an inappropriate way.[33] Marshall too was concerned about his inappropriate use of paragraphs. He asked generally that Wayne would "amend any obvious impropriety in this or any other respect which you may discover."[34] Naturally though, this would entail more costs for Wayne through delays in marketing.

By mid–1804, Marshall completed the second volume, focusing on Washington's early life. The problem he saw by this stage in the process after volume two was published was that due to the accelerated production schedule (even though still technically behind schedule), and the continuing lack of time, the quality of the work was suffering in both content and accuracy. The first two volumes were not successful at all. At best, Wayne broke even, and his customers were requesting refunds due to delay and the careless editing of the volumes.

The reaction of the reading public to Marshall's work was predictable. Not one sale beyond the subscribers occurred at first. While not interested in large numbers in Marshall's work, Americans were still fascinated by Washington's life. Weems' 1800 biography was a far less serious—and in most places totally untrue—work but it was vastly more popular that Marshall's. Weems had had no access to Washington's writings from Bushrod like Marshall had. In this instance, the American public of the first decade of the nineteenth century seemed much more seduced by the Washington myth; the national, heroic Washington. This heroic Washington was designed as someone who could make you feel good about your country and yourself. Marshall's work, by comparison, while it didn't make you necessarily feel bad, was ponderous, cold, laborious, and redundant.

As to the public perception of Washington, one of the most unusual dichotomies concerning him and his death developed over the six years between 1799 and 1805. It was during this time that Washington died and Marshall (and Weems, and Ramsay) began publishing his biography. Also, Washington and Marshall's political foe Thomas Jefferson became president. More interestingly, for a nation which seemed to reach the depths of emotional despair after Washington's death, by 1805 they seem to have nearly forgotten him as a real person, if sales of Marshall's biography were any indication. Naturally, there were mitigating circumstances with Marshall's work (the cost, the long period of writing, the negative commentary from Jefferson) that no doubt impacted sales. Yet, for the country's savior, for its unquestioned hero, the work seemed destined for good sales—especially coming from a respected professional like Marshall. However, this did not happen. Americans overwhelmingly rejected Marshall's work, and ironically sought out Weems' moral biography in much greater number. Market analysis did not exist at the time so there is a great deal of speculation involved, but it would seem that American's were much more interested in the imaginary version of Washington that Weems created than the much more accurate personal portrait that Marshall produced.

Americans were interested in projecting their beliefs and aspirations onto Washington in an effort to promote themselves with an image of citizenship and virtue as a potentially obtainable goal for themselves. And if they could not reach this goal, they still had the image of Washington to admire and could still feel superior and proud of a country theoretically founded on the qualities that they wanted him to embody. Why muck that up with the more accurate or nearly accurate work that Marshall was offering?

Some good news arrived by the end of 1804—royalties. Marshall and Bushrod could count slightly over $4,000 each in payment received from Wayne.[35] Also, by February 1805, Marshall had delivered the manuscript for volume four. The completion of the next to the last volume was surely a relief. Just as helpful for Marshall's stress level was the completion of the Justice Samuel Chase impeachment trial. Associate Justice Chase was being tried in what many saw as a political trial orchestrated by President Jefferson to rid the Supreme Court of Federalist appointees. Had Chase been convicted, Marshall had every reason to believe he would have been next to face impeachment.

In addition to the Chase impeachment, Marshall was dealing with the one case most everybody today knows from high school history: *Marbury v. Madison.* The case, decided in 1803 just as the writing project was moving into rapid gear, was also a major reason for delays and errors in volume one.

While the fourth volume and the threat of impeachment passed, Marshall was left to ponder volume five. He was keenly aware of the criticism that the first four volumes were an "unattractive rehash of what had already been better told."[36] The fifth volume, generally considered the best of the series, was finished in the summer of 1806 and published in the fall of 1807. By this late date, even the overly optimistic Mason Weems had virtually given up on Marshall and moved on to selling other titles by different authors.

Evaluation

One major problem with volume one as already noted was the lack of an appearance by George Washington. Instead, volume one consisted of "the voyages of discovery, the settlements and explorations of America, and the history of the colonies until the Treaty of Paris in 1763 ... treated in dull and heavy fashion."[37] In response to criticism, Marshall in part blamed "the impatience ... of subscribers which had so hastened him."[38] In Marshall's view, the impertinence of the public forced him into compromises in his work. Largely though, throughout the project, Marshall was resolute in the face of criticism and constant pressure from Wayne.

Marshall's work did improve as he progressed through the five volumes. He clearly took into account the criticisms concerning the earlier volumes as he prepared the succeeding volumes, but not to the point that his unique folksy style was fully eradicated by volume five. In fact, identifying the author of volume one as the author of volume five would not be difficult as the continuity of workmanship is evident throughout. Still, the grammar and other inconsistencies he was criticized for early in the project did improve over the course of the work.

As a biographer present or past, John Marshall is alternately praised and criticized. His earnest efforts at composition were not what drove most of the debate however. Rather, Marshall's work as a biographer has been portrayed from varied perspectives. On one hand, Marshall is seen as a forthright amateur who became overwhelmed by the work after agreeing to undertake the task. Conversely, Marshall is seen as—while still an amateur—highly accomplished. His desire to use original manuscripts would be seen today as the symbol of responsible scholarship. Although his impartiality could still be questioned, his methodology was sound. Throughout the long gestation period his approach and commitment waivered and altered, and in some respects it could be said he never really finished the work, even after nearly thirty years of effort.

Marshall has not fared too well from modern-day reviewers. His work has been shown to be in more cases than not extensive copying of earlier works on the same subject. Most stop short of labeling Marshall a plagiarist. Instead, he comes across—in a more genteel description—as engaging in "unacknowledged borrowings."[39] While these misgivings exist in great number, it is just as easy to find supporters who, while acknowledging irregularities in how history is generally crafted, nonetheless, praise Marshall for his use of the original sources made available to him by Bushrod Washington. While there is plenty of blame or criticism that can accurately be leveled against Marshall, he cannot be criticized for his use of Washington's manuscripts. This act of utilizing original sources, while not unique to historians, singles out Marshall in fact for much praise and credit.[40]

John Marshall specifically dismissed the notion that his work was little more than plagiarism in the preface to volume one. Perhaps sensitive to the possibility of the charge of scholarly neglect and hoping to quiet any comments of that nature from the start, Marshall wrote,

> Doddesly's Annual Register, Belsham, Gordon, Ramsay, and Stedman have, for this purpose, been occasionally resorted to, and are quoted for all those facts which are detailed in part on their authority. Their very language has sometimes been employed without distinguishing the passages, ... by marks of quotation, and the author persuades himself that this public declaration will rescue him from the imputation of receiving aids he is unwilling to acknowledge, or of wishing, by a concealed plagiarism, to usher to the world, as his own, the labours of others.[41]

The issue confronted by the reputation of Marshall, or Jared Sparks, or any early pioneer in any profession is of course a comparison to modern-day practices. Naturally, in virtually every instance, this is completely unfair. Yet, it has and no doubt will continue as a proven source of debate for the few professional descendants who still recognize their (the early pioneer professionals') early contributions to a specific field, in this case John Marshall.[42]

All in all, Marshall's experiences as an author and historian would bedevil him to the end of his life in 1835 in one form or another. Through revisions, updates, clarifications, and abridgements, Marshall's work literally never ceased. For what he envisioned as a five-year project at best, he instead submitted himself to a nearly thirty-five–year odyssey.[43] This was not all for naught though; a contemporary one-volume abridged version is still available in print as of 2014. First editions of his five-volume set routinely sell for over $10,000.

Conclusion

Marshall was particularly strong in recounting events in which he had first-hand experience, such as the winter at Valley Forge and the Battle of Monmouth in New Jersey. Both of these events today loom large in Revolutionary era mythology, and both have been the subject of countless stand-alone historical studies over the years. Nonetheless, it is really to Marshall that credit must go for bringing the story of these two (and other) events to the attention of the reading public. More than any other section of Marshall's *Life,* the sections on the conduct of the war are the most nonpartisan (and best written) aspects of the entire work. Furthermore, it is in no small part due to Marshall that the course of Revolutionary historiography over the next two centuries was set in motion.[44]

Marshall's Supreme Court colleague Joseph Story wrote a review in 1828 wherein he praised Marshall's "close investigation, caution, patience, and steady devotion to the weight of evidence."[45] At the turn of the twentieth century, the scholar Herbert Osgood wrote of "well balanced judgment of the great jurist," while admitting that Marshall did borrow occasionally from other authors.[46]

The controversies that dogged Marshall would also envelop his successor in the Washington enterprise—Jared Sparks. While their respective "crimes" were not exactly the same, they and many others of their period have been banished from consideration today. Their fate has become oblivion with their very names regularly scoffed at in modern historical circles. Indeed, modern historians would certainly not consider themselves to even be in the same career field as someone like Ramsay, Marshall, or Sparks. Very much like a modern physician would cast dispersions on collegial ancestors, contemporary historians are far too ready to dismiss their professional forebears.

Over the nearly five years of composition, Marshall maintained a rigorous, disciplined schedule. During a period when some of the most momentous challenges came before the Supreme Court, Marshall held to his work on the *Life.* Indeed, Marshall delivered nearly seventy-five opinions from the period 1801 to 1807. Without exaggeration, Marshall was an extremely busy man during these five or six years.[47]

Absent from this larger picture of composition is Bushrod Washington. The picture that emerges during the years of writing is that of Marshall being left to the composition and business aspects of dealing with the publisher and in turn the public. While on the surface this is the picture that emerges,

Bushrod did in fact work much more on the later volumes. He created the contents pages, reviewed and edited the narrative, and helped to craft some of the language when necessary. Bushrod also intervened at the request of an exasperated publisher Caleb Wayne imploring Bushrod to try and get Marshall to work quicker. Bushrod was not always quick to act. This reticence on the part of Bushrod will be seen again twenty years later, when Jared Sparks enters the stage to work on his edited version of Washington's papers.

Bushrod and Marshall had a unique working relationship, which only developed more as the years went by. Aside from their work as colleagues on the Supreme Court, they became partners in the publishing process. Marshall was the writer; Bushrod though provided the two most important items that Marshall needed. Bushrod lent his last name, "Washington," and most importantly, George Washington's vast collection of papers, which he inherited.

Bushrod Washington

He was the single largest benefactor of the estate of the most famous man in the world. Largely forgotten today, Bushrod Washington's contribution to two main aspects of American history cannot be overlooked. As a largely loyal colleague of Chief Justice John Marshall on the Supreme Court, Justice Washington was part of some of the most foundation-building cases in constitutional law argued up to that time. Washington also was actively involved in trying to promote his uncle's legacy: first, as a willing partner with John Marshall in Marshall's work as a biographer; and, second, as a grudging partner with Jared Sparks in his project to edit and publish Washington's papers nearly twenty years after Marshall started his work. His contributions are more than enough to warrant a stand-alone biography, and perhaps someday he will be removed from his uncle's shadow long enough for a creditable treatment of his life to be written.

Just months after his uncle's death, Bushrod realized the obligation and trust which he held in his uncle's papers. His scholarly inclinations enabled him to recognize that he had a responsibility to posterity and to those currently alive who would benefit from a more detailed understanding of his uncle George.

To his friend, Dr. Morse, Bushrod wrote on February 18, 1800 (barely two months after his uncle's death):

So soon as I found myself the legatee of the papers of my late uncle General Washington, I presumed that the public would expect from me the history of a life so conspicuously employed as he was in the civil and military affairs of this country. Your observations have impressed me very fully with the propriety of having such a history prepared for publication as speedily as circumstances will admit. A diffidence of my own talents for such an undertaking, together with weak eyes and want of time will probably forbid me from attempting it; but I trust that the selection of a fit character may be in my power, and this I shall endeavor to make immediately.[48]

Bushrod Washington was born at Bushfield, the family estate in Westmoreland County, Virginia, on June 5, 1762, with his uncle George in attendance. Westmoreland County at the time sat between the Chesapeake Bay on the east and swamp land on the west. Today, the Chesapeake Bay still borders on the east, but Washington, D.C., now borders on the west. Bushrod was a colonial by birth at the end of the French and Indian (or Seven Years) War, a conflict in which his uncle George gained a considerable reputation. His father was John Augustine Washington. John was a younger brother of George and a member of the Virginia House of Burgesses. His mother was Hannah Bushrod, a member of a prominent Virginia family.

The Washington and Bushrod families' rise in the colonies were nearly identical.[49] Through hard work, advantageous marriage, and social and political connections, they prospered considerably throughout the eighteenth century, so much so, that even before mid-century, in 1743, the estate named Mount Vernon was created by Lawrence Washington, George's half-brother. It was George's full brother, John Augustine Washington, who married Hannah Bushrod and brought the two families together. John and Hannah lived for several years at Mount Vernon while George was away in the French and Indian War.[50]

Young Bushrod came into a world on the edge of great change brought about by events relating to the imperial policy of a world power. This same power denied his uncle George a military commission as a colonel in the British Army, despite his contributions during the French and Indian conflict. The year of his birth the British and French signed the Peace of Paris, ending the French and Indian War, which marked the beginning of the end of Britain's control over her thirteen colonies in North America. Three years after his birth, in 1765, the British imposed the first of a series of Acts designed to generate revenue to offset the high costs incurred during the recently ended French and Indian War.

Even on their plantation, Bushrod's family would have felt the impact of the new British measures—whether directly by paying the new taxes or indirectly by feeling indignant over the tax. Certainly through his father's exposure as a delegate, the Washingtons became part of the population in the colonies who were concerned over the new approach to colonial administration. In fact, in Leedstown, Virginia, a gathering of protesters in February 1766 included Bushrod's father, John Augustine.[51] They drafted several resolutions to express their displeasure. From 1760 to 1765, George served in the House of Burgesses with John, and the brothers no doubt shared information on the Stamp Act and its fallout.[52]

Bushrod spent his formative years in much the same manner as his peers. He was an introverted and bookish child who was privately tutored in the classics at the home of Richard Henry Lee. This experience provided Bushrod with exposure to the broader world, particularly England. Richard Henry Lee was educated in England and provided Bushrod with the benefits of a more cosmopolitan approach to life. There is no indication that he possessed any greater or lesser talents than others his age, other than his scholarly inclinations. He was, though, known as a small boy, often sickly. Much later in life, he was described as "about common height, of slight figure, sallow complexion, and straight brown hair ... one of his eyes apparently sightless, and the other having more than the fire of an ordinary pair."[53] Physically, he clearly did not take after his uncle George. Furthermore, Bushrod was described as "easy in manners, and affable, unaffected, unpretending, and as far as possible from stateliness."[54]

Bushrod entered William and Mary College in 1775 and graduated in 1778—the third year of the American Revolution, and returned home. He went back to Williamsburg in 1780 to study law with George Wythe at William and Mary, was elected to Phi Beta Kappa, and met another student who would become a lifelong friend and colleague—John Marshall.[55]

Bushrod appears to have enjoyed his time in Williamsburg. In a letter to his mother in July 1780, he wrote "my situation here ... is I confess as agreeable as I could wish having my choice in the Society of Gentlemen whose characters are good and examples edifying."[56] For most of the war, Bushrod seems to have been able to remove himself from the tragedy and hardship taking place around him. This was in part due to the fact that no active theater of war was nearby.

This changed in early 1781, when General Cornwallis entered Virginia and settled in Petersburg. Bushrod joined the local militia under Colonel John Mercer, which was part of Lafayette's larger army in Virginia. Bushrod was present at the Battle of Green Spring from which Cornwallis began his march to Yorktown.[57] At Yorktown, Lafayette's army—including the Mercer militia—joined forces with George Washington's Continental Army to defeat Cornwallis and effectively end the Revolution. Bushrod witnessed this event and demobilized shortly afterward and returned home.[58]

Return to the Law

After his brief military career, Bushrod furthered his legal studies by gaining admittance to the law office of James Wilson of Philadelphia in 1782 through the financial support of his father and uncle. Uncle George in fact went so far as to recommend Bushrod to Wilson, who was cautious about taking on a student. "Permit me to recommend my nephew to you," Uncle George wrote to convince Wilson of the ability of his nephew Bushrod.[59]

Uncle George was keen to encourage Bushrod to make the most of his opportunity in Philadelphia. He wrote to Bushrod, "Let the object, which carried you to Philadelphia, be always before your Eyes."[60] Bushrod seems to have taken his studies seriously and his uncle's admonition to heart. He wrote his mother that he intended "to devote my whole time to law."[61] Between the time spent with the legal scholar George Wythe in Williamsburg and James Wilson in Philadelphia, Bushrod, by 1785, possessed one of the finest legal educations available in the newly independent United States.

James Wilson

When young Bushrod Washington arrived in Philadelphia to begin his legal studies, Wilson was already an established figure of great stature, highly regarded as a jurist and as a historian. Although Wilson never wrote history for public consumption in book form, he laced his arguments with continual references to English history, principally political history. In his work as a legal historian and scholar, Wilson turned to his history books as often as he turned to his legal books. Wilson's library, from which Bushrod drew instruction, included important names in legal theory such as Montesquieu, Hobbes, Coke, Blackstone, and Grotius, among many others.[62] While Wilson was capable of preaching a torrent of legal philosophy in an instant, he seems not to have passed this predilection to Bushrod.

This reliance on historical precedent no doubt had its impact on Bushrod. After completing his studies with Wilson, in the 1790s he produced his own historical compilations on Virginia legal cases, which required a reliance on historical editing. More importantly, Bushrod was exposed to the possibilities of historical writing through Wilson's extensive inclusion of history in his work. This exposure left an impression on Bushrod in his eventual role as the inheritor and keeper of his uncle George's papers. These papers had unquestioned historical importance and the sensitivity Bushrod witnessed in Wilson's office was a part of his desire to see the collection utilized in a historical manner.

Wilson was one of the foremost legal scholars in the country and had a thriving practice. He was from Scotland and carried many of the elements of the Scottish Enlightenment thinking in his theories and legal work. As a student, Wilson himself had studied law with John Dickinson of Delaware, who had studied at the Inns of Court in London.

Wilson strove throughout his life to bring together the various elements of an emerging American consciousness. "Wilson attempted to blend the ideas of liberty and the rule of law with the new idea of popular sovereignty."[63] As one of only six men to sign both the Declaration of Independence and the Constitution, he had as much to do with the intellectual underpinnings of the American founding as any man. Wilson not only signed both of America's founding documents, he was instrumental in drafting both. Records indicate he was a seminal figure during the debates in 1776 and in 1787. Wilson's agile mind allowed him to address "the law in broad, often bold strokes that encompassed philosophy, psychology, and political theory."[64] Much of his writing outside of the law was reflected by his research about the law as well. In the new nation, virtue was of paramount importance for being a citizen. Wilson, through his writings, was most closely associated with those who saw citizenship as a "close relationship among public virtue, moral commitment to the public interest, and respect for the will of the people based on their intrinsic good."[65]

Starting a Practice

After concluding his studies with Wilson in April 1784, Bushrod returned home to Westmoreland County, where he married Julia Anne Blackburn and opened a law office. His practice did not thrive, though he did survive by making a respectable living on his own without assistance from his famous family. For the next four years, Bushrod was involved in politics and family matters that kept him confined to the Westmoreland County area. His father's death in 1786 left Bushrod, as the eldest, to run the estate and dispose of the property. He also paid many visits to Mount Vernon, where he and his uncle George spent considerable time discussing the political events of the day.

In 1787, the year of the Constitutional Convention, Bushrod was elected to the Virginia House of Delegates. The next year he served in the Virginia constitutional ratifying convention. In this capacity he argued and voted in favor of ratification of the federal constitution drafted in Philadelphia under the watchful eye of his uncle George at Independence Hall. James Madison, as a member of the same ratifying convention in Virginia, commented that Bushrod was "a young gentleman of talent."[66]

Following his less than anticipated success at a law practice in Alexandria, Bushrod moved to Richmond. This move allowed him to renew his friendship with John Marshall. Due to the frail health of his wife, and his own not too robust health, the Washingtons rarely socialized. Being industrious though, Bushrod edited, between 1790 and 1796, the Reports of the Virginia Court of Appeals. Bushrod also did legal work for his uncle. Throughout the spring of 1798, George Washington was involved with land purchases in Kentucky from Henry Lee. In a letter dated January 19, 1798, George Washington wrote to Bushrod that he "must request the favor of you to investigate this matter."[67] This work, which Bushrod undertook, involved not only reviewing the actual deeds, but also researching the exact location, size, tax responsibilities, and so forth.

While still practicing law in Richmond, Bushrod received a letter from President John Adams appointing him to the Supreme Court. By the letter from President Adams of December 20, 1798, Bushrod Washington became one of the youngest appointees to the United States Supreme Court. At 36, Bushrod was picked to replace his old law teacher, James Wilson, who had died. Bushrod's career on the Supreme Court lasted over thirty years, until his death in November of 1829 in Philadelphia.

On the Court

Bushrod Washington served as an associate justice of the United States Supreme Court from 1798 until 1829—one of the longest in history. His term coincided most closely with that of his Richmond friend John Marshall. While on the Court, Bushrod was a consistent ideological ally of Marshall. Bushrod was by all accounts a supporter of the muscular constitutional interpretation indicative of the Marshall Court. Rarely did he deliver an opinion contrary to Marshall. In fact, Bushrod disagreed with Marshall just three times, while writing seventy majority opinions and only one dissenting opinion.[68]

An able ally of Marshall, Bushrod himself contributed significantly to the development of American constitutional law. Among his most important contributions was the case of *Corfield v. Coryell* in 1823. In his opinion, Bushrod spelled out several fundamental rights that greatly impacted later constitutional jurisprudence. In particular, Bushrod highlighted rights dealing with the privileges and immunities clause of the Constitution. Specifically, Bushrod's opinion upheld the rights of states to presume certain privileges for its residents exclusive of nonresidents, and that laws delegating such privileges did not violate Congress's role in interstate commerce regulation.

In addition to his career as a Justice, Bushrod served in several high-profile capacities in the young country. For several decades, Bushrod served as the president of the American Colonization Society. In this role, he oversaw the efforts of his organization to lobby Congress for funding to establish a colony in Africa for black Americans; primarily those enslaved, but those who were free too. The money authorized would be used for purchases of land in Africa, transportation and other costs associated with the venture. His work with the Society was heavily criticized by abolitionists and some proponents of slavery.

Mount Vernon

Bushrod's stewardship of Mount Vernon was not very successful. After his uncle George's death, Martha lived on the third floor of the mansion until her death in 1802. Bushrod handled her legal affairs just as he did for his uncle George. During those three years, the decay of the house which had started even before George's death accelerated. The money necessary to keep a home the size of Mount Vernon upright was enormous, even with free labor. Bushrod, while he inherited the structure, did not inherit much actual cash to use for repair. In addition to repair and upkeep, the mansion Bushrod and his wife moved into was "emptied of everything" as a consequence of an estate sale held on July 20, 1802.[69] Bushrod purchased a few pieces, but nowhere near enough to fit out a mansion like Mount Vernon. Bushrod was forced to take a loan from prosperous friends in Philadelphia to furnish his version of Mount Vernon.

For the first twenty years he owned the property, it lost money. Bushrod had a job; he was not available most of the year to run the plantation. Overseers and managers could only do so much. A full-time presence was required. His wife Anne's various illnesses also contributed in occupying Bushrod's time and keeping him away from being a hands-on plantation owner.

Although his law practice was prosperous by now, it was not on a level to sustain Mount Vernon. Nor was his salary as a justice enough to support such an estate. Furthermore, his farms were not profitable, and Bushrod was thus forced to sell many of the slaves he inherited to raise money for the estate. This move further incensed abolitionists who wondered why the president of the Colonization Society could not set an example by letting his slaves become colonists in Africa.

While he consciously avoided the public spotlight that could easily have been his due to his name, Bushrod still could not avoid the obligations of his fortunate birth. His contributions to John Marshall's biography were enough to secure a place in American history. Yet, it would be Bushrod's work with Jared Sparks which garnered the most attention from later researchers.

Part IV

· · · · · ·

The final part of this work will focus on Jared Sparks. Referenced many times in the previous sections, Sparks straddles the mid-nineteenth century world of history as a figure of both the old-school and new-school of historiography.

Through his prodigious efforts he nearly single-handedly changed the course of American history writing without setting out to and perhaps without consciously knowing he did. In some ways his contribution is best ascertained after the passage of time. Yet, a backward glance runs the risk of judging Sparks too much by contemporary standards.

Whatever his faults might have been, Sparks proved more reliant on source material than any historian before him. His story is not well known and more of it needs to be told. The look presented here is nowhere complete but it can serve as a start.

10

Jared Sparks and the Writing of The Life and Writings of George Washington

••••••

Sparks in Context

Jared Sparks today is clearly not a household name as far as American history is concerned. He lived and worked with other Boston literary luminaries such as contemporaries and near contemporaries George Bancroft (1800–1891, a lifelong friend he met while a student at Philips Exeter Academy) and William Prescott (1796–1859), among many others. As a professor, he taught and influenced a generation of later historians, including Francis Parkman (1823–1893). However, during his life, and throughout the "heroic model" (or great man) period of historical writing in the United States, Sparks cut a wide swath. His desire to see historical research and writing improved in the United States was evident in his correspondence. After researching at the British Museum in 1840 (when the British Library was still housed there), for example, he wrote, "When shall we see the like in the Athenaeum," in comparing the higher number of researchers in London to the lower number of researchers at the private Boston library and research center.[1] Lamenting the state of American libraries and repositories was a life-long hallmark of Sparks. His extensive travels abroad made him acutely aware of the long road ahead for his own country in preserving not just their own past, but the accumulated knowledge residing in nearly every library in Europe worth its name.

Boston during the nineteenth century produced some of the most compelling writers in America. In part this was due to the one literary magazine which provided them a consistent outlet for their work. Boston historians "had a practical monopoly on the writing of American history, possessing what was, in effect, their own house organ, the most important intellectual quarterly in America during the middle years of the nineteenth century, the *North American Review*," significantly, owned and edited during the early years by Jared Sparks himself.[2] Another practical aspect of why New England historians were so productive was simply the habit of the region not to throw things away. The ill-defined Yankee frugality in some measure helped in the research of the past.

Sparks was in the vanguard of American historians and to a certain extent set standards which others were to follow and refine into the modern discipline of history we recognize today. Garry Wills writes that the "nineteenth century was marked by the move from philosophical or 'conjectural' history to archival research."[3] Sparks was at the forefront of that transformation. And it was his work and approach that place him at the intersection of the great shift in historiography. While his work today is often criticized as being clouded with gushing patriotism and of editing controversial life episodes into more generous scenes, as was common at the time, he did render a tremendous service to historical writing by producing nearly seventy volumes during his career and selling nearly 600,000 copies of his works. The sheer productivity of Sparks created such an enormous body of material that he virtually set himself up as a target for critics.

Sparks' success was due in part to the sensitivity that had developed in the public consciousness over historical topics related to the Revolutionary period. This awareness of the Revolution was in part heightened by the passing of many veterans, and Sparks was able to tap into this wellspring of emotion purely by coincidence. In this way he was in fact the recipient of the accumulated attempts that began with historians like Ebenezer Hazard and David Ramsay. Much like authors trying to write about Washington when he was still alive and facing the difficulties of his still-living presence, writing about the Revolution while so many veterans were still alive was fraught with problems as well. It was only when more began to pass away that historians could approach the topic with more independence of thought.

What Sparks brought to the evolution of the field was a much broader scope and significance of effort that was not available to his predecessors in part because there was either no country established or it was too young. By the time Sparks became active as a writer with the *North American Review*, the country was already on its fifth president (James Monroe).

Over a career spanning nearly fifty years, Sparks became familiar with nearly every individual who was prominent in the broad field of American writing.

He traveled extensively in Europe, England, and the eastern United States to collect his material. Sparks held important positions in academia, and the magazine he edited, the *North American Review*, is still in circulation as of 2014. His immense contributions (rarely have his efforts been surpassed) though have resonated so little over the decades that he is virtually unknown today. Yet, his legacy lives on in his magazine, and more importantly, every editorial paper's project that is in existence today.

In a Nutshell

Looking off in the distance, with a book in his right hand, a finger held between the covers marking a page as though he was momentarily diverted from reading to strike a pose, the portrait of Jared Sparks by Thomas Sully from 1831 is both formal and intimate, but also rough and detached. Sparks' face seems to emerge from the shadows, revealed and cloaked, still slightly concealed though behind a look both determined and unsure simultaneously. He is a young man sure of his place yet still needing to convince himself—and others. Consciously or not, Sully captured the dual qualities of Sparks as a historian who straddled the precipice between the past and the future of a profession he spent his life developing.

Jared Sparks represents the culmination of the accumulated efforts of his predecessors engaged in American historical editing and writing. Sparks was a seminal, albeit controversial, figure in American historiography. He was appointed professor at Harvard to the first department of history established by an American institution of higher learning.[4] This appointment alone put Sparks at both a culmination point and a starting point. It was a culmination in the sense that he represented the end of the nonprofessional historian and the beginning in the sense that the scholarly historian was at the start of their professional ascent in the academic world and the popular imagination. Michael Kraus, writing in the 1950s, summed up Sparks this way: "The long wait of Americans for native historians came to an end when Sparks and [George] Bancroft appeared. More than any others they established American historical writing on a firm footing."[5] Kraus continued, "Though his [Sparks'] work was eventually superseded, the vast range of his activity altered completely the character of our historical literature and indicated the direction that much contemporary and later research was to take."[6]

Sparks also had the benefit of coming onto the scene when the accumulation of manuscript resources as a scholarly endeavor was truly beginning to gain momentum in the United States. Prominent men, and men hoping for prominence, joined together to herald a new movement within the country to preserve the literary remains of the founding generation and of the era immediately preceding the Revolution and immediately following. In this way, Sparks was as much in the right place at the right time as he was a pioneer in the field.

As editor, Sparks strove in his work to utilize prerogative as an editor "without changing the author's meaning and purpose."[7] In the final analysis, after a career editing more manuscripts than anyone up to that time, "in searching for and assembling the sources Sparks exceeded all his predecessors."[8]

By comparison, James Savage, editor of the journal of Jonathan Winthrop, worked approximately the same time (1820s–1840s) that Sparks composed his edition of Washington's writings. Savage's work was very much admired. "As a contemporary of Sparks he pointed the way toward more exacting standards of research, founded on primary sources critically evaluated. Both Savage and Sparks developed a consciousness of historical method."[9] While Savage and Sparks strove to engage the American public in a new approach to American history, it would be Sparks who would push the boundaries beyond anything that had occurred prior to his time by the sheer volume of original material that he dealt with.

Also, it would be Sparks who would have to deal with recrimination on a transatlantic scale. More than likely this was mainly due to the familiarity of the topic Sparks worked on: George Washington. However, there can be little doubt that some professional jealousy from other writers aimed at Sparks was not far from the initial reason. Although immensely prolific (see appendix four), Sparks has come down to us as not just the compiler of Washington's papers, but, to his many critics, as a biased or reckless editor, as will be discussed. While his shortcomings are lamentable, even though understandable, his efforts still earn him the thanks of anyone who claims the mantle of historian to this day, whether they acknowledge that debt or not.

The Project in Brief

The correspondence between Bushrod Washington and Jared Sparks is unique in American historical literature. In his efforts documenting President Washington's papers, Sparks wrote to Bushrod Washington, the president's nephew who had inherited his papers. Although Bushrod Washington initially declined to give Sparks the help he requested, he eventually consented to allowing Sparks access to his uncle's materials. As Sparks himself wrote in the preface to his stand-alone one-volume biography of President Washington, "Whoever would understand the character of Washington, in all its compass and grandeur, must learn it from his own writings and from a complete history of his country during the long period in which he was the most prominent actor."[10]

Sparks had developed a plan of publishing the collected works of George Washington and corresponded with innumerable people in America and Europe to obtain copies of the president's correspondence. However, the letters Sparks produced himself during his ten-year project on George Washington are nearly as important as the papers of Washington which Sparks sought to collect. Sparks' written letters with the Washington family, not to mention the innumerable letters he sent to archival repositories in America and Europe, gather to hundreds of pages. In a bound volume of letters at the Morristown National Historical Park, hundreds of pages of correspondence detail the relationship between Sparks and the Washington family.[11] The collection of Sparks' letters chronicles one of the earliest attempts to gather, through primary sources, the literary remains of a major historical figure. When Jared Sparks began his project officially with a letter to Bushrod Washington in 1826, he may not have thought that a chunk of his correspondence with Bushrod and his descendants would end up bound together in a leather volume and stored as part of an archival collection. In many ways the collection of letters itself constitutes a vivid, narrative, semi-drama dealing with the composition of the Washington manuscripts into a readable and digestible set.

The correspondence Sparks had with Justice Washington represents his attempt to logically take his search to one of the relatives of the late president, and the one who inherited his papers. This effort was time-consuming, and Bushrod Washington consented to help Sparks only after he had already traveled throughout the original thirteen colonies collecting copies of the president's writings and had proven he was serious in his effort. Bushrod Washington also felt much more comfortable with the project once his writing partner from twenty years earlier, John Marshall, was involved and actively encouraging Sparks.

Bushrod was faced with a young, smart, and energetic Jared Sparks with a plan far beyond anything he and John Marshall attempted twenty years prior. Initially, Bushrod was not only concerned about the level of work Sparks was proposing, he was concerned as well about being called upon to assist Sparks in much the same way he was with Marshall. By 1826, Bushrod was in no physical condition to even consider such an undertaking, not to mention his extensive workload as a justice. Yet, Sparks was convincing; he had done an extraordinary amount of work already and was going to publish something whether Bushrod granted access to the material or not. In a final effort to persuade, Sparks wrote,

> I will engage to execute the work according to the plan proposed in my former letter taking upon myself the charge and responsibility of the literary part, and the business of finding a publisher and superintending the publication; and I will agree then to divide with you equally the property of the copyright, or the profits of sales.[12]

Sparks attempted to remove every possible burden (and fear) from Bushrod in exchange for access to the manuscripts he held. Sparks even asked Bushrod to withhold whatever letters he deemed too sensitive for Sparks to see or publish to ensure the reputation of President Washington and the family. (This decision would come back to haunt Sparks as being far too lenient for the historical record.)

Sparks in no way underestimated the level of work he was entering upon in 1826 and willingly dedicated the time it would take to see his efforts through to publication. Only a topic such as Washington would have been considered important enough to induce someone to devote his life for the foreseeable future to a literary undertaking such as he proposed. Without the stature of Washington to rely on to help open doors and acquire access to papers, Sparks would have faced a formidable challenge indeed.

The Search

During 1825 Sparks wrote hundreds of letters to colleagues and acquaintances concerning access and knowledge about Washington's writings not kept at Mount Vernon. Sparks wrote surviving founders like Thomas Jefferson. An advocate for history and historical writing as already discussed, Jefferson responded to a letter from Sparks seeking support by saying, "I am happy to be informed of the historical work which you are about to undertake because I know that whatever you undertake will be well done."[13] Sparks also wrote to individual state archives inquiring about any collection of Washington's papers that may have been held in state repositories. While he received many positive responses, he did get distressing replies such as one from New Hampshire: "There can be little doubt the office once contained *many* of his [Washington] letters, but everything of that description has, till within a few years, been regarded ... as a part of the useless lumber of the office, and treated accordingly."[14] In other words, the material was tossed. Responses like this spurred Sparks to action in an effort aimed at preservation as much as at scholarship.

Sparks would spend the summer of 1826 on a tour of the former southern colonies in an attempt to obtain information on the extent of material available outside of Mount Vernon. Sparks' reputation and contacts opened many doors, so many that Sparks was able to write to Bushrod on September 12, 1826, when Bushrod was still vacillating over allowing Sparks access to his uncle George's papers,

> I am very confident of procuring nearly everything which can throw light on the public character and transactions of General Washington.... My only regret is, that the work must at last be imperfect, my great purpose defeated, my hopes but

partially realized, and a reasonable expectation of the public disappointed [if I am not allowed access to your uncle's papers].[15]

On his journey through the former colonies Sparks met John Marshall, at his home in Richmond. Marshall talked favorably with Sparks about his proposed project and how he might go about gaining access to the necessary materials, especially from Bushrod. Marshall, one of Bushrod's closest friends, and the Chief Justice of the United States, provided Sparks with another powerful colleague ready to assist him.

Another example of reaching out to living founders was Jared Sparks' correspondence with James Madison in 1827, when Madison was one of a handful still living.[16] Fortunately for Sparks, Madison was still in a physical and mental state to be able to interact with Sparks in a meaningful and fruitful way. One particular question Sparks felt compelled to ask was what the state of agitation for independence among the members of the Continental Congress was when Madison was a member of the Virginia state assembly. Madison stated "my entire belief that they were not" in response to a question on whether there was unanimity on declaring independence.[17] Madison continued, "I can only say therefore, that, so far as ever came to my knowledge, no one of them ever aroused, or was understood to entertain, a pursuit of independence at the assembling of the first congress, or for a very considerable period thereafter."[18] Madison was a good sounding board for Sparks as well, due to his advocacy for the writing of history. A scholar of the study of history in his own right, Madison had written "It has been the misfortune of history that a personal knowledge and an impartial judgment of things rarely meet in the historian."[19] Madison was echoing the need for objectivity in the field of history writing, a lesson Sparks understood but yet did not fully follow.

Sparks was very much in Madison's debt. He wrote to Madison, "I would not weary or trouble you, but when you recollect that there is no other fountain to which I can go for information; I trust you will pardon my importunity."[20] Madison happily played the role as one of the few remaining leaders of the Revolution still alive and alert enough to assist Sparks. In such a capacity he was invaluable in helping Sparks understand the nuances of the Revolutionary period and also what topics should be left alone and not publically revealed. As a former secretary of state and president, Madison was uniquely qualified to pass judgment on those topics best left undisturbed. Sparks was acutely sensitive to the matter of how delicate some of the topics still were even in 1830. The sensitivity to this particular issue would come to haunt Sparks by 1850.

Americans had come to understand by 1830 their founding in terms that they felt most comfortable with. And like most other nations, needed a founding forged in war and brought forth through peace. Taking too many liberties with the cherished, received wisdom of that founding was fraught with dangers. Sparks was well aware his project had the potential to disrupt many accepted "truths" of the Revolutionary period and thus sought to limit those chances by scrupulously avoiding any hint of controversy. As we have seen, he assured Bushrod Washington he would tread lightly, and he also informed James Madison of his cautious approach, even though Madison felt the need to still reiterate the point.

The Beginning

Jared Sparks was born in Wellington, Connecticut, on May 10, 1789. Raised in a poor farming household, Sparks very early displayed exceptional intellectual acumen and was assisted financially by friends who acknowledged his academic ability and made it possible for him to attend Philips Academy in Exeter, New Hampshire. He entered Harvard in 1811 and graduated in 1815. Throughout his college career he was an exceptional student who thrived in scholarly pursuits. His talent was quite broad—he was as adept in science as in the humanities. He taught school during his Harvard years and earned a living as a tutor in mathematics at Harvard after graduation. His first entry into the world of literary production occurred in 1817, when he started a job with the *North American Review* two years after that publication began operation.

During this time Sparks was also studying theology. He was a Unitarian in faith and felt he had an obligation as an educated, reasoning man to put himself at the disposal of a congregation. In 1819, he moved to Baltimore to take up duties as a Unitarian minister. He was firmly convinced that the liberal, less orthodox version of Unitarianism was well suited for the needs—as he saw the needs—of the upper south. He quickly gained enough attention in political circles to be appointed chaplain of the United States House of Representatives in 1821—a post he did not pursue but which became his through his ever widening set of influential acquaintances. The life of a minister who was hoping to establish a foothold for a relatively new religion, in the United States anyway, eventually became too much even for Sparks' ability. The pressures and constant debate involved did not ultimately suit his temperament. He returned to Boston in 1823 after less than five years in the ministry. Even while in Baltimore and Washington though, Sparks continued to write articles for the *North American Review*, and his reputation grew as a writer and emerging scholar.

In late summer 1823, Sparks purchased the *North American Review* from its five partners. Sparks instituted several changes with his new magazine, including the idea of paying writers for their articles. Within five years, he could count 3,200 subscribers. Sparks sold one-fourth of the magazine in 1826 and the other three-fourths in 1830. The seven years that the *Review* was under Sparks' control it prospered considerably. Not just financially either; the *Review* earned a reputation for scholarship and dependable writing which Sparks fostered and demanded of contributors, including himself.

Sparks published his first book in 1828, a biography of the explorer John Ledyard. Ledyard was widely admired for his expeditions in Africa, Asia, and the South Pacific. Yet, he had nothing to do with the American Revolution or the founding of the United States—the topic Sparks would spend much of the rest of his life articulating and the period or theme he is most remembered for. As such, the book is something of an oddity in the Sparks canon of published works (see appendix 4).

Starting Washington

Sparks never left a clear description of how he came about the idea for an edition of Washington's writings. As a scholar of math and science, and as a Unitarian minister, history would not necessarily seem a topic to interest Sparks. He may have been inspired by his colleagues and his reading to oppose the general atmosphere of the time as captured by John Adams in a letter to Thomas McKean in 1813; Adams wrote, "Can you account for the apathy, the antipathy of this nation to their own history? Is there not a repugnance to the thought of looking back? While thousands of frivolous novels are read with eagerness and got by heart, the history of our own native country is not only neglected, but despised and abhorred."[21] For Sparks, if in fact he was thinking along the same lines, George Washington represented "the history of our own native country" that Adams wrote about.

As early as 1816, Sparks asked for and received a sample of Washington's penmanship from his friend William Sprague. Sprague, a fellow minister with a strong sense of history and collecting, was at Mount Vernon as a guest, hoping to obtain samples of Washington's writing for his collection.[22] His enthusiasm in letters to Sparks about being at Mount Vernon evidently created a stir in Sparks for the literary remains of America's founders as a souvenir.[23]

This interest only grew as Sparks moved away from the ministry to editing and writing in Boston. In 1824, a colleague who owned a printing office, Charles Folsom, confided in Sparks an idea he had for an edition of Washington's writings. Sparks had sought to assist Folsom by writing a letter to Bushrod Washington requesting access to George Washington's papers for Folsom. Bushrod denied the request. In the reply letter back to Sparks from Bushrod however, Sparks wrote a short paragraph to himself (or posterity?) where he mentions his aspirations toward a work of his own. At the bottom of Bushrod's letter denying access to Folsom, Sparks wrote:

> The preceding letter was written in reply to an inquiry which I made on account of a publisher [Folsom] who contemplated publishing an edition of George Washington's writings. I have myself thought of this plan for some time. At present we cannot find the writings of Washington without looking through many books and documents, and it would certainly be desirable to have all the works of this great man brought together.[24]

Jared Sparks had two advantages that Charles Folsom did not. One, Sparks already had a career in literature and was an accomplished writer with a respectable portfolio. Secondly, Sparks had an enormous network of contacts in the literary and political world. He was widely known for his work on the *North American Review* and for his time as a minister, especially when he was the chaplain of the House of Representatives.

There was also a huge difference in Folsom and Sparks' plans. Folsom sought an undefined study of Washington that attempted to portray him as a rather one-dimensional character who single-handedly won the American Revolution. Sparks however sought to provide a more broad brush approach to the life and legacy of Washington. Certainly not comprehensive by today's standards though, Sparks' plan was to segment the various components of Washington's career in an effort to present a larger, better articulated, image of Washington.

In 1826 as mentioned, Sparks began on a course of work that, for better or worse, set the tone for the rest of his life. Over the spring and summer, Sparks traveled throughout the original thirteen colonies researching and gathering information. He met more important figures in American life and corresponded with as many more as he met. He secured valuable contacts in manuscript repositories and found a vast collection of material for his purposes. Most importantly, over the summer of 1826, Sparks began a relationship with two men who would change the course of his life—Bushrod Washington and John Marshall.

As a reminder, Bushrod Washington was not unfamiliar with Jared Sparks. Sparks had written a letter to him on behalf of Charles Folsom in 1824, requesting that Folsom be given access to the late president's papers for a study of his writing that Folsom had contemplated. Bushrod declined the request in part because he (Bushrod) had a vague notion that he would attempt an edited version of his uncle's papers. This should in no way be confused with the work John Marshall composed over twenty years earlier—*The Life of George Washington*. After being refused by Bushrod, Folsom simply abandoned his project. Sparks however, was not deterred. His plan to edit Washington's correspondence had been germinating for several years before he set out on his tour of the former colonies as a scholar and his sending of his own letter to Bushrod basically requesting the same access for himself that Folsom had requested.

By comparison, essentially, Sparks had a plan and Folsom did not. In the first of a multitude of letters (January 26, 1826) written by Sparks to Bushrod and later to other Washington family members, Sparks describes in vivid and moving detail his developed plan for his edition of Washington's writings (see appendix one).

After his January 26, 1826, letter to Bushrod became publicly known, the proposed project received favorable reviews from many prominent men—among them Justice Joseph Story, Edward Everett, and Daniel Webster. (Joseph Story was a very prominent New England scholar and jurist. An associate justice on the United States Supreme Court, he had considerable influence with Bushrod and Marshall as a major figure in American legal history. Story was also a writer in his own right and well known outside of New England.) Not only did Sparks receive support for the project, but those offering support felt he (Sparks) was the best person to undertake the task. Justice Story was so enthusiastic that he personally spoke on Sparks' behalf with his Court colleagues Bushrod Washington and John Marshall. Story even advised Sparks to think about reviewing Marshall's recently published book on the history of Colonial America. This one volume was originally the first volume of Marshall's *Life of Washington* before it was spun off as a separate work. Story advised Sparks that "his work on the Colonies ought, by the bye, to be reviewed by some able hand."[25] This was a not so subtle hint that Sparks could help his cause with Bushrod by giving Marshall's work a favorable review in his magazine, thus encouraging Marshall to support Sparks' project with Bushrod.

While quoted and discussed above, the first letter from Sparks to Bushrod Washington bears repeating as it articulates for the first time the aspirations of an American historian. These aspirations reached a crescendo whereby from the pen of Jared Sparks would be crafted more than just a narrative; out of these ideas, came an academic discipline. Sparks would establish the ground rules which—although amended and updated—guide every history department in America today. Bushrod, John Marshall, and Joseph Story are critical, necessary ingredients to this development as well. Without their blend of rejection and acceptance, Sparks may have given up seeking access to Mount Vernon. Without access to Mount Vernon, Sparks would not have achieved the status he did as historian and scholar. He would have been successful, but not as much as he eventually became.

The material at Mount Vernon was vast and constituted the largest collection of Washington's writing concentrated in one place. State governments, individuals, and the federal government all held their own collections that had accumulated during Washington's busy life. Justice Story felt that Bushrod deemed the material at Mount Vernon as a "sort of family inheritance, and that no person ought to be permitted to have anything to do with the publication unless he stands in his own intimate confidence."[26]

Unfazed, Sparks made plans to move forward with the project in the expectation that eventually he would secure access to the Mount Vernon material. For Sparks, "Washington's public letters and papers [were] the property of the nation."[27] Bushrod's response of March 13, 1826, left little doubt of his intentions. Bushrod, older and wiser from his publishing experience with Marshall, was hesitant to delve into another similar venture. Ten days later, on March 26, 1826, John Marshall wrote to Sparks to commend him on his project. Marshall wrote, "I am gratified at the expectation of seeing his works ushered to the world by a gentleman whose literary reputation ensures full justice to his memory."[28] Marshall was as optimistic and supportive as Bushrod was pessimistic and unresponsive.

If Sparks' first letter to Bushrod was like an architectural drawing, the second letter was a masterpiece of writing designed to convince Bushrod that he was indeed cheating himself and history—"The day must of course come when all these papers will find their way to the public in some form or other. The voice of the country, the genius of history, will demand them. As this will in the nature of things happen, is it not better that they should be published under your own eye, with your inspection and guidance?"[29]

On September 12, 1826, Sparks wrote to Bushrod concerning the latter's March 13, 1826, letter. Notwithstanding Bushrod's unwillingness to assist, Sparks wrote, "I had already made such progress in the undertaking, that I could not reconcile myself to the idea of abandoning it."[30] Sparks had by late summer 1826 "visited all the southern and middle states" and "procured copies of all General Washington's letters" available outside of Mount Vernon in the former colonies that he could find.[31] Sparks by this time was planning to tour the New England states and finish at "the office of the Secretary of State at Washington."[32] Sparks did not mince emotions when he declared to Bushrod that, essentially, I don't need you: "In short, I am confident of procuring nearly everything, which can throw light on the public character and transactions of General Washington."[33]

Over the winter of 1826–1827, Bushrod made his decision to allow Sparks access to the manuscripts. Sparks, boarding at Mrs. Clark's on F Street in Baltimore at the time, was elated. Sparks wrote on January 16, 1827, that he would not pressure him (Bushrod) for immediate access to Washington's papers, but would wait until he was "most at leisure" to meet with him.[34]

Sparks and Bushrod agreed to meet in early March to begin a discussion on the work at Mount Vernon. On March 28, 1827, Sparks put at the beginning of a letter to Bushrod (on circuit duty in New Jersey) "Mount Vernon"—Sparks had finally arrived. Not just physically *at* Mount Vernon, but also in the sense of having achieved his goal. Aside from John Marshall, no other historian had been granted such unprecedented access to the collection; and at Mount Vernon on top of it all. He was not only working with Washington's manuscripts, he was working with them *at* Mount Vernon; what could have been better? Sparks relayed that after two weeks of work he was dismayed at how he had underestimated the amount of material in Bushrod's possession. This would mean much more work for Sparks than planned, but with "patience, assiduity, and a lively zeal in the work to conquer all obstacles" he promised to see his project through to completion.[35]

By April 1827, Sparks, a month into his work at Mount Vernon, was contemplating a decision that would haunt him and his reputation to this day. In an effort to ensure the near sanctity within which Americans held Washington, and in an effort not to upset Washington descendants or descendants of other Revolutionary era figures, Sparks contemplated modifying, or polishing, the language of certain pieces of correspondence. He also considered revising grammar and spelling, to ensure a more refined, articulate Washington was presented to readers through his letters. This approach was considered for letters Washington sent and received.

On April 17, 1827, Sparks wrote Bushrod to assure him that the concern about propriety was well understood. Sparks clearly began to take a cautious approach through conversations with Bushrod who voiced his concerns. Sparks wrote, "In publishing the letters received by General Washington, I am fully aware of the delicacy you mention, and trust my judgment will guard me against any indiscretion which shall afford reasonable grounds of complaint."[36] The issue that future generations would criticize Sparks for was mainly a deal he struck to have access to the manuscripts. Bushrod and many others were concerned that if the aspirations written by their ancestors during the Revolution or other periods of America's founding were put into print for mass circulation, that carefully and finely crafted reputations would be potentially damaged. Sparks continues, "I do not think it necessary for much delicacy to be used, except where there is manifest danger of giving undue offense to some living person, or of commuting an act of unkindness or injustice to the character of the dead."[37]

Removal

In a massive and detailed letter in April 1827 to Bushrod on his findings and progress at Mount Vernon after one month, Sparks reported several key developments, among which was the sheer volume of material, which Sparks had to admit he underestimated. Among the most prominent was the fact that Sparks had come to the conclusion that "the papers [should be] removed to my own study in Boston."[38] Also, Sparks was growing concerned about over-staying his welcome at Mount Vernon and about employing copyists to create transcriptions of all the correspondence and how much this would cost and how long it would take.

The April 1827 letter—aside from the indications toward editing—is unique for multiple reasons; the final one being Bushrod's note at the bottom of the letter. Bushrod wrote "On the 29th April, I answered this letter and agreed to the removal of the papers on the terms proposed, unless the C. Justice should think the measure improper."[39]

One of Sparks' arguments for the transfer was the practical concern of fire. When Sparks was at Mount Vernon working, he observed that the original letters were kept with bound copies—both of which would probably be lost in the event of fire. "In point of safety there would actually be a gain in having these transcripts deposited in some place separate from the originals, for an accident by fire at Mount Vernon would now endanger the whole, whereas the loss of one part only would be of comparatively small moment."[40]

Sparks planned to transport and care for the manuscripts in a thorough manner. "I will procure boxes to be made, in which they shall be carefully packed, and will take them to Boston by land under my own charge, and at my own expense. They shall also be brought back at my expense, and I will pledge myself that all the papers shall be returned, unless presented by accident not in my power to control."[41]

During the journey home to Boston with the papers, Sparks reported his progress to Bushrod to ease his concern for the papers. On June 4, 1827, Sparks wrote to Bushrod en route to Boston that he had received numerous positive indicators concerning the overall project in the various towns he had passed through on his way to Boston. A letter supporting Sparks' project from his friend Justice Joseph Story had been reproduced and widely distributed in newspapers and thus spread the early word concerning the George Washington papers project.

In bringing the manuscripts back to Boston for extended study, Sparks was treated to a hero's welcome. In a bizarre show of approbation, his friends and literary colleagues treated him almost as a conquering hero who brought home war trophies. Indeed, moving nearly 40,000 manuscripts—many copies—safely to Boston from Mount Vernon was a logistical feat in and of itself, but the reception afforded Sparks was completely out of place with the aspirations and designs for which Sparks had the manuscripts in the first place. Today it would seem totally inconceivable to attempt such a transfer in private hands. The liability—both financial and moral—would be overwhelming. Professor John Bassett, writing in 1917, summed it up thus:

> The Washington papers were kept in a fireproof building while in Boston, and Sparks had an index made. When he finished with them they were returned to the owners without loss or damage. His use of the collection called attention to its value, and in 1834 it was purchased by the national government and deposited in the library of the state department. It now [1917] forms the most precious part of the manuscripts collection of the Library of Congress.[42]

It is not hard to imagine Bushrod reacting with a sense of relief at getting Sparks out of his home, even at the risk of releasing the manuscripts. Although Mount Vernon was a large house, it had boxes of papers spread throughout, which required Sparks to remain relatively mobile as opposed to being stationary in one place of the mansion. From Sparks' perspective too, the prospect of being able to work ensconced in the comfort of his own study must have been appealing. The thought of a blistering Virginia summer just around the corner was probably not eagerly anticipated either on his part. So, overall, both Bushrod and Sparks had compelling reasons to mutually agree to the transfer of the manuscripts. Even so, Sparks wrote to Bushrod prior to his departure, "I can hardly imagine a more charming spot, then this [Mount Vernon] has been for the last five weeks."[43]

Sparks had written several letters to Justice Story in May 1827, before leaving Mount Vernon, about the progress of the project and the overall plan for the volumes. In typical Sparks fashion, the letters to Story are long and detailed. In them he describes the same plans he proposed to Bushrod and indicates that he's more convinced than before he started that the project will be a success.

Similar to Marshall's biography, pre-publication hype started early for Sparks' project too. The *National Intelligence*, a newspaper from Washington, D.C., among many others, published notice of Sparks' project in early 1827. Even Bushrod took notice while away from Mount Vernon attending to Court matters. Bushrod wrote Sparks that "public curiosity is highly wound up and will, I doubt not, be most abundantly gratified when the work comes out."[44]

By August 1827, Sparks was able to tell Bushrod that agents were working "in different parts of the United States" selling subscriptions.[45] It is tempting to wonder how Bushrod felt about the prospects of subscription sales given his experience with John Marshall twenty-five years earlier and the disappointing sales they experienced. Yet, if he felt cynical about the prospects for worthwhile sales, he never indicated as much.

It was also in the August 1827 letter to Bushrod that Sparks voiced his first concerns about the project. Although already selling subscriptions, Sparks had yet to find a publisher who would "allow us what I think a fair compensation."[46] As a last resort Sparks suggested he would use his position at the *North American Review* to ensure ultimate publication. Even this option was fraught with risk for Sparks though. He would have to assume financial responsibility up front for all the work in the hope of some future reimbursement. These letters to Bushrod read almost as though Sparks was attempting to get Bushrod or even Marshall to provide capital to get the publication process started. Bushrod never exhibited any inclination of providing financing of any kind throughout any part of the project, and Sparks never did ask directly. Sparks was not suggesting anything of that nature (although it may have come across that way), and they cleared that point up in letters toward the end of 1827. Sparks was beginning to feel the best route for publication was indeed through his office at the *North American Review,* regardless of the cost.

Abroad

During most of 1828 and half of 1829, Sparks was researching in Europe. It was this trip, if any other evidence was needed, that ensured Sparks would always be associated with the vanguard of nineteenth-century historians. Aside from his assiduous research in the United States, which in and of itself placed him at the pinnacle of research historians, Sparks "became the first American to search the archives of Britain and France for new materials on his subject."[47] As such, "Sparks was part of the great tradition of nineteenth century historiography."[48] Sparks' mission to Europe also highlighted the need for countries, including the United States, to better collect, arrange, and provide access to their records. His mission identified the need to ensure that all documents, regardless how sensitive, should be made available to researchers.

Sparks arrived in Liverpool, England, on April 15, 1828. He took rooms at the Adelphi hotel and began to acquaint himself with England and its people through some of the letters of introduction he carried. He made his way to London, arriving there on April 24, where he continued to make introductions through the letters provided him by colleagues in the United States before he left.

Encountering Problems

In 1828, the State Paper Office was the main repository for official British government correspondence. While each department kept many of their own papers, some were consolidated at the State Paper Office, and as such that office served as an unofficial British national archive. The office had some power over other departments regarding access to the papers.

Robert Peel, Home Secretary in 1828 when Sparks arrived in London, was in the process of updating policies concerning State Papers access, and in particular papers relating to the American conflict during the Revolution. Peel had stated in January of 1828 "that the State Paper Office needed centralized control ... so that it would be impossible for controversial document[s] to be examined by researchers."[49] Naturally, this is what Sparks had specifically gone to look at in Europe. Unbeknownst to Peel, his actions were destined to eventually bring him into conflict with Sparks' work. The steps that the State Paper Office employed under Peel to prevent unwanted access were extremely thorough. It even had a provision that "not even the endorsement of the Prime Minister was sufficient to enable the researcher to circumvent" the new rules.[50]

Peel's name and position first came to Sparks' attention on May 10th in 1828; Sparks made an annotation in his travel diary referring to Peel as someone he would need to contact regarding access to the State Paper Office. In his journal, Sparks described his first encounter with the new rule:

> The State Paper Office is under the particular charge of the secretary of the Home Department, but is customary for all the secretaries to consult such papers in that office as they want in the regular prosecution of business. But as my application goes beyond this limit, Mr. Huskisson thinks he cannot with propriety grant a permission which is the particular province of the secretary in the other department.[51]

On May 8, after nearly a week doing preliminary work at the British Colonial Office, Sparks was retroactively denied access to the volumes he had been researching already. After much protesting, Sparks consented to fill out the new, appropriate forms to request to see certain specific papers. This was somewhat senseless to Sparks as he wasn't sure himself what he would find, and the whole point of research was to examine material of an unknown content in the hopes of finding useful information. Essentially, Peel was severely restricting research by allowing access to specific manuscripts only. This meant researchers would have to know ahead of time what documents would have the information they were looking for.

For all the commotion caused by Robert Peel and his new rules, the issue deflated almost as quickly as it began. Receiving communication from the Colonial Office as to how to proceed with Sparks' request, Peel initially berated staff at the Colonial Office for already having provided Sparks with access to some manuscripts. Having thought about it more, Peel then decided to free himself from the matter by telling the Colonial Office it was up to them if they wanted to grant Sparks continued access. Peel apparently was concerned about the potential diplomatic repercussions of denying Sparks access, particularly with the impressive network of supporters Sparks had arrayed on his behalf in both England and America. By early June, Sparks was back at the Colonial Office researching the papers he desired. He had lost about a month of work dealing with Robert Peel and others over access to "sensitive" documents. Sparks' persistent effort nonetheless paved the way for future historians to work with original manuscripts pertaining to the delicate issue of the American Revolution. In itself, this was a major advancement for scholarship.

Diversions

When not engaged in his work, Sparks found time to acquire a large circle of friends and acquaintances. Mostly drawn from the aristocratic, literary, or political realm, Sparks came to be seen as more than just "an American." Many of his new contacts were genuinely interested in his project and found it quite exciting and unique. Those less inclined to the historical aspects of Sparks' project found the literary portion to be just as captivating. Beyond his intellectual ability, Sparks was a charming and sought after conversationalist. He had little difficulty in securing coveted invitations to dinners and other gatherings of the important people in Europe and England. The letters of introduction he carried were almost unnecessary, as word spread of the American scholar who had such a commanding presence and such a confident persona with an easy grasp of the most intricate intellectual topics of the day. In a word, he was a natural as a guest.

The Continent

On June 16, 1828, Sparks crossed the English Channel and arrived in Belgium to begin work in European archives. From Belgium, Sparks made his way to Germany, stopping in Bonn before proceeding to Leipzig. At Bonn, Sparks was the toast of the university. Not only was he learned, outgoing, and charming, he was also American. Such a combination was rarely seen at the celebrated German institution. Part of Sparks' goal while in Europe was to inquire about possible European editions of his soon-to-be-completed work, efforts which would prove fruitful several years later. He generally found acceptance of the plan and was readily encouraged to visit specific publishers with his proposal. While at the universities, he discussed his project but did little research with manuscripts. In fact, most of his time in Germany was devoted to discussing future translations and publishing ventures. Given the lax state of international copyright law at the time this was not surprising. Yet, he found the interaction with scholars in the forefront of the awakening academic historical field to be stimulating and rewarding. (For further discussion of Sparks in Germany see the epilogue.) Sparks received a ready reception among the foremost proponents of the quickly emerging fields of historiography where the Germans were considered the leaders. He was seen as a forerunner of the positive historic advancement being made in America.

Sparks spent most of the rest of 1828 in France, specifically Paris. He worked closely with the elderly Marquis de Lafayette and utilized the Marquis' influence and his own personal papers in his research. Sparks had by this time created quite a stir among the intellectual circles in Europe with his expansive and bold plan and engaging personality and intellect. He did much on his own to dispel the ethos and myth of the uneducated or uncivilized American. In many ways Sparks was the perfect cultural ambassador to Europe precisely when America needed one the most.

Sparks returned to the United States on May 11, 1829. His trip had been a success on many levels. Not only did he accomplish his research goals, he had established an American intelligentsia presence, which later in the nineteenth century—and early twentieth—would see hundreds of American artists establish themselves in Europe.

Recognizing the significance of Sparks' trip, fellow historian George Bancroft wrote to Sparks on June 4, 1829,

> Right welcome to America again. Let me join my congratulations with those of your friends, who see you visibly, on the great success which report attributes to your expedition. It falls to the lot of few men to identify themselves with a leading object of curiosity and interest. I may say, apart from the feelings which give me a personal interest in your success, I am sincerely rejoiced at your unwearied efforts, and the valuable and honorable results which have crowned them.[52]

While He Was Away

Sparks returned from Europe a bona fide literary figure—this even though his major work still lay ahead of him. It should be remembered that during the years 1826–1830, when Sparks was plunging headlong into the Washington project, he was also deeply involved in preparing his biography of the American explorer John Ledyard. In addition to this he was editing a diplomatic history of the United States based on primary sources and similar in approach to his Washington project. As if that were not enough, Sparks embarked on a biography of Gouverneur Morris, a major figure of the Founding era, which he agreed to undertake as part of a deal with Morris' widow, whereby Sparks would gain access to the valuable collection of Morris' papers for his Washington project.[53]

Finally, Sparks was still editor of the *North American Review,* a task which required much original work beyond the compiling and research of historic manuscripts. Sparks happily relieved himself of his duties at the *North American* by selling his three-quarter share to Alexander Everett. With this money, and some of his royalties and advances he was able to finance his continued Washington research, including the travel.

Sparks also had assistance in the preparation of the Washington material when he was away from his home. His friend Samuel Eliot "arranged the early Washington letters, hired copyists, and had personally supervised copying."[54] Sparks also received help from another friend, the Rev. Thaddeus Harris. "Week after week Harris sorted through the papers until he had them 'arranged in exact chronological order, by the year, month, and day of the month and done up in suitable bundles well tied together.'"[55]

The Next Phase

To keep on schedule with his expectations, Sparks next needed to find a publisher. As discussed earlier, Sparks dreaded this task because he felt so many publishers were not necessarily unscrupulous, but rather motivated purely by profit. Sparks was far more idealistic in his venture than most writers would have been. He had to make money of course, but the transmission of knowledge took priority. And Sparks was not aware of a publishing firm that shared his approach. After extensive searching, he realized that he had to make a decision because there was no option remaining at the *North American* since he sold his shares. In March 1832, he signed a contract with Hilliard, Gray, and Company of Boston. The agreement called for a twelve-volume set to be titled *Writings of George Washington.*

Being a committed perfectionist with what had become his life's work, Sparks spared no expense in creating not just books, but works of art.[56] He specified the binding shop, he commissioned art work, chose the typeface and size, and selected the leather for the cover.[57] As the former editor of the *North American Review,* Sparks knew books. He knew the process of putting words on paper, bound in leather, to create a work of art. He knew the entire process, from start to finish. At the end of the Washington project, he had "edited and prepared for publication 2,643 letters and documents, produced 1,065 pages of appendices, compiled a 154-page index, and wrote a full-length life of Washington, by any standard a noteworthy accomplishment."[58] When the final volume appeared in 1837, Sparks had produced "twelve massive volumes, well printed and illustrated, with more than 6,000 pages containing primary sources available for the first time, with hundreds of footnotes and other explanatory material placing the documents in perspective, plus a full length biography tying the whole set together."[59] This output demanded suitable attire.

The End

To add to his work load, after Bushrod Washington's death in 1829, Sparks had to contend with a new owner of the Washington papers. Bushrod had left the papers to his nephew, Congressman George Corbin Washington. In 1832 Congressman Washington asked Sparks for a detailed account of the papers he had in his possession in Boston. Sparks provided the congressman with a detailed list and also reminded him of the contract by which he could have the papers until he was finished with his work.

All was in order with Congressman Washington and the loan of the papers until 1834. Sparks learned then that the federal government had an interest in obtaining the Washington archive primarily for the purpose of establishing pension records. The only other complete set of pension information was destroyed by fire in the early nineteenth century. In the summer of 1834, the Washington archival collection, most of it in the physical possession of Sparks in Boston, was sold by Congressman Washington to the federal government for $25,000.[60] Over the next three years, Sparks ensured he had the access he needed to the papers while still allowing Congressman Washington to move forward with the physical transfer of most of the papers from Boston to the capital.[61]

11

The Harvest of Sparks' Washington

······

Regardless how much mud is thrown at the *Writings of George Washington* today, the published volumes when they appeared were magnificent—from every perspective. No one had ever attempted such a project before, and Sparks was rightly pleased with his efforts. Most importantly, by 1837, "the books' income had reached \$30,741," a gratifying sum for a man of modest means.[1] The summer of 1837 also marked the fulfillment of Sparks' ten-year contract with Bushrod Washington and John Marshall. By this time however, both Bushrod and John Marshall had passed away, and their heirs collected their respective shares of the proceeds. After ten long years of work and hundreds of letters and promises, Sparks had kept his word. Sparks was indeed an established author and scholar, as well as a businessman. Yet, the income did not end in 1837. Over the years the set would be reissued, and thanks to Sparks' publishing acumen he always turned a profit. In fact, "by the 1850s Sparks was still sending payments to the Washington and Marshall families" for their share of the royalties.[2]

Sparks had proven that a scholar, a historian, could indeed earn a respectable living. Although he came from Boston, Sparks proved further that one need not have independent financial means to pursue a career in scholarly endeavors. Unlike some of his friends and colleagues, like George Bancroft or William H. Prescott, Sparks was not a man of leisure with ample family money to support him.

Success followed on success. Sparks furthered his notoriety with his single volume *Life of George Washington*. This work too provided steady income, which was all for Sparks and not part of the profits he shared with the Washington and Marshall families. His success was not only confined to the United States. In Europe too, his work sold well, and by 1840, earned him a reputation among the intelligentsia who had remembered him as a promising figure from his earlier visit. Both French and German readers proved quite receptive to the work.[3] Success in Germany was particularly gratifying. Germany was the center of historical scholarship, and gaining the recognition of the academics there was a unique and distinctive honor for Sparks.

One incident however marred his reception in France. Sparks had arranged with Francois Guizot, a respected scholar in his own right, to handle the French edition. Guizot had managed to overlook the omission of Sparks' name on the title page, and Sparks was certainly not amused. Furthermore, Guizot had independently written an essay on Washington which proved quite popular and led to Guizot being equated with the French edition of Washington's writings rather than Sparks.[4] In the end, there was little Sparks could do.

A work of erudition like Sparks produced was bound to attract those who benefitted from loose copyright laws. Within two years of publication, Sparks was in Federal Circuit Court in Boston. Sparks' good friend and colleague, Justice Joseph Story, presided in an unmistakable case of copyright infringement even according to the loose copyright environment of that time. In November 1839, Sparks easily prevailed against Charles Upham—a man Sparks knew well—who was forced to cease his actions on behalf of the pirated version of Sparks' work. Upham laid low for eleven years before he shipped the stereotype plates from his pirated edition to England, where publisher George Willis gladly printed and sold the set.[5]

Copyright law was still a far from settled field of law at the time. Sparks recognized this and did what he could when he first published his edition. Sadly, the United States and England didn't have reciprocal recognition of copyright law. Consequently, Sparks lost thousands of dollars to pirated versions of his work, particularly in England.

Copyright

The first true copyright law in England pertaining to authors did not appear until 1709 in a statute by Queen Anne. Prior to that time, for hundreds of years, copyright had only protected printers and publishers. England led the legal and literary world in copyright protection and enhanced the duration of that protection throughout the eighteenth and nineteenth centuries. In fact, "between 1735 and 1875, no less than thirteen parliamentary acts governed the legal application of copyright in the United Kingdom."[6] Toward the end of the nineteenth century, in 1886, England once again took the lead with other European countries in establishing the principal of reciprocity with the creation of the Berne Convention of 1886. This treaty effectively ended the common practice of piracy engaged in by publishers, particularly in dealing with foreign authors. During this same period however, the United States "continued to regard the work of a foreign (i.e., non-resident) author as unprotected 'common' property."[7] The United States continued to allow pirated editions of foreign authors to be legally printed until 1891, "when the United States finally agreed to discontinue sanctioning literary piracy."[8] Foreign authors such as Charles Dickens had petitioned for decades to get the Congress to accept international copyright conventions.[9] Even American writers such as Mark Twain complained bitterly that American publishers should not be allowed to pirate foreign works royalty free because that took away from the ability of American writers to get published in the country with royalties. For publishers, it was cheaper and more profitable to pirate foreign works rather than take on American works. Essentially, this practice had a negative impact on American literary talent, or so Twain and others contended.

Throughout the formative period of American literature,

> The interaction of the three modes of thought in the nineteenth century was often awkward. The typical British publisher wanted protection for his copyrights ... to keep his business competitive with practical, protectionist Yankee publishers, while the average British author desired to have his or her natural right in intellectual property acknowledged the world over, a concept inherent in the French model of copyright.[10]

The first American copyright law was passed in 1790. This act had little practical impact as it lacked an enforcement mechanism and allowed for the importation of pirated material. Few authors took advantage of the new law either. Throughout the 1790s and into the early nineteenth century, efforts were made to lobby Congress to strengthen copyright laws and confront the issue of pirated editions from overseas. Attempts were made to place high tariffs on books and printed materials imported into the United States, but these efforts too were largely ignored. It was not until 1830 that "Congress finally pass[ed] international copyright laws that made pirating of foreign imprints illegal by extending copyright protection to foreign authors."[11] At this time, 1830, "only one book in three sold in the United States came from an American press."[12] This legislation worked both ways in that it stopped foreign printers from publishing pirated American works, and it prevented American printers from publishing pirated foreign works.

America's protectionist attitude toward copyright lingered, especially with Canada, until 1986. The reason for the protracted literary dispute stemmed from an error in 1842 in a piece of British legislation which left the colonies [i.e. Canada] out of a provision that was designed to prevent American publishers from flooding British markets with cheap, pirated editions of works of

British authors. This loophole most noticeably impacted Canada, where Britain "acknowledged the futility of trying to stem the tide of American books washing across the world's longest undefended border."[13]

Professor Sparks

Teaching was never far from Sparks' mind. In 1835, he wrote to his friend George Ticknor, who was traveling in Europe,

> I have an idea of a project for teaching history by direct instructions and lectures, and I am desirous of procuring from abroad whatever may aid me in such a design. As you will naturally look into some of the principal universities, you may perhaps pick up now and then a syllabus of lectures of a plan for instructing in that department, or a printed course of lectures, or pamphlets and books illustrating the subject, which I shall be glad if you will send to me.[14]

Sparks was the most famous historian in America at the time, and his 1832 address to the Phi Beta Kappa Society, entitled "Some Characteristics of History as a Subject of Study, and particularly the History of the United States," made him even better known at his alma mater. After declining the initial offer to teach, Sparks was approached again in 1838 by Harvard President Josiah Quincy. Quincy had a dramatic offer: Sparks was to become the McLean Professor of Ancient and Modern History, "the first such history professorship, other than ecclesiastical, ever established in an American college or university."[15] The benefactor of the new endowment, John McLean, stated in his will "that the incumbent should deliver annually a course of public lectures in his department, for the benefit of the students of Harvard College, to such classes and at such times as the president and fellows might appoint."[16] Not a very tall order in terms of a workload. Sparks would be free to develop the department as he saw fit. In addition to Harvard, Sparks was asked to sketch out a department of history for the University of New York in 1835.

In an age which recognized the public intellectual, Sparks found great success, recognition, and appointments to professional organizations (see appendix five for a partial list of historical societies of which Sparks was a member). Sparks was also in great demand as a speaker, and his public lecture engagements became much more frequent as the 1840s and 1850s progressed.

12

The Bitter Harvest of Sparks' Washington

••••••

The decade of the 1840s was a period of great acclaim for Sparks as a scholar. He filled his time by teaching, researching, writing, and traveling. He was so successful that in 1849 he was appointed president of Harvard College. Yet, during the moment of his greatest professional accomplishment, he found himself under attack from nearly every quarter over a variety of topics pertaining to his *Washington.*

William Reed in 1847 had published a biography of his grandfather Joseph Reed. The elder Reed had been a private secretary to Washington, and the grandson had filled the biography with numerous letters and manuscript material. The younger Reed was a correspondent of Sparks,' and the two shared a mutual interest in memorializing the Revolutionary period. In fact, William Reed helped Sparks with the letters between Washington and his grandfather when Sparks was compiling his volumes.[1] William Reed's biography was in many ways inspired by Jared Sparks and was in no way intended as a "corrected" version of Sparks' work. Both men knew this. The biography Reed produced was nonetheless compared to Sparks' edition by a gentleman in New York. In a side-by-side comparison to Reed's version, Sparks' tendency to cautiously overedit became more apparent.[2] In an editorial on February 12, 1851, a writer known as Friar Lubin wrote a damaging critique of Sparks and his method in the New York *Evening Post.* Lubin, a pseudonym for John Bigelow (an editor and part owner of the *Post*) was blunt and accusatory of Sparks and left no doubt what he thought of Sparks' life work.[3] Not only was Sparks accused of editorial malfeasance, but his judgment in selecting which documents to feature was challenged too.

Sparks chose not to respond to the editorials. He had no reason to. His methods and criteria had already been outlined in great detail and excruciating minutiae to Bushrod Washington, John Marshall, Joseph Story, and to the general public in the preface to the *Washington Papers*. He had nothing to hide or respond to. Sparks himself stated this in a letter he wrote to Horace Binney in December 1852:

> The plan adopted for editing Washington's writings was explained at the outset, in the fullest and clearest manner, and I knew that I had faithfully executed the plan according to my best ability and judgment. The task of making a selection of the most valuable materials from so large a mass of papers, and of reconciling the discrepancies of different copies, was as difficult as it was arduous.[4]

Sparks continued in another letter:

> As to the general merits of the controversy, I have only to add that the mode of editing unpublished letters is a fair subject of criticism. But when an editor sets out certain principles with fullness and precision, the criticisms ought to proceed upon that basis, and not run into censures of him for not doing what he did not pretend to do. Hence it was unjustifiable in the critics to condemn my editorial labors with so much asperity, and at the same time to keep out of sight the explanations I had so largely and explicitly given in the introductory part of the work. This mode of proceeding was neither honorable nor just, since its only tendency was to pervert public opinion by making false impressions and exciting distrust.[5]

If anything, Bigelow was guilty of not being aware of how Sparks had prepared the public for what they would be receiving in his volumes. Bigelow seemingly came out of nowhere; perhaps as an attempt to make money for the *Post* by generating controversy with the most famous historian in the country, maybe even the world. Yet, Sparks let the year of 1851 pass by. When all appeared clear, Sparks was again assailed in the *Post* in December 1851. This time, the attack originated in England; and this time it came from a friend.[6]

Lord Mahon

Most damaging in many respects were the attacks that were hurled at Sparks from England. Philip Henry Stanhope, Lord Mahon, picked up on the *Post* editorial and wrote his own essay comparing the Sparks and Reed publications. Drawing nearly the exact same conclusion as Bigelow did (although Mahon claimed he came to his conclusion independent of Bigelow), the Lord Mahon exposé hurt Sparks more because it damaged his international reputation. Sparks valued his status as a revered historian because he felt above all other people claiming that title he had truly earned his. His investment of time, money, and physical stamina had worn Sparks down considerably. As already described, his workload and output was prodigious—nearly unimaginable. Yet, it would not fall to Sparks to be able to enjoy the fruits of his labors just yet.

Lord Mahon's charge against Sparks was as follows:

> I am bound, however, not to conceal the opinion I have formed, that Mr. Sparks has printed no part of the correspondence precisely as Washington wrote it; but has greatly altered, and, as he thinks, corrected and embellished it. Such a liberty with the writing of such a man might be justifiable, nay, even in some respects necessary, if Washington and his principal contemporaries had been still alive; but the date of this publication (the year 1838) leaves, as I conceive, no adequate vindication for tampering with the truth of history.[7]

Unfortunately, Sparks didn't defend himself well. He relied on colleagues to respond for him and tried to remain above the fray—the strategy proved ineffectual.

Sparks embarked on a quixotic defense "instead of simply admitting to omissions and alterations in the letters—which had been acceptable practice during the time he produced his monument—Sparks defended himself with uncharacteristic naiveté and some deception."[8] Sparks took the whole affair far too seriously. Rather than enjoin an academic discussion about the profession, Sparks chose to strike back in a manner not suited to his temperament. Much like a child being suddenly put upon by a school-yard bully, Sparks reacted in a way he was bound to lose—he chose to fight, and Sparks was no fighter. Sparks indeed felt he was being attacked by much larger forces than just academic disputation:

> Again, I had the best evidence for believing that Mahon was put upon his false track by meddlesome and interested persons in this country, with some of whom he had before been in correspondence. There was a scheme on foot, an editor's and publisher's project, for bringing out a new collection of Washington's writings, and it was thought that the best preliminary steps would be to ruin my edition. Hence the vehement and reckless attacks that first appeared in the newspapers. Under these circumstances, I thought it not worth while to go any further with Lord Mahon than to show him to be utterly in the wrong, as to every essential point which he made a ground of censure, and to rebuke in courteous terms his somewhat lofty airs and pretensions; taking care also not to divert the reader's attention by branching off into collateral topics, to which I was sometimes tempted by his presumptuous and overweening confidence.

Not satisfied, Sparks responded again in April 1852,

> To decide what papers should be selected in preference to others, where nearly all of them were in certain degree important and valuable, was felt to be a responsible, delicate, and difficult task, requiring a discriminating judgment and perfect impartiality in estimating their contents. Moreover, it was precisely one

of those cases in which any two minds, acting under different impressions, though aiming at the same end, would be likely often to differ.[9]

As a transitional figure, Sparks was bound to draw the ire of historians more radically devoted to a new approach. For Bigelow and Mahon, both vehement proponents of new scientific history, Sparks was simply too antiquated. His approach belonged to a previous era. He fit more snugly in a time when historical writing was more about subjective analysis as opposed to objective analysis. Sparks himself is certainly partly to blame for his acknowledged lapses of judgment in the editing process. Yet, each one of those identified lapses had represented a compromise which Sparks felt necessary to make in order to achieve the support of those few remaining Revolutionary era participants, and even more critically their descendants.[10] In his *Life and Writings of Jared Sparks,* Herbert Baxter Adams summed up the fracas thus:

> Mr. Sparks did exactly what he undertook to do, and was required to do by his agreement and understanding with Judge Washington and Judge Marshall. Mr. Sparks edited Washington's papers with some literary discretion, with a due regard to the interests of the living as well as of the dead. He proposed to issue in attractive, readable, popular form, a series of twelve volumes of good selections from a great mass of historical and biographical materials concerning the father of his country. It was a patriotic and literary undertaking, not a mere antiquarian reprint or an indiscriminate collection of documents.[11]

While an excuse, it is also a non-excuse, depending on one's interpretation. This is exactly what Sparks argued himself too. He wrote, "It is a matter, however, upon which there may be an honest difference of opinion, according to the views which individuals may entertain, without impeaching any one's integrity or motives; but the New York critics seem to have lost sight of candor and justice."[12]

Sparks received support from a wide spectrum of notables during the early 1850s in response to the Reed/Mahon strictures. United States Senator Charles Sumner, the famous abolitionist from Massachusetts, wrote in April 1852, "I begin by expressing my sincere satisfaction in your recent letters, which, it seems to me, amply vindicate your judgment and integrity in editing the papers of Washington."[13] Francis Parkman, himself a famous historian known for *The Oregon Trail,* published in 1849, and a former student of Sparks, wrote "I thank you for the copy which you sent me of your reply to the strictures on the writings of Washington. I had already read the letters as they appeared in the papers, and it seems to me that they must prove satisfactory to any person who is not blinded by interest or prejudice. I hear them spoken of in this manner."[14] William Hickling Prescott was another historian who came to Sparks' defense. Finally, James Mackee, librarian of the State Department, where Washington's papers were kept since their purchase by the federal government in 1834, wrote to Sparks, "No one cognizant of such facts would justly charge you with mutilating, suppressing, or altering the papers you have so faithfully and honorably edited."[15]

Over the course of three years, Bigelow, Mahon, Reed, and Sparks (sometimes acting through surrogates) traded point and counterpoint without inflicting a fatal blow on either side. The key fact all along was that Sparks was forced in many cases to use Washington's Letter Books, which were copies often at variance with the actual letters. Washington himself employed copyists to make transcriptions of his letters and papers, and in many cases these copyists altered or improved the originals, many times with Washington's approval. Actually, Washington himself started the trend of altering the manuscripts. Referring to the Reed letters which started the whole affair, Sparks wrote:

> I relied entirely on the transcripts furnished to me by himself [William Reed], which proved in many parts to be erroneous. His book is anything but ingenuous. He [Bigelow] prints the two texts in parallel columns, and leads the reader to understand that every variation between them was an editorial change made by me, whereas nearly all of them are discrepancies between the originals in his possession and the letter-books from which my text was drawn.[16]

The matter for Sparks seemed over until late in the 1850s, when one of the most respected authors in Europe and America defended Sparks one more time. Washington Irving, near the end of his life, and struggling to complete a biography of his namesake, wrote that the Sparks edition "could 'safely be relied upon for historical purposes.'"[17]

No Ill Will

Even with the uproar, Sparks was too much the gentleman and scholar to hold misjudgments against someone. When Lord Mahon reached out to Sparks via their mutual friend George Ticknor in January, 1853, Sparks welcomed the overture.

> It has given me concern to have found myself engaged in controversy with Mr. Sparks. I am told that he is coming on a visit to England. Pray, if you happen to see him, be so good as to say to him from me, that I hope the paper-war which has passed between us may not, in his opinion, preclude me from having the honor to call upon him on his arrival, and making his acquaintance. While I adhere to my own opinions and understand him as unreservedly to adhere to his, respecting editorship, I do not feel that difference as at all irreconcilable with my general sentiments towards him, as a fellow-laborer in the field of literature, of esteem and regard.[18]

In fact, Sparks and Mahon continued to share their writing with each other for mutual review and enjoyment. They came to share aspects of their literary lives over the next several years and came to a general understanding of bygones are bygones. They also each sponsored the other for membership in academic societies in their respective countries. It would have been fascinating had the two decided to come together and form some sort of society for historiography in connection with historical manuscripts. Unfortunately, they both were getting old, and tired.

Sparks had had enough. He retired from the Harvard presidency in 1854. He continued to write, research, and above all travel. He watched in horror as his beloved country nearly tore itself apart during the Civil War. He died peacefully in Cambridge, Massachusetts, on March 14, 1866.

Legacy

Even during his lifetime, Jared Sparks was a figure of controversy. His level of culpability for his "crimes" against the historical profession (both the nineteenth- and twentieth-century versions) is a topic which will no doubt continue to be debated and highly scrutinized for years to come. Sparks himself certainly did not set out to be a controversial figure. Like many of his predecessors in the field, Sparks was inspired by the American story and how best to preserve it. Building on the framework established by such figures as Ebenezer Hazard, David Ramsay, and Mercy Otis Warren, Sparks was able to make a living at his vocation and became quite wealthy and well known as a historian and scholar.

Sparks was an exceptional individual, and his knowledge was recognized as one of his many positive qualities. His understanding and willingness to entertain multiple perspectives earned him many loyal friends and admirers. Sparks' reputation also helped to challenge the attitudes many in England and Europe had concerning American intellectual endeavors. His work, and in fact his character, helped to smooth the way for a future generation of historians and researchers later in the nineteenth century, much as his persistence with Robert Peel in England to gain access to the British archives helped future researchers gain access to manuscripts.

With much of the Revolutionary generation dying off during his early years of writing, Sparks' project seemed on multiple levels to keep the aspirations and goals of that era alive and well. Aside from his pioneering work in historical writing, Sparks served this second function mostly by default. His efforts did not rekindle interest in the Revolutionary period so much as keep a slow, fading fire burning by reaching out to many who had first-hand recollections.

Due to his good timing, Sparks did not have to re-interest anyone because the link, albeit tenuous, was still present.

While initial reviews of his work were positive, even glowing, these reflected the strange status Washington held in the American psyche. In one respect, Sparks was almost bound to get initial good reviews; his subject matter ensured it. Yet, by 1837, the last of the Founding Fathers had died, and America could cautiously move into the realm of critical self-reflection. Yet in criticizing Sparks' work, it would seem that a reviewer might be attacking Washington himself—which in turn then would have been by extension an attack on the country.

In the end, Sparks indeed had altered Washington to reflect the type of hero Sparks had envisioned him to be. The public already had this exalted, manufactured view of Washington, so in a way Sparks simply gave his readers what they wanted. He was totally open about his methods though. He fully explained his editing methodology in the way modern editors explain their methods.

To this day, Sparks is dismissed by the historical community for the aggressive style of editing he employed with Washington's letters. In large measure this is like dismissing Washington because he owned slaves, or dismissing any person's life work because they followed the overriding impulses of their time. Sparks was even advised on his editing methodology. In 1828, President John Quincy Adams advised Sparks that he should "correct freely all blunders in orthography and grammar ... in Washington's letters."[19] His friend Samuel Eliot told Sparks he had a "duty" to protect Washington's image by correcting his letters.[20] Sparks likewise followed this practice in his other works, including the *Diplomatic History* and in his biography of Gouverneur Morris.

An opposing point of view came from Sparks' friend Charles Folsom, who cautioned that editors and copyists should "retain the bad spelling and false syntax [found in] original papers [and] should retain all such peculiarities of the author ... to show his quality and education, as well as the fashion of the times."[21] Supreme Court Justice Joseph Story, Sparks' personal friend, also found the level of editing somewhat unnecessary. Story was concerned with the attitude of the public and how they would respond to the changes, regardless of how minor they might be. Americans not familiar with the type of editorial processes professionals like Sparks employed might have a difficult time determining genuine from non-genuine. This could be even more complicated with a figure like Washington.[22]

Sparks was still very much a scholar and gentleman of the Enlightenment period. Regardless of how much he moved the study of history into the nineteenth century, he still clung, consciously or not, to the attitudes of that period which many of his countrymen had left behind. The idea of intuiting history was nothing new, and in a sense that is what Sparks would be accused of. He intuited, or divined, what Washington or other figures would have said had they had the proper opportunity, or perhaps a better education. The greatest of all eighteenth-century historians, Edward Gibbon, was well aware of the unique qualities of fact and nonfact intuition. Gibbon wrote,

> The confusion of the times and the scarcity of authentic memorials oppose equal difficulties to the historian who attempts to preserve a clear and unbroken thread of narration. Surrounded with imperfect fragments, always concise, often obscure, and sometimes contradictory, he is reduced to collect, to compare, and to conjecture; and though he ought never to place his conjectures in the rank of facts, yet the knowledge of human nature, and of the sure operation of its fierce and unrestrained passion, might on some occasions, supply the want of historical materials.[23]

Garry Wills has recently written that part of the reason writers like Sparks did what they did was because "the eighteenth century was a period of absolute monarchs and church authorities who kept their records sealed, handed out official versions of events, and censored or outlawed competing versions of the truth."[24] While Sparks will always be remembered for his work to unseal official records in England and Europe (not that it was a big problem in the United States), he will also be remembered for his less than successful attempts to recreate the language of the historical figures he wrote about. If we take Gibbon as a guide, Sparks indeed never did put his conjectures "in the rank of facts." Rather, Sparks was clear in his introduction to make certain his editorial methods.

Conclusion: The Benefits of History

••••••

Since the dawn of writing, history has played an important part in the repertory of written works.[1] The concept or idea of a heroic age in historical writing is a real phenomenon which serves a powerful social, cohesive goal. Just as American historians sought to create a new concept of unity in the meaning of a United States, so they also sought to develop a framework upon which to construct that concept. The need therefore for a heroic or inspirational story about the beginnings of a society or government provide a choice opportunity for historians to bring together multiple elements of unity, greatness, and uniqueness in an effort to fashion a national identity. This pattern of history was used to establish the contours of a society and government and dates to the earliest writing known to exist. It therefore seems a perfectly ordinary human response to have historians or writers construct the agreed upon versions of national identity. Tales of glory and heroism were put down on clay by the ancient Sumerians and are easily decipherable to this day. Recording the great works of a monarch are some of the earliest examples we have of what today we recognize as history. History designed to record, to inspire future generations, or to warn potential enemies; all these motivations and more drove our literate ancestors to put "pen to paper."

Yet, how different is the history written four thousand years ago from today? Do we not seek to warn our foes, record our deeds, or inspire future generations? Of course we do; and much more besides. In many ways, the history produced today is not really that much different regarding motivation as that produced five millennia ago. We can certainly argue that elements of objectivity are clearly and without question more ascendant today all the while with subjective writing not far behind.

Another way of putting it is to see the human element of creativity at work in objective history. The humanistic strain seeks to separate history from mere chronicling to truly attempt to represent a time, place, and a people, free of judgment or moralizing or enveloping patterns of nationalism. While these types of works are great for producing antiseptic, sterilized, comfortable versions of history, they do little to advance the understanding of the past as a human endeavor. Rather, comfortable history seeks to justify the elite through vignettes designed to celebrate their own peculiar characteristics at the expense of other peoples, therefore making the elites feel more superior to others.

The concept of "others" has been a strong motivating force in historical writing. Without an "other" there is generally no need to expound upon one's perceived greatness. To this day the concept is quite strong and molds the writing and learning of both scholars and the reading public.

Most successful societies feel the need to transmit the key elements of their success to future generations. They impart key elements to their own citizens of course to propagate the society; to others (noncitizens) as both a boastful narrative and as a means of persuasion. In the two centuries covered by this work (1650–1850), events transpired that had consequences far beyond British North America. Debates raged over government, religion, and economics; in essence, the rights of man. Epic struggles ultimately decided through arms foretold the fortune of the world we inhabit today.

At the turn of the eighteenth century, America was powerful enough to recognize itself as unique. America was unique regarding outlook and of having been spared the horrific wars that tore Europe and England apart in the seventeenth century. This turned out to be a critical point. America, safely insulated for the most part, began to develop its own understanding of an organic life and culture. Without the opportunity to keep a safe distance from war, America could have been doomed before it began.

The dreams and aspirations of the earliest seventeenth-century settlers gave way to the realities of distance and new peoples. In an attempt to reflect that the best was yet to come, writers, not yet historians, sought to portray their new home in America as a work in progress. That positive outlook was reinforced countless times before 1700. The writers and historians crafted a story whose time frame was the future, not the past. In many respects, the earliest historians were future oriented, not looking to the past. This approach started to change during and especially after the Revolution when America was able to write its own story and begin to craft a national ethos built on facts, and not dreams. It is a transformation in approach that is still being perfected today.

Without a past to reconstruct, early American historians could rely only on a vision of the future—yet with a genuine sense of singularity from England or Europe. The buildup of the inevitable (as the writers prophesied) aspects of American greatness was the method employed to secure a past for the colonies. The adventures and hardships of the early settlers had to be redeemed in some manner by a future generation. This future generation had an enormous burden to carry by thus being weighted by the hand of their ancestors whether they liked it or not. This redemptive quality also played nicely into many of the quasi-religious approaches to history that continually hovered around the edges of historical writing that tried, but never succeeded, in gaining a strong following outside fragmentary groups easily influenced by such writing.

History can thus be seen as a civic virtue, a foundation upon which a society, a culture, or even a civilization appears in its best light and most often for the benefit of its own people. In this instance, historiography is more than narrative or chronicle; it becomes a pattern, in a written form, of how to remember the past. History is thus rendered a monument of words, just as inspiring and moving as a monument of stone.

For history to be truly meaningful though, it must be free of nationalism, patriotism, or societal egomanias. As John Marshall's publisher, C. P. Wayne, mentioned to him, he needed to tone down the Americanism if he hoped to reach a larger audience.

Currently, the debate on the universality of history is being carried out in multiple ways across the world. One of the most famous examples involves the Elgin Marbles at the British Museum. Greece has tried for years to have the Marbles from the Parthenon repatriated to their native land from England. Greece even built a museum especially for the Marbles as an attempt to pressure the British Museum to act. Thus far, the British Museum has not. What the British Museum has done however is lay down the perspective under which they claim the Marbles.

The current director of the British Museum, Neil MacGregor, has framed the argument for the Marbles' staying in Britain in terms of the universality of human history. Rather than granting the nationalistic overtones for Greece of the Marbles, MacGregor argues that it is his museum's "duty to 'preserve the universality of the Marbles and to protect them from being appropriated as a nationalistic political symbol.'"[2]

Can George Washington be seen as a universal symbol of history? Or, is George Washington simply a nationalistic symbol? These are large questions and not easily answered—if they can even be accurately answered. Washington, like the Elgin Marbles, the Magna Carta, or any other potent symbol of national pride, can never fully be judged in terms purely objective. History is more than names and dates; history more likely then is relative to perspective. In this light, history is still a process, but not necessarily a destination. We promote our museums and historical sites as though history was a destination determined by those running such institutions. Naturally, history must be more than this if it is ever going to survive in the public sphere.

Or, as Lord Acton was later to write concerning the *Cambridge Modern History,* of which he served as the first editor when it began publishing in 1902, wrote: "Contributors will understand that ... our Waterloo must satisfy French and English, German and Dutch alike; that nobody can tell, without examining the list of authors, where the Bishop of Oxford [Stubbs] laid down his pen, and whether Fairbairn or Gasquet [a Catholic cardinal], Liebermann or Harrison took it up."[3] To further the point, history, to be true, meaningful history, needs to belong to everyone. History needs to be understood to have an impact. If it is not understood by others, it is not history. Without the human element that is recognized by humans, it is myth. Contrary to the popularity of written history with a singular focus designed for immediate consumption within a particular group, it needs to be understood by others to stand the test of time. As J. G. A. Pocock states, "What explains the past legitimates the present and moderates the impact of the past upon it."[4] This in a way ensured the somewhat mystical or supernatural components surrounding the American founding. Professor Pocock alludes to this when he comments, "Part of the history of a society is the history of what it has done; to which we may add the history of what it says it has done, and the history of how it has come to say it—to tell this particular history."[5]

Telling a "particular history" is where so much of history goes astray. Particular history is history designed for one group of people. It is a historical approach which nearly defies historiography in that it approaches a psychological impression of a particular group of people marketed as history. A historical process that is identifiable by all societies is necessary for a true definition of history. Without that consensus definition, history does not exist. What does exist in its place is platitudinous gratification designed to gratuitously garner the approbation of the largest number of members of a particular group of people. In this case, "a historian in a more civic society may believe that he is writing the truth, when he is in fact writing what asserts the beliefs and the interests of a party or a class."[6] The most sincere form of history comes about by the historian who prepares a history which exposes the immense struggles existing within the community they write about. As Professor Pocock explains,

> In two ways, therefore, historians are likely to discover that there can be more than one history of events within the society, and that any event may be part of more histories than one, since those who remember it differently live in the histories they remember. The historian who has access to both lives in a multiplicity of histories, and informs his society that its history is contested, debatable and multiple.[7]

History is thus identity; a powerful motivation for establishing and maintaining a sovereign conception of self or nationhood. Ultimately, history is so complex because we are so complex. We are all living a multitude of histories bound up into the present. History "will be told to, of and by the members of that society, in terms which must be partly those of the public language that society has formed for itself and has a particular need and capacity to speak, write and understand."[8]

One-dimensional history produced for internal consumption also is usually terribly simplified. Lost in the rush to prop up "core values" is the intensely complex nature of history. Simply put, history is about people, and people are not simple. Longing for or desiring simple history

> is perhaps to miss the point of the past—that it is *complex,* and therefore demands our care and attention. Every history is provisional, an attempt to say something in the face of impossible complexity. There is a weight of responsibility here on the historian: never to try to claim that his or her account is the *only* way of telling the story. But there is responsibility for the reader also: not to discount histories, because they are imperfect, but to engage them as the true stories they can only be.[9]

Simply put, there is no such thing as a "definitive" history.

Epilogue: The German Influence on Sparks

••••••

German institutions were at the forefront in the nineteenth century of historiography as a developing, serious discipline. While the overall theme of this work is the rise of American historiography in the large sense, one component of that theme has to do with the larger movement in historical criticism that was forming in Europe, particularly in Germany. It has been seen that one of the major motivations during the development of American writing throughout the eighteenth century was the impetus of prophecy relating to the future destiny or greatness of the American colonies—and later states. This determination to predict was as strong as the eventual desire to succeed.

Europe and European (including Britain) ways of thought and acting and living were obviously bound to impact Americans. Even after independence, no one seriously believed that Americans could simply turn their collective backs on European ways and go about their business. One area in which this was particularly true was the realm of scholarly thought and activity.

In particular, German universities were at the forefront of a virtual revolution in the study and writing of history. At the turn of the nineteenth century, German intellectuals were quickly exploring the field of historiography in an effort to move away from the simplified name and date approach, which had dominated the field as long as could be remembered. In some ways the elements that precipitated the professionalization of academic history in Germany helped to fuel the American imitation of the German development. The strong components of local and regional history written in the colonies through at least the mid-eighteenth century were in fact an abbreviated version of what occurred in Germany over a much larger span of time. Germany was not unified

165

as a political state until the late nineteenth century and thus had over a millennium to perfect the art and pattern of regional historical writing. The American colonies on the other hand, by comparison, seem to be accelerated in the extreme. Yet, whether the impetus was nurtured over centuries or decades, the end result was highly similar, and most scholars and academics in the United States by the early nineteenth century recognized this loose similarity, while not actually making a direct comparison.

Perhaps the most influential of all the academic German historians of the nineteenth century was Leopold von Ranke. The English historian Lord Acton described Ranke and his influence as "the representative of the age which instituted the modern study of history. He taught it to be critical, to be colourless and to be new. We meet him at every step, and he has done more for us than any other man."[1] For all the accolades showered on Ranke, he of course had his limitations. But, for the purposes of American historians studying in Germany, and studying the German approach heavily influenced by Ranke, his contribution, both directly and indirectly, was indeed extensive. Certainly the most direct way the connection can be made is by highlighting the notable American historians who studied in Germany and then returned home to institute some version of what they learned.

One such historian was Henry Adams, grandson and great-grandson of American presidents. Adams, "who, like most notable nineteenth- and early-twentieth-century American historians, had trained in Germany, introduced such a seminar at Harvard in 1871 (there was another at Johns Hopkins) and supervised several of the earliest Harvard PhDs in the early 1870s, half a century before such seminars began to be introduced in England."[2]

In multiple ways, Jared Sparks was one of the first Americans to recognize the gradual shift in historical emphasis occurring in the intellectual community. Sparks gained this awareness in part through his work at the *North American Review*. It was on the pages of the *Review* that a new approach represented the first effort by Americans, which gained the respect and attention of Europeans. The *Review* encouraged a "climate for the study and the discussion of the then evolving forms of Romantic literature and philosophy."[3] Sparks himself had indeed first gained recognition as an intellectual through his efforts at the *Review*. Yet, as described, for all of his awareness and acceptance of new approaches to historical writing, Sparks still held strongly to many of the qualities of earlier historical writing.

Sparks' fortuitous living in Boston enabled him to tap into the strong currents of thought gathering in that city which allowed "for the dissemination of radical ideas and philosophies and the controversy surrounding liberal religious and political doctrines."[4] Sparks further gained from the specific area of radical thought being pursued in the *Review* and in Europe. History as a separate academic discipline was beginning to make progress, and the efforts put forth by pioneers like Sparks drew attention. The *Review* thus served as a vehicle that provided a venue for Sparks and others to work through their theories and attempt to find a new approach to historical study.

In addition to the new approach to historical study which the *Review* represented, the publication also brought the concept of a literary periodical the serious attention it needed. The concept of a journal held specific connotations—especially in the southern states. Publishers and writers faced a reading audience "with the very popular belief that literature and criticism were both amusement and diversion"—not serious writing.[5] In the north the view was nearly the same, with the exception that serious writing had an air of quaintness to it that did not generally exist in the south.[6] In instances, serious writing to the general, potential, reading public was viewed as barely worth the time or effort to read or even compose.[7]

Yet, the early editors pressed on. The desire in the United States to emulate European manners and customs extended naturally to intellectual pursuits. And as a result of the interest shown to European publications of a similar vein, the American version received some much-needed attention. It was on the pages of the European journals that the new approach to "a study of philosophical history" came to gather a following. Among the Americans most impacted by this development was Jared Sparks.

In the period between Sparks' two periods as editor, the *Review* moved more and more purposefully to becoming a "distinctly literary and historical publication."[8] This transformation paralleled the awakening in Sparks to his own latent understanding and developing conception of history. It was however the German ingredient which brought the Americans, including Sparks, to more fully appreciate the possibilities of a journal devoted to intellectual pursuits in history and literature.

This awareness in the United States by 1825 owed a considerable amount to the earliest pioneers in historiography—Charles Brockden Brown primary among them. While Brown helped set the stage in the United States, he had no impact whatsoever in Europe. His work was far too early, and he was not associated with the literary elite of Philadelphia in the way Sparks would be in Boston twenty-five years later. The European development of philosophical historiography was organic in the sense it grew out of the ashes of the French Revolution and ultimately the horrors of the Napoleonic Wars.

If the American Revolution is considered in the sequence, the fifty years from 1775 to 1825 saw an unprecedented change in world social, political, and economic understandings, which challenged traditional methods of interpreting historical events. Much like Charles Brockden Brown in 1800, the philosopher of history by mid-century had moved well beyond the simplistic nonhuman responses to world events.

> Even if one agrees that the development of modern historiography should be viewed as a seamless web extending back to the Renaissance, it was not until the late nineteenth century that the cognitive superiority of historical writing based on critical use of source materials, archival research, and a historicist view of human society was able to establish itself.[9]

It is abundantly clear that the rise of American literary philosophical history had its roots in the rise of German Romantic thought at the turn of the nineteenth century. This development in historical understanding reached American readers through travelers and the few students who studied at German universities. For "out of the New England historical and cultural setting, the criticism of German Philosophical thought accurately reflected the urgent contemporary need for a debate on the direction and meaning of American history."[10] This new approach ultimately permeated all facets of intellectual pursuit and in the historical realm ultimately led to the appointment of the first chair of history in the United States at Harvard. Jared Sparks was the first holder of the position. The time had arrived by the end of the first quarter of the nineteenth century for America to take a stand on an intellectual par with Europe. The old cultural nemesis written about by so many writers over the previous two centuries had finally come to be laid to rest.

Appendix 1: Jared Sparks to Bushrod Washington, January 26, 1826

••••••

The first letter (nearly ten pages) from Jared Sparks to Bushrod Washington spells out in grand detail the ambitious plan he has arrived at "after very mature reflection" for the publishing of President Washington's collected papers. He meticulously outlines the plan which will consist of three parts: (1) Official Letters; (2) State Papers, & other official documents; (3) Private Correspondence.

As Sparks states, his ambition is to "make every statement & allusion clearly understood and exhibit, in connexion [sic] with the letters, a thread of history as continuous and perfect as the nature of the subject will admit." Near the end of his letter, Sparks writes that it is his desire that his project will serve "both as a tribute due to the name of Washington, and a repository for the perpetuating the most valuable treasures of American history." Sparks vowed to "engage resolutely" in his project and promised to "spare neither industry nor expense" to produce a work which is "creditable to the fame of Washington, to our literature, and our national history." It is striking that Sparks held to his plan over a ten-year project.

Boston, January 26, 1826

To the
    Hon Bushrod Washington,
        Sir

You may recollect, that nearly two years ago I wrote you concerning a design, which a friend of mine then had, of publishing an edition of "General Washington's Works." As he did not carry his purpose into execution, I was myself led to examine the subject, and have read with great attention such of the writings of General Washington, as I have been able to obtain. I have also made numerous inquiries, respecting his official letters to the Governors of the states, during the revolution,

169

and to the principal officers of the army. The result of my investigation has been, that there is in existence a vast number of unpublished letters written by him, which are of the highest importance as containing materials for a correct history of the country, and as exhibiting in a still more imposing light, than has yet been done, the extraordinary resources and powers of the author's mind, and the controlling influence of his opinions and character, in gaining the independence, and establishing the free governments which are now the glory and happiness of his countrymen, and the admiration of the world.

Under this conviction, and after very mature reflection and extensive enquiry, I have resolved, should such a project meet your approbation, to collect and publish all the works of General Washington, both such as have already appeared in print, and such as are to be found in manuscript. My plan is to accompany the whole with a full body of notes and historical illustrations, and to arrange the material under the following divisions,

Part 1 Official Letters

This division will embrace all General Washington's correspondence which may be strictly called official; that is, his letters to the Governor of Virginia, while engaged in the French War; his letters to the President of Congress, and the committee on the army during the revolution; his letters to the governors of the states and committees appointed to correspond with him by different legislatures; his letters to the officers of the army, and the other individuals engaged in public affairs; and such of his letters, while president of the United States, as may be deemed of an official character.

The two volumes of "Washington's Official Letters," first published in London, in the year 1795, embrace those only which were addressed to the president of Congress from the time he took command of the army in June, 1775, to the end of the year 1778, about three years and a half. These were copied in the Secretary's office at Philadelphia, by a person who took them to London, and published them, with the apparent design of continuing the series. But the sale did not probably encourage him to fulfill his intentions as he is still living in London, and nothing in addition to the above two volumes has appeared. These letters were doubtful correctly copied, but they are printed with many omissions, which were thought necessary to accommodate them to the state of public feeling at the time. I do not find, that any of the letters to Congress, after the year 1778, have been printed; nor any of the vast numbers, which he wrote to the governors of the states; nor any of those sent to officers of the army, except in a few instances, where memoirs of the general officers have been written.

I have learnt from the secretaries of several states, that many letters from General Washington are on file among the public papers, copies of which can be obtained without difficulty. The same thing I have also ascertained, in regard to the papers left by some of the leading officers of the army. Many letters from the Commander in Chief are found among them. In the library of the Massachusetts Historical Society, is a volume of [?] letters by General Washington, collected from the papers of Governor Hancock, & deposited there by his widow. In the same library is also a series of volumes of manuscripts, which belonged to Governor Trumbull, & which contain all General Washington's correspondence with him & gentlemen in New Hampshire has a full copy of the proceedings of the committee of Congress, which visited the army in 1780, to consult with the commander in chief on important affairs. In this manuscript volume are contained fifteen letters from General Washington, unpublished letters of his are also deposited in the library of the New York Historical Society. In short, it would not be easy to calculate the number which may be gathered from different sources, by a thorough & persevering examination.

When these are collected, my purpose is to arrange them in chronological order and to add such explanations by way of notes, as will make every statement & allusion clearly understood and exhibit, in connexion with the letters, a thread of history as continuous and perfect as the nature of the subject will admit. In constructing the notes, many valuable material may be drawn from the letters written in reply to those of General Washington very few of which have ever been published. To what extent these may be obtained, can be known only by future enquiry. Copies of these written by the Governor, & other authorities of the states, are unquestionably preserved. All other sources of information will likewise be resorted to, on which premise in any way to aid the execution of my plan.

Part II State Papers, & other official documents

In this division will be brought together his messages to Congress, addresses, general orders to the army, and whatever other papers there may be of a public nature, which cannot be properly ranked under the division of official letters.

The notes and illustrations here will principally relate to the political state of the times; to the opinions, views, and purposes of the author, to his wisdom in devising measures of the most salutary kind, and his influence and the weight of his character in carrying them into effect, to his agency in directing the progress of events, and leading them to the best ends in establishing the new government on a solid foundation; and, indeed, to whatever may elucidate the history of his political life.

Part III Private Correspondence

In this department much discretion must of course be exercised. It is not to be supposed, that all his private letters, nor all that can be collected, are suited to publication. There is much even here, however, that is not only curious, but valuable. His agricultural correspondence with Sir John Sinclair, & Mr. Anderson, which was published in England, will come under the head; and many letters, which here appeared from time to time in public papers and journals; as well as numerous others in manuscript, known to be in the hands of individuals. Of this description of letters, I should not be disposed to print any, except such as you, & other judicious persons, may deem in accordance with the dignity of the work, as containing interesting facts, or developing traits of the author's mind and character.

The notes under this division will be few & short, explaining such parts of the letters as may require it, & detailing such particulars and incidents, as may come to my knowledge, respecting the private pursuits, and the characteristic habits & opinions of the writer.

I have thus, Sir, in a few words as possible, disclosed to you my plan. In making to you this frank and explicit exposition, I have two objects in view. First, as it is a thing in which you, as an individual, are more deeply interested than any other person, it is highly proper for me to ascertain, whether you approve my undertaking, and are willing to promote it by your counsel & aid, before I take any public meas-

ures for prosecuting it. And secondly, it is of the utmost importance for me to know
whether you will consent that access may be had to the papers of General Washington in your possession.

I am aware, that there is some delicacy in the second point, nor should I venture
to make the inquiry were I not encouraged to do it by many gentlemen, to whom
I have explained my designs, on whose judgment I can rely, & to whom the fame
of no man is dearer, than that of Washington's. These have professed, one and all,
to regard my project as one of a magnitude and importance which justify me in
making even such an application; and whatever may be your view, as to the expe-
diency of allowing the papers to be examined, I cannot doubt you will duly appreciate my motives, & freely excuse any thing that may to you have the appearance of
impropriety in the liberty I take. It was the habit of General Washington to preserve
copies of his correspondence. While in the army he kept regular letter books for
this purpose; and from many circumstance I infer that the same was done in respect
to most of his private letters. In his correspondence with Mr. Anderson, for instance,
he sent a duplicate of a letter which he found had not reached its destination.

Now, as it is to be presumed, that General Washington's letters have been preserved with great care, by the persons into whose possession they may have fallen,
it can hardly be doubted, that a public advertisement would bring nearly all of them
to light, and those in the archives of the legislatures of the states may be had by
direct application; yet, after every effort is made, there must be deficiencies, particularly in regard to letters among the papers of the general officers of the army,
whose descendants may desire to retain them for a first publication in a future biographical notice of the person to whom they were written. And some will also necessarily be overlooked; that are in the offices of the secretaries of the States, by
reason of the masses of papers with which they will be connected. The only possible
mode of supplying such deficiencies, is by examining the copies of correspondence
left by General Washington. If you agree with me, therefore, as you most certainly
will, that if such a work is to be executed, it should be done in as complete and perfect a manner as possible, I think you will not fail to see, in a clear and convincing
light, the force of these hints.

Again, there are other documents of the highest value among the papers of General Washington, many of which cannot be supposed to exist any where else, and
these are the letters received by him during his whole public life. It would seem
that he was as remarkable for retaining the original of all letters sent to him as for
preserving copies of his own. In almost every letter to Congress he mentions copies
of letters enclosed, which he had received from public person and the originals of
which, were kept by himself. In some cases, it is not likely the writers of these preserved copies in others, where copies were taken at the time, they have doubly been
lost in the vicissitudes through which they have passed, so that at the day it is prob-
able, that the only copies in being are the single ones among the papers at Mount
Vernon. Yet these letters unfold many of the leading principle and moving stirrings
of the revolution; they afford the very best materials of history, and, in a work, are
absolutely essential to illustrate the work of General Washington.

With these views of the subject, I shall leave it to your better judgment to decide
in what light it is proper for you to regard my proposed undertaking. As to myself,
it only needs be added, that I have been chiefly influenced by a deep conviction of
the importance of such work, both as a tribute due to the name of Washington,

and a repository for perpetuating the most valuable treasures of American history, which, in their present scattered state are subject to be swept into oblivion by every wind that blows, exposed to the mercy of accident, & the consuming power of the elements. My thoughts have been more or less occupied with the plan for the last two years, as a literary enterprise it falls in with my inclination and pursuits; but the labor of collecting materials so widely diffused, & of preparing them in the way I propose for the press, is one of which no adequate conception can be formed by any person who has not had some experience in work of a similar kind. But I have resolved to engage resolutely in the task, if I undertake it at all, and to spare neither industry nor expense in endeavoring to execute it, as far as my ability will allow, in a manner creditable to the fame of Washington, to our literature, and our national history.

For further information, as to my purposes and qualifications, permit me Sir, to refer you to Judge Story with whom I have conversed on the subject, and who manifests a lively interest in the plan of collecting into one body all the writings of General Washington. With Mr. Webster and Mr. Wheaton I am also acquainted, and I doubt not they will readily answer any inquiries, you may wish to make respecting my character and pursuits.

I shall write to Judge Marshall, and I hope you will do me the favor to show him this letter, that he may fully understand my views and motives.

I have the honor to be, Sir
    With great respect,
        Your Ot. Servant—Jared Sparks

Appendix 2: Bushrod Washington to Jared Sparks, March 13, 1826

......

The second letter from Bushrod Washington to Jared Sparks spells out, in ambiguous terms, the fact that Justice Washington and Chief Justice Marshall have, "for some years past" been engaged in a similar, albeit less encompassing, project. Justice Washington states, "It is our intention to publish many of the letters" relating to the affairs which President Washington involved himself in as a military commander and as a statesman.

Washington March 13th 1826.

Sir

Your letter of the 26th January was handed me by Mr Justice Story, and I owe you an apology for the delay which has taken place in answering it. The truth is that, although living under the same roof, the important cases which the Judges have had to examine and discuss in conference diverted the attention of the C. Justice & myself from the subject, insomuch, that it is but lately that we had an opportunity of conversing upon it.

The only answer which it is now in my power to give to your proposal will be contained in the following statement of facts.—A part of the work which you contemplate writing has for some years past engaged the attention, & commanded the labour, of the C. Justice & myself. It is now completed, and we expect in the course of the next summer to put to press about three volumes of what we judge to be the most interesting of Genl. Washington's letters, written during the war of the revolution, and subsequent to its termination. It is further our intention to publish many of the letters addressed to him by the governors of the several states, foreign officers & others during those periods.

The letters written by him prior to and during the French war, are, many of them, copied, and will be published at some future period. I am Sir very respectfully Your mo. Ob. Servt.

Bushrod Washington

Appendix 3: Washington Papers Contract

••••••

The contract or agreement signed by Jared Sparks, Bushrod Washington, and John Marshall is transcribed here. In the agreement, Justice Washington (and Chief Justice Marshall) agreed that Sparks would "have free access to the said papers of the said General Washington at Mount Vernon, with full permission to examine and to take copies." Sparks however, cannot remove letters from Mount Vernon without written permission. Sparks agreed to "take upon himself the charge and responsibility of the literary part of the said work," and to basically engage fully and completely in the enterprise. Sparks would pay up front the cost associated with the research and publishing. These costs would be reimbursed to Sparks from proceeds from the sale of the work. Justice Washington and Chief Justice Marshall would share in the profits once Sparks is reimbursed. The copyright was to be shared two ways between Sparks on one side, and Justice Washington and Chief Justice Marshall on the other.

Articles of agreement entered into this seventh day of March in the year eighteen hundred and twenty seven between Jared Sparks of the state of Massachusetts of the first part, and John Marshall of the city of Richmond and Bushrod Washington of Mount Vernon, both of the state of Virginia witness, that whereas the party of the first part proposes to prepare for publication and to publish an edition of the Works of General Washington according to a plan proposed by the party of the first part in a letter from him bearing date the 26th day of January in the year eighteen hundred and twenty six addressed to the said Bushrod Washington one of the parties of the second part, which work the said party of the first part now engages to execute according to the plan proposed in the said letter (reference whereto is here made as part of these articles) the said party of the first part taking upon himself the charge and responsibility of the literary part of said work and the business of finding a publisher and of superintending the publication, it is hereby covenanted and agreed by and between the aforesaid parties in manner and form following, that is to say;- First, the said party of the first part covenants and agrees in consideration of having access to all the papers in possession of the said Bushrod Washington, which were devised to him by his uncle the said General Washington, and permission to take copies on extracts from the same, subject to the qualification herein after mentioned, to prepare for publication and to publish an edition of General Washington's Words, according to the plan proposed by the said party of the first part in the letter before mentioned (which letter is now distinguished by the name's of the parties to this agreement being endorsed thereon), and to execute the said work according to the said plan, and to take upon himself the charge and responsibility of the literary part of the said work, and the business of finding a publisher, and of superintending the publication thereof and to secure the copyright thereof.—Second, the said Bushrod Washington covenants and agrees, that the said party of the first part shall have free access to the said papers of the said General Washington at Mount Vernon, with full permission to examine and to take copies or extracts of the same at Mount Vernon, but not to remove the said papers, or any or either of them to any other place without the leave of the said Bushrod Washington first obtained in writing, or, in case of his death, of the person to whom or to whose care they shall and may be committed by the said Bushrod Washington by his will or otherwise, it being fully understood and agreed by the parties to this agreement, that any paper may be withheld which the parties of the second part both or either of them, do not deem suited or proper for publication; and the parties of the second part further covenant and agree to deliver to the party of the first part, with a view to facilitate his labors, the copies of letters from and to the said General Washington, which they have caused to be made, free of any change.— Third, the said Jared Sparks on his part covenants and agrees, that the parties of the second part shall be equally interested with himself in the property of the copyright or copyrights to the said work, and in the profits of the sales, after the expenses of the said Sparks, the said party of the first part, which have been or shall hereafter be incurred in procuring materials for the historical illustrations of the said work, shall be deducted from the said profits of the sales; that is to say, the said Sparks of the first part is to be entitled to a moiety of the property in the said copyright or copyrights, and to a moiety of the profits of sales of the said work, after the said deduction is made, and the said parties of the second part to the other moiety of the said copyright or copyrights, and of the said profits of sales after the said deduction is made.

Bushrod Washington [seal]
John Marshall [seal]
Jared Sparks [seal]

Appendix 4: Major Works
by Jared Sparks

••••••

1. *Life and Travels of John Ledyard*—1828.
2. *The Diplomatic Correspondence of the American Revolution*—1829–1830 (12 volumes).
3. *The American Almanac and Repository of Useful Knowledge*—1830.
4. *The Life of Gouverneur Morris*—1832 (3 volumes).
5. *The Life and Writings of George Washington*—1834–1837 (12 volumes).
6. *The Works of Benjamin Franklin; with Notes, and a Life of the Author*—1836–1840 (10 volumes).
7. *The Library of American Biography*—1834–1838 (10 volumes); 1844–1847 (15 volumes).
8. *Correspondence of the American Revolution*—1853 (4 volumes).

One final note: During 1833–35, while Sparks was working on the Washington papers project, he boarded at the Craige house in Cambridge, Massachusetts. Today, this house is known as the Longfellow National Historical Site. It became the home of Henry Longfellow and his family several years after Sparks had left and after the owner Mrs. Craige died. Longfellow and Sparks worked as colleagues at Harvard. Coincidently, the Craige home, before the Craiges owned it, was also the headquarters of General Washington after he was appointed commander in chief of the Continental Army in 1775.

Appendix 5: Literary and Historical Societies to Which Jared Sparks Was Elected[1]

••••••

Phi Beta Kappa Society, Harvard University, August 16, 1812.

Maryland Academy of Sciences and Arts, July 22, 1821.

American Academy of Language and Belles-Lettres, Washington, D.C., April 5, 1822.

American Academy of Arts and Sciences, May 25, 1825.

Massachusetts Historical Society, August 29, 1826.

Columbian Institute, Washington, D.C., October 7, 1826.

American Antiquarian Society, October 23, 1827.

Michigan Historical Society, August 30, 1830.

Indiana Historical Society, December 11, 1831.

Pennsylvania Historical Society, March 20, 1834.

Golden Branch Society, Phillips Exeter Academy, November 7, 1834.

American Philosophical Society, April 21, 1837.

Antiquarian Society of Copenhagen, October 30, 1837.

Antiquarian Society of Athens, June 20, 1838.

Kentucky Historical Society, July 30, 1838.

Historical and Geographical Society of Brazil, December 1, 1839.

Georgia Historical Society, July 8, 1840.

National Institution, Washington, D.C., August 22, 1840.

Illinois Literary and Historical Society, December 18, 1843.

Scientific and Literary Society, Palermo, February 11, 1844.

Connecticut Historical Society, April 3, 1844.

Maryland Historical Society, April 4, 1844.

Missouri Historical and Philosophical Society, January, 1845.

Royal Academy of Sciences, Berlin, February, 1845.

American Colonization Society, March 22, 1845.

New Jersey Historical Society, September 4, 1845.

New England Historic-Genealogical Society, October 7, 1846.

Royal Academy of Sciences, Turin, November, 1849.

New Hampshire Historical Society, July 12, 1850.

Ohio Historical and Philosophical Society, May 26, 1852.

Newport Historical Society, November 23, 1853.

Society of Antiquarians, London, February 15, 1854.

Wisconsin Historical Society, March 6, 1854.

Old Colony Historical Society, April 3, 1854.

Iowa Historical Society, March 4, 1857.

Moravian Historical Society, July 13, 1857.

Chicago Historical Society, November 24, 1857.

Historical Society of Tennessee, January 5, 1858.

Historical Society of New Mexico, January 30, 1860.

Vermont Historical Society, 1860.

Appendix 6: George C. Washington to Jared Sparks, 1849

••••••

Among the numerous charges brought against Sparks over the years is that he corrupted the collection from Mount Vernon by giving, selling, or otherwise causing portions of the collection to go unaccounted for. While it is true that Sparks occasionally gave letters as mementoes to colleagues and interested individuals, he never gave anything that was deemed as overly valuable intrinsically. Also, Sparks made a copy of everything parted with. Finally, it should be pointed out that when Sparks arrived at Mount Vernon in 1827, the family had been in the practice of handing out mementoes themselves for over twenty-five years.

The issue came up with the Washington family over a decade after the completion of the work. Inquiring about the current location of material deemed as lost, in 1849 George C. Washington (grandnephew of the president and three-term congressman) had written to Sparks asking his recollection of the material, if any. Sparks responded to the letter by George C. Washington in a letter which pointed out the problems with organization that already existed at Mount Vernon when he arrived over twenty years earlier:

Dear Sir,

Your letter of the 27th ult. has come to hand. The missing "Diaries," & "Cash Memorandum Books," which you mention, I have never seen, nor any others except those which I returned to you. When I packed the papers for removal at Mount Vernon, Judge [Bushrod] Washington was not at home, being absent attending the Court. The papers relating to the Revolution, which were on the lower floor of the office, were in tolerably good order & condition; but the private papers, & those before & after the Revolution, were in a room over the others, thrown loosely into open boxes, & in a state of confusion. I took all I could find, as I was authorized to do by the Judge. The deficiency of the Diaries I observed at the time, but no more of them ever came to light. An important volume of the "Orderly Books" was also missing, but neither Judge Washington nor Judge Marshall could give any intelligence about it, although the latter thought he had used it in writing the "Life."

I have recently been informed, that one of the volumes of the "Diary," (I think for the year 1790, but am not certain) is now in possession of Mr. Bogart of New York, but how it fell into his hands I know not. I have never seen it. I have the impression, also, that I have heard of another volume somewhere, but I do not now recollect where it was said to be.

The loss of the Diaries I considered a serious misfortune in drawing up the Memoir of the Life, especially those of the period of the Presidency. You know there was a rumor, that papers relating to the latter part of this period were secretly taken from the office after the General's death. I once mentioned this subject to Judge Washington. He replied cautiously; "We have never charged any person with such an act," intimating, as I thought, that his suspicion was strong. I suppose there was no positive proof except the absence of papers, which there was good reason for believing had been left by General Washington.

Sparks, Jared, 1849. Letter to George C. Washington. Historical Manuscript Collection, Mount Vernon Ladies' Association, George Washington's Mount Vernon Estate, Museum & Gardens, Mount Vernon, VA.

Chapter Notes

• • • • • •

Preface

1. Giles Gunn, ed., *Early American Writing* (New York: Penguin Books, 1994), xv-xvi.

2. Ibid., xv.

3. Michael Kraus, *The Writing of American History* (Norman: University of Oklahoma Press, 1953), 51.

4. This is not to say that it was totally dependent on Europe for inspiration—"though often provincial and countrified, [American writing] is rarely colonial in the sense of being dependent on its mother country." Everett Emerson, ed., *Major Writers of Early American Literature* (Madison: University of Wisconsin Press, 1976); "Religion remained the most written about subject in pre–Revolutionary America." Joseph J. Ellis, *After the Revolution, Profiles of Early American Culture* (New York: W. W. Norton & Company, 1979), 3.

Introduction

1. Jane Austen, *Northanger Abbey and Persuasion* (Oxford: Oxford University Press, ND), 108.

2. Ibid., 109.

3. While Jane Austen may have struck upon the temper of the majority of her reading audience, roughly thirty years prior to Austen, Abigail Adams, writing ca. 1786 to her son Charles, stated: "I am very glad you have engaged in the reading of History. You recollect I dare Say how often I have recommended to you an acquaintance with the most important events both of ancient and modern times. You have begun properly by attending to that of your own Country first. It would not be amiss if you was to read Hubbards history of the Indian Wars and Neals history of Massa. Those with Hutchinsons will give you a just Idea of the first Settlement of America and the dangers perils and hardships which our Ancestors encountered in order to establish civil and Religious Liberty." (Spelling and grammar kept as in the original letter.) C. James Taylor, ed., *The Adams Papers Digital Edition.* (Charlottesville: University of Virginia Press, Rotunda, 2008).

4. Arthur H. Shaffer, *The Politics of History: Writing the History of the American Revolution, 1783–1815* (New Brunswick, NJ: Transaction Publishers, 2009), 3.

5. Among the historians of this period prior to Jared Sparks can be included Jedidiah Morse, Hugh Williamson, Noah Webster, David Ramsay, Mason Weems, John Marshall, Hugh McCall, and Edmund Randolph. Ibid., 9. This list is only partial and omits women such as Judith Sargent Murray and Mercy Otis Warren, or other men such as Charles Brockden Brown.

6. Ibid., 8. "American historians of the first national generation reached maturity during or soon after the attainment of Independence."

7. Sparks viewed instruction in history far beyond anything that existed at that time. Rather than simply memorizing names, dates, and events, Sparks advocated for the analysis of history; the study of pertinent documents; and the writing of essays. His outline included "(1) The nature of historical testimony; (2) The

sources of history; (3) The origin and progress of historical literature; (4) Modes of writing history in different times and countries; (5) Critical remarks on the works of the most approved historians; (6) Judgment to be formed of histories in regard to the character and qualifications of the writers, the periods in which they wrote, and the events they narrate; (7) Best methods of studying history, and the previous knowledge requisite for pursuing the study to advantage." Herbert Baxter Adams, *The Life and Writings of Jared Sparks: Comprising Selections From His Journals and Correspondence.* vol. 2 (New York: Houghton, Mifflin and Company, 1893), 36.

8. In his 1917 work *The Middle Group of American Historians*, John Spencer Bassett wrote of the difficulties of ascertaining an objective understanding of the historians writing during and immediately after the Revolution. Particularly in terms of the biography, Spencer wrote: "A man bought a biography because it set forth his own political sentiments or his ideas of noble character." Spencer continues, "We were all partisans of our own cause in the contest with Great Britain and, whether we wished to know its simple history or to read the biographies of its leaders, we demanded narratives that stimulated self-satisfaction." John S. Bassett, *The Middle Group of American Historians* (New York: Macmillan Company, 1917), 15.

9. Shaffer, *The Politics of History*, 8.

10. John Burrow, *A History of Histories: Epics, Chronicles, Romances and Inquiries from Herodotus and Thucydides to the Twentieth Century* (New York: Alfred A. Knopf, 2008), 426.

11. "The War of 1776 Gave Rise to National Historical Writing in America." David Dirck Van Tassel, "Recording America's Past: American Historical Writing, 1607–1889" (PhD diss., University of Wisconsin, 1955), 45.

12. Moses Coit Tyler, *The Literary History of the American Revolution,* vol. I (New York: Frederick Ungar Publishing Co., 1966), vii.

13. Trevor Colbourn, *The Lamp of Experience: Whig History and the Intellectual Origins of the American Revolution* (Indianapolis, IN: Liberty Fund, 1998), 235.

14. Shaffer, *Politics of History,* 145.

15. Ibid.

16 Russell Blaine Nye, *The Cultural Life of the New Nation, 1776–1830* (New York: Harper & Row, 1960), 249.

17. Lester J. Cappon, ed., *The Adams-Jefferson Letters: The Complete Correspondence Between Thomas Jefferson and Abigail and John Adams* (Chapel Hill: University of North Carolina Press, 1987), 391.

18. Van Tassel, "Recording America's Past: American Historical Writing, 1607–1889," 149.

19. Jeremy Belknap gained such a reputation that by 1786, a young John Quincy Adams, then a student at Harvard, wrote to his father John, "America, appears to hasten towards, perfection, in the fine arts; and any Country, would, boast of a Belknap, as an historian, a Dwight as a Poet, and a West as a Painter." Not only was John Quincy promoting the historian Belknap, but the humanities in general. This was directly keeping in line with the laments of previous generations' writing about their hopes and fervent belief that America would someday have culture to rival Europe. C. James Taylor, ed., *The Adams Papers Digital Edition* (Charlottesville: University of Virginia Press, Rotunda, 2008).

20 C. James Taylor, ed., *The Adams Papers Digital Edition* (Charlottesville: University of Virginia Press, Rotunda, 2008). Spelling and grammar presented as in the original letter.

21. Ibid., 69.

22. As quoted in Van Tassel, "Recording America's Past: American Historical Writing, 1607–1889," 70.

23. Colbourn, *The Lamp of Experience,* 197.

24. Ibid., 196.

25. Ibid., 199.

26. Ibid.

27. Van Tassel, "Recording America's Past: American Historical Writing, 1607–1889," 162.

28. Ibid., 149.

29. Ibid., 153.

30. Ibid., 150.

31. During this time (early 1790s) Jefferson was also involved with William Waller Hening. Hening conceived the idea to prepare and edit a history of the laws of Virginia. With access to Jefferson's unparalleled library at Monticello, Hening spent years putting his work together. In the end (1823), he had published over twenty volumes of historical material relating to Virginia's legal history. Other states, notably Maryland, New Jersey, and Massachusetts, also had individuals who compiled similar studies. Fred Shelley, "Ebenezer Hazard: America's First Historical Editor," *The William and Mary Quarterly* 12, no. 1 (January 1955), 388–390.

32. Thomas Jefferson, *Writings* (New York: Library of America, 1984), 661.

33. Ibid.

Chapter 1

1. Michael Kraus, *The Writing of American History* (Norman: University of Oklahoma Press, 1953), 7.

2. Giles Gunn, ed., *Early American Writing* (New York: Penguin Books, 1994), xviii.

3. Kraus, *The Writing of American History*, 8.

4. Ibid., 12.

5. Samuel Eliot Morison, *The Intellectual Life of Colonial New England* (New York: New York University Press, 1956), 178.

6. Kraus, *The Writing of American History*, 14.

7. David Dirck Van Tassel, "Recording America's Past: American Historical Writing, 1607–1889" (PhD diss., University of Wisconsin, 1955), 19.

8. Ibid., 18.

9. Kraus, *The Writing of American History*, 45.

10. Ibid., 46.

11. Ibid., 44. Colden was also one of the first historians to enter into the fray concerning the writing of history and the need for accurate and authentic narratives. Colden wrote,

He that first writes the History of matters which are not generally known ought to avoid as much as possible, to make the Evidence of the Truth depend entirely on his own Veracity and Judgment; For this reason I have often related several Transactions in the Words of the Registers. When this is once done, he that shall write afterwards need not act with so much Caution; Histories wrote with all the Delicacy of a fine Romance, are like French dishes, more agreeable to the Pallat than the Stomach, and less wholsom than more common and courser Dyet.

12. Moses Coit Tyler, *The Literary History of the American Revolution,* vol. I (New York: Frederick Ungar Publishing Co., 1966), 10.

13. Morison, *The Intellectual Life of Colonial New England*, 181.

14. Ibid. Morison further writes that Hubbard's "style is pedestrian where it is not obscure; Hubbard had an unfortunate trick of prolonging sentences, clause after clause, until they reached the length of a paragraph." Ibid., 181. Hubbard did however possess a quality concerning the "beauties of nature that is rare among colonial writers, especially in the seventeenth century, when nature was an enemy to be subdued rather than enjoyed." Ibid., 182. In one passage, Hubbard writes:

In May you shall see the woods and fields so curiously bedecked with roses, and an innumerable multitude of other delightful flowers, not only pleasing to the eye, but smell, that you may behold nature contending with art, and striving to equal, if not excel many gardens in England. Nay, did we know the virtue of those plants and herbs growing there (which time may more discover), many are of opinion, and the natives do affirm, that there is no disease common to the country, but may be cured without materials from other nations.

As quoted in Morison, *The Intellectual Life of Colonial New England*, 183.

15. Van Tassel, "Recording America's Past: American Historical Writing, 1607–1889," 20.

16. Harvard historian Samuel Eliot Morison was exuberant when he described the strides made by New England historians in the post–Puritan mold:

Thus, before the puritan century came to an end, political literature had begun; and in these tracts of the Revolution of 1689, we can already discern the qualities of the literature of 1765–1775. A generation that had produced little but sermons, theological tracts, and histories of Indian wars, was nevertheless prepared for political disputation; and, during the next seventy years, New England writers showed the same skill in baiting royal governors and showing up Tory sophistry, as formerly they had employed in fighting the Indians and beating the devil.

Morison, *The Intellectual Life of Colonial New England*, 209.

17. Ibid., 24.

18. Ibid., 26.

19. Kraus, *The Writing of American History*, 47. Prince further states, "I would not take the least iota upon trust; if possible, I examined the original authors I could meet with.... I cite my vouchers to every passage; and I have done my utmost ... to find out the truth, and ... relate it in the clearest order." Ibid., 48.

20. Morison, *The Intellectual Life of Colonial New England*, 182.

21. Kraus, *The Writing of American History*, 40.

22. Trevor Colbourn, *The Lamp of Experience, Whig History and the Intellectual Origins of the American Revolution* (Indianapolis, IN: Liberty Fund, 1998), 7.

23. Ibid.,179.

24. Quoted in Colbourn, *The Lamp of Experience,* 179.

25. Kraus, *The Writing of American History*, 38–39.

26. Joseph J. Ellis, *After the Revolution, Profiles of Early American Culture* (New York: W. W. Norton & Company, 1979), 4.

27. Ibid., 7.

28. Ibid.

29. Ibid., 5.

30. The poem reads:
There shall be sung another golden age,
The rise of empire and of arts,
The good and great inspiring epic rage,
The wisest heads and noblest hearts.
Not such as Europe breeds in her decay;
Such as she bred when fresh and young,
When heavenly flame did animate her clay,
By future poets shall be sung.
Westward the course of empire takes its sway;
The first four acts already past,
A fifth shall close the drama with the day;
Time's noblest offspring is the last.
As quoted in Ellis, *After the Revolution,* 6.

31. Ibid., 4.

32. Ibid.

33. Ibid.

34. Tyler, *The Literary History of the American Revolution,* vol. I, 26.

35. Colbourn, *The Lamp of Experience,* 5.

36. As quoted in Carl L. Becker, *The Heavenly City of the Eighteenth-Century Philosophers* (New Haven, CT: Yale University Press, 1960), 95.

37. As Ralph Waldo Emerson stated in 1837 in his American Scholar speech: "If there is any period one would desire to be born in, is it not the age of Revolution; when the old and the new stand side by side and admit of being compared; when the energies of all men are searched by fear and by hope; when the historic glories of the old can be compensated by the rich possibilities of the new era?" Ralph Waldo Emerson, *Essays & Lectures* (New York: The Library of America, 1983), 68.

Chapter 2

1. Trevor Colbourn, *The Lamp of Experience, Whig History and the Intellectual Origins of the American Revolution* (Indianapolis, IN: Liberty Fund, 1998), 5.

2. As quoted in Peter Gay, *The Enlightenment: An Interpretation. The Science of Freedom.* (New York: W. W. Norton and Company, 1977), 369.

3. Ibid.

4. Ibid., 370.

5. Carl L. Becker, *The Heavenly City of the*

Eighteenth-Century Philosophers (New Haven, CT: Yale University Press, 1960), 92.

6. Ibid., 93.

7. Colbourn, *The Lamp of Experience,* 25.

8. David Dirck Van Tassel, "Recording America's Past: American Historical Writing, 1607–1889" (PhD diss., University of Wisconsin, 1955), 42.

9. As quoted in Michael Kraus, *The Writing of American History* (Norman: University of Oklahoma Press, 1953), 90.

10. Colbourn, *The Lamp of Experience,* 192.

11. Ibid., 226.

12. Moses Coit Tyler, *The Literary History of the American Revolution* ,vol. I (New York: Frederick Ungar Publishing Co., 1966), 6.

13. Ibid.

14. Ibid., 9.

15 As a measure of the lengths to which some clergymen infused religion into the political contest on both sides, the following is excerpted from *The Bible and the Sword* ..., by John Fletcher. It reflects a Methodist view as to why the English must suppress the American rebels:

In this hour of tremendous danger, it would become us to turn our thoughts to heaven. This is what our brethren in the colonies are doing. From one end of North America to the other, they are fasting and praying. But what are we doing? Shocking thought! We are ridiculing them as fanatics, and scoffing at religion. We are running wild after pleasure, and forgetting everything serious and decent at masquerades. We are gambling in gaming houses; trafficking for boroughs; perjuring ourselves at elections; and selling ourselves for places. Which side then is Providence likely to favour? In America we see a number of rising states in the vigour of youth and animated by piety. Here we see an old state, inflated and irreligious, enervated by luxury, and hanging by a thread. Can we look without pain on the issue?

From Ellis Sandoz, ed., *Political Sermons of the American Founding Era, 1830–1805* (Indianapolis, IN: Liberty Fund, 1990), 563.

16. Ibid., xiii-xiv.

17. Colbourn, *The Lamp of Experience,* 18.

18 Russel Blaine Nye, *The Cultural Life of the New Nation, 1776–1830* (New York: Harper & Row, 1960), 250.

19. Samuel Eliot Morison, *The Intellectual Life of Colonial New England* (New York: New York University Press, 1956), 135.

20. Colbourn, *The Lamp of Experience,* 20.

21. Fred Shelley, "Ebenezer Hazard: Amer-

ica's First Historical Editor," *William and Mary Quarterly* 12, no. 1 (January 1955), 384.

22. Stephen William Schuster IV, "To Build a Monument: Jared Sparks and *The Writings of George Washington*" (PhD diss., Texas Christian University, 1977), 52.

23. Ibid.

24. The historical society (and literary society) movement is in and of itself quite fascinating, particularly in the United States where the "newness" of the political system had yet to produce the heroes which dominated European historical and literary societies. Refer to appendix 5 for a list of societies to which Jared Sparks was elected.

Chapter 3

1. John S. Bassett, *The Middle Group of American Historians* (New York: Macmillan Company, 1917), 15–16.

2. Michael Kraus, *The Writing of American History* (Norman: University of Oklahoma Press, 1953), 67.

3. David Dirck Van Tassel, "Recording America's Past: American Historical Writing, 1607–1889" (PhD diss., University of Wisconsin, 1955), 44.

4. Bassett, *The Middle Group of American Historians*, 2.

5. Van Tassel, "Recording America's Past: American Historical Writing, 1607–1889," 42.

6. Ibid., 43.

7. Kraus, *The Writing of American History*, 56.

8. Leon Jackson, "Jedidiah Morse and the Transformation of Print Culture in New England, 1784–1826," *Early American Literature* 34, no. 1 (1999), 3.

9. Robert E. Spiller, Willard Thorp, et al., eds. *Literary History of the United States* (London: Macmillan Company, 1969), 131. "This is the corpus of literature of the American Revolution—a couple of thousand little books with their pretentious and formidable titles, intended for instant circulation, designed to change men's minds, addressed to urgent problems, sometimes touching the universal issues that confront men everywhere, any time, in civil society." Ibid.

10. Moses Coit Tyler, *The Literary History of the American Revolution,* vol. I (New York: Frederick Ungar Publishing Co., 1966), 54.

11. Ibid.

12. Kraus, *The Writing of American History*, 58.

13 Ibid.

14. Russell Blaine Nye, *The Cultural Life of the New Nation, 1776–1830* (New York: Harper & Row, 1960), 242.

15. Ibid.

16. Jackson, "Jedidiah Morse and the Transformation of Print Culture in New England, 1784–1826," 3.

17. "The American Revolution, in particular, provided poets and writers with distinctively native subject matter, fraught with tragic, epic, and narrative possibilities, loaded with heroes and villains." Nye, *The Cultural Life of the New Nation, 1776–1830*, 244.

18. In a footnote, Nye quotes an English publication, *Blackwood's Magazine*, as writing

There is nothing to awaken fancy in that land of dull realities. No objects carry the mind back to contemplation of a remote antiquity. No moldering ruins excite interest in the history of the past. No memorials commemorative of noble deeds arouse enthusiasm and reverence. No traditions, legends, fables, afford material for poetry and romance.

Nye, *The Cultural Life of the New Nation, 1776–1830*, 242.

19. Jackson, "Jedidiah Morse and the Transformation of Print Culture in New England, 1784–1826," 3.

20. "A man bought a biography because it set forth his own political sentiments or his ideas of noble character.... We were all partisans of our own cause in the contest with Great Britain and, whether we wished to know its simple history or to read the biographies of its leaders, we demanded narratives that stimulated self-satisfaction." From Bassett, *The Middle Group of American Historians*, 15.

21. Kraus, *The Writing of American History*, 68–69.

22. Tyler, *The Literary History of the American Revolution,* vol. I, 39.

23. Trevor Colbourn, *The Lamp of Experience: Whig History and the Intellectual Origins of the American Revolution* (Indianapolis, IN: Liberty Fund, 1998), 89.

24. Ibid.

25. Ibid., 104.

26. Ibid., 105.

27. Quoted in Colbourn, *The Lamp of Experience,* 107.

28. Ibid., 108.

Chapter 4

1. Arthur H. Shaffer, *The Politics of History: Writing the History of the American Revo-*

lution, 1783–1815 (New Brunswick, NJ: Transaction Publishers, 2009), 8.

2. It was also during the Revolution that some sought to recover the enthusiasm associated with pre–Revolutionary America by bringing back the ideas of America's destiny with cultural greatness. This action clearly put them on one side of the war or the other. Joseph J. Ellis, *After the Revolution: Profiles of Early American Culture* (New York: W. W. Norton & Company, 1979), 11.

3. John S. Bassett, *The Middle Group of American Historians* (New York: Macmillan Company, 1917), 12.

4. David Dirck Van Tassel, "Recording America's Past: American Historical Writing, 1607–1889" (PhD diss., University of Wisconsin, 1955), 47.

5. Shaffer, *The Politics of History: Writing the History of the American Revolution,* 3.

6. Ibid., 9.

7. For a contemporary look at this practice, see the article "The Real Cuban Missile Crisis" in *The Atlantic.* It can be found online at http://www.theatlantic.com/magazine/print/2013/01/the-real-cuban-missle-crisis/309190 (visited 1-11-2013).

8. Shaffer, *The Politics of History: Writing the History of the American Revolution,* 4

9. "…one should remember that the use of history as a politic weapon had deep roots in Anglo-American culture." Ibid., 31.

10. Van Tassel, "Recording America's Past: American Historical Writing, 1607–1889," 52.

11. Ibid.

12. Michael Kraus, *The Writing of American History* (Norman, OK: University of Oklahoma Press, 1953), 62.

13. Tassel, "Recording America's Past: American Historical Writing, 1607–1889," 59.

14. Ibid., 145.

15. Ibid., 74.

16. John Adams, writing late in life, opined that the history of the Revolution would not be an easy topic; he wrote, "Who shall write the History of the American Revolution? Who can write it? Who will ever be able to write it? The most essential documents, the debates and deliberations in Congress, from 1774 to 1783, were all in secret, and are now lost forever." As quoted in Edmund C. Burnett, ed., *Letters of the Members of the Continental Congress,* vol. I (Gloucester, MA: Peter Smith, 1963), iii.

17. Shaffer, *The Politics of History; Writing the History of the American Revolution,* 105.

18. Ibid., 1.

19. Ibid., 119.

20. This practice has created the most havoc for archivists and historians. However, collectors also fret over early versions of later redrafted manuscripts—this naturally has to deal with valuation on the open market.

21. The *Columbian* newspaper as quoted in Van Tassel, "Recording America's Past: American Historical Writing, 1607–1889," 71.

22. Ibid.

23. While "only" a woman, she did not let this stop her from researching in one of the most respected institutions in Boston at the time, the Athenaeum. She was the only woman given such deference for many years. It is a sign not only of her tenacity, but of the respect she was held in by the much better known men who regularly utilized the library. Van Wyck Brooks, *The Flowering of New England* (New York: E. P. Dutton & Co., Inc., 1952), 125.

24. Ibid., 82.

25. Leon Jackson, "Jedidiah Morse and the Transformation of Print Culture in New England, 1784–1826," *Early American Literature* 34, no. 1 (1999),18.

26. Ibid. 18.

27. Kraus, *The Writing of American History,* 81.

28. Ibid.

29. Mark L. Kamrath, *The Historicism of Charles Brockden Brown: Radical History and the Early Republic* (Kent, OH: Kent State University Press, 2010), 81.

30. Edmund C. Burnett, ed., *Letters of the Members of the Continental Congress,* vol. I (Gloucester, MA: Peter Smith, 1963), 182.

31 Fred Shelley, "Ebenezer Hazard: America's First Historical Editor," *William and Mary Quarterly* 12, no. 1 (January 1955), 45.

32. Russel Blaine Nye, *The Cultural Life of the New Nation, 1776–1830* (New York: Harper & Row, 1960), 250.

33 Samuel Eliot Morison, *The Intellectual Life of Colonial New England* (New York: New York University Press, 1956), 128.

34. Shelley, "Ebenezer Hazard: America's First Historical Editor," 47.

35. Quoted by Shelley from a letter from Hazard to Jonathan Trumbull. Ibid., 48.

36. Julian P. Boyd, *The Papers of Thomas Jefferson, Volume I, 1760–1776* (Princeton, NJ: Princeton University Press, 1950), 164.

37. Shelley, "Ebenezer Hazard: America's First Historical Editor," 49.

38. Ibid., 51.

39. Ibid., 52.

40. Ibid., 55.

41. Edmund C. Burnett, ed., *Letters of the Members of the Continental Congress,* vol.VI (Gloucester, MA: Peter Smith, 1963), 67–68.

42. Shelley, "Ebenezer Hazard: America's First Historical Editor," 55.

43. Ibid., 56. William Gordon would eventually move to England, where he produced a four-volume history of the United States. Gordon sent a copy to Washington in 1789 and detailed his writing method to Washington as being quite liberal with sources. It turned out that Gordon had actually copied nearly verbatim the *Annual Register* in one of the most egregious cases of plagiarism known. Kraus, *The Writing of American History*, 72.

44 Martha Washington also spent the winter of 1779–1780 with her husband in Morristown. When she returned to Mount Vernon in July of 1780, she wrote to her cousin to ask that he send his daughter to be with her at Mount Vernon as Martha was upset over the state of the General's condition of despair when she left Morristown. Original letter in the Morristown National Historical Park archival colletion, part of the Lloyd W. Smith Collection.

45. Shelley, "Ebenezer Hazard: America's First Historical Editor," 66.

46. Ibid., 67.

47. Ibid., 68.

48. Ibid., 44.

49. Ibid., 45.

50. Men such as Abiel Holmes, Timothy Pitkin, James Grahame, George Bancroft, James Savage, John Palfrey, and Herbert Osgood—among others—can be said to have profited from Hazard's pioneering work. Ibid., 70.

51. Van Tassel, "Recording America's Past: American Historical Writing, 1607–1889," 165.

52. Kraus, *The Writing of American History*, 100.

53. Ibid., 101.

Chapter 5

1. Mercy Otis Warren, *History of the Rise, Progress and Termination of the American Revolution Interspersed with Biographical, Political and Moral Observations,* vol. 1, ed. Lester H. Cohen (Indianapolis, IN: Liberty Fund, 1994), xvi.

2. Ibid.

3. Ibid., vol. 1, xvii.

4. Michael Kraus, *The Writing of American History* (Norman: University of Oklahoma Press, 1953), 78.

5. Ibid., 79.

6. Ibid.

7. Warren, *History of the Rise, Progress and Termination of the American Revolution,* vol. 1, ed. Cohen, xix.

8. Ibid., vol. 1, xxi.

9. Lester J. Cappon, ed., *The Adams-Jefferson Letters: The Complete Correspondence Between Thomas Jefferson and Abigail and John Adams* (Chapel Hill: University of North Carolina Press, 1987), 453.

10. As quoted in Christine M. Lizanich, "'The March of This Government': Joel Barlow's Unwritten History of the United States," *The William and Mary Quarterly* 33, no. 2, Third Series (April 1976), 315.

11. As quoted in Lizanich, "'The March of This Government': Joel Barlow's Unwritten History of the United States," 316.

12. As quoted in Lizanich, "'The March of This Government': Joel Barlow's Unwritten History of the United States," 317.

13. Emory Elliott, *Revolutionary Writers: Literature and Authority in the New Republic, 1725–1810* (Oxford: Oxford University Press, 1982), 94.

14. Ibid., 95.

15. "Barlow was aware that he was living through a time in which European writers and intellectuals were consciously rejecting the sacred history, the biblical types, and the religious language that had been an unquestioned part of American writing before 1776. For sophisticated readers in the 1790s the uses of such language without irony or a hint of embarrassment was certain to reveal the writer to be a fool." Ibid., 112.

16. Ibid., 110.

17. As quoted in Lizanich, "'The March of This Government': Joel Barlow's Unwritten History of the United States," 320.

18. Elliott, *Revolutionary Writers: Literature and Authority in the New Republic, 1725–1810,* 102.

19. Arthur Shaffer, "John Daly Burk's "History of Virginia" and the Development of American National History," *Virginia Magazine of History and Biography* 77, no. 3 (July, 1969), 337.

20. The term exceptionalism, or exceptionalness, has been resorted to many times in this work (and is quite common in today's discourse) in an attempt to describe the way, or manner, in which early historians sought to depict the development and rise of the United States. Yet this concept was precisely what Brown challenged. This is not to say that eighteenth-century histo-

rians had used the term or even considered it in the way it has come to be used. Rather, use of the term today to describe the past approach is simply a convention of convenience to indicate the idea behind the word in the eighteenth century.

21. Mark L. Kamrath, *The Historicism of Charles Brockden Brown: Radical History and the Early Republic* (Kent, OH: Kent State University Press, 2010), 9.

22. Ibid., 5.

23. Ibid., 6.

24. Charles F. Hobson et al., eds., *The Papers of John Marshall*, vol. VI (Chapel Hill: University of North Carolina Press, 1990), 304.

25. Kamrath, *The Historicism of Charles Brockden Brown: Radical History and the Early Republic*, 17.

26. Ibid., 10.

27. Ibid., 84.

28. The Charles Brockden Brown Society was founded only in 2000.

29. Robert E. Spiller, Willard Thorp, et al., eds. *Literary History of the United States* (London: Macmillan Company, 1969), 181.

30. Ibid., 182.

31. An interesting side note is that Brown was influenced by the British philosopher William Goodwin. Goodwin's wife, Mary Wollstonecraft, famously wrote the *Vindication of the Rights of Women*, while their daughter, Mary Shelley, is known for her work *Frankenstein*. Brown's novel *Wieland* in 1798 is considered to have provided some food for thought as Mrs. Shelley wrote *Frankenstein*.

32. Russel Blaine Nye, *The Cultural Life of the New Nation, 1776–1830* (New York: Harper & Row, 1960), 240.

33. Kamrath, *The Historicism of Charles Brockden Brown: Radical History and the Early Republic*, 72.

34. Ibid., 73.

35. Ibid., 75.

36. Ibid., 83.

Chapter 6

1. Russel Blaine Nye, *The Cultural Life of the New Nation, 1776–1830* (New York: Harper & Row, 1960), 251.

2. Ernest E. Leisy, *The American Historical Novel* (Norman: University of Oklahoma Press, 1970), 214.

3. Cathy N. Davidson, *Revolution and the Word: The Rise of the Novel in America* (Oxford: Oxford University Press, 1986), viii.

4 Leisy, *The American Historical Novel*, 22.

5. Ibid., 25.

6. Ibid., 28.

7. Ibid., 35.

8. Inventories from Boston booksellers in the late seventeenth century indicate fiction was available for purchase, everything from romance to the legend of Dr. Faustus. See Samuel Eliot Morison, *The Intellectual Life of Colonial New England* (New York: New York University Press, 1956), 131.

9. Leisy, *The American Historical Novel*, 42.

10. Ibid., 62–63.

11. Ibid., 69.

12. Joseph Plumb Martin, *A Narrative of Some of the Adventures, Dangers and Sufferings of a Revolutionary Soldier, Interspersed with Anecdotes of Incidents That Occurred Within His Own Observation*, George F. Scheer, ed. (Acorn Press, 1979), viii. Scheer writes that in the interests of history, "the *Narrative* was first brought to my attention one evening several years ago by Francis S. Ronalds, Superintendent of the Morristown National Historical Park, who had discovered it in the private collection of Lloyd W. Smith, of Morristown, which is now part of the Park Library. After some investigation of its authorship, he had become convinced that it was the work of Joseph Plumb Martin, and he was enthusiastically rediscovering it for a number of historians. I found the narrative so engrossing and its infectious humor so diverting that I thought is should be brought to the attention of modern readers." Ibid.

13. David Chacko and Alexander Kulcsar. "Israel Potter: Genesis of a Legend." *William and Mary Quarterly* 41, no. 3, Third Series (July 1984), 366.

14. Ibid., 368.

15. Ibid., 367–368.

16. Ibid., 372.

17. Ibid., 378.

18. Ibid., 386.

19. Ibid., 389.

20. Herman Melville, *Pierre or The Ambiguities, Israel Potter: His Fifty Years of Exile, The Piazza Tales, The Confidence-Man: His Masquerade, Uncollected Prose, Billy Budd, Sailor: An Inside Narrative* (New York: Library of America, 1984), 431.

Chapter 7

1. Jill Lepore, "His Highness George Washington Scales New Heights," *New Yorker,* September 27, 2010, 3.

2. Ibid., 1.

3. Ibid.

4. Ibid., 2. Lepore goes on further to say that "since 1990, major American publishing houses have brought out no fewer than eighteen Washington biographies, a couple of them very fine, to say nothing of the slew of boutique-y books about the man's military career, his moral fortitude, his friendship with Lafayette, his faith in God, his betrayal by Benedict Arnold, his "secret navy," his inspiring words, his leadership skills, his business tips, his kindness to General William Howe's dog, and his journey home to Mount Vernon for Christmas 1783." Ibid., 2–3.

5. "To a degree historians idealized Washington in the way leaders in other new states have been idolized, but they resisted the temptation to follow their contemporaries and turn him into a demi-god. Reluctant to criticize him, they came close to hero-worship, but their writings did not glorify him as much as their society." Arthur H. Shaffer, *The Politics of History: Writing the History of the American Revolution, 1783–1815* (New Brunswick, NJ: Transaction Publishers, 2009), 140. Shaffer seems to contradict John Adams, who stated: "I have been distressed to see some members of this house disposed to idolize an image which their own hands have molten. I speak here of the superstitious veneration that is sometimes paid to General Washington."

6. Theodore J. Crackel, ed., *The Papers of George Washington Digital Edition* (Charlottesville: University of Virginia Press, Rotunda, 2008).

7. Ibid.

8. Richard Norton Smith, *Patriarch: George Washington and the New American Nation* (Boston, MA: Houghton Mifflin Company, 1993), 301.

9. George Washington Farm Ledger 1797–1799, Morristown National Historical Park. Lloyd W. Smith Collection. Rare Books.

10. George Washington Farm Ledger 1797–1799, Morristown National Historical Park. Lloyd W. Smith Collection. Rare Books. James Anderson was Washington's manager at Mt. Vernon. He was hired in 1797 after Washington retired. It was Anderson who started the distillery at Mt. Vernon as a profitable solution to the surplus wheat crop. Robert F. Dalzell and Lee Baldwin Dalzell, *George Washington's Mount Vernon: At Home in Revolutionary America* (Oxford: Oxford University Press, 1998), 222.

11. "The Richest U.S. Presidents." *Forbes* magazine.

12. Dalzell and Dalzell, *George Washington's Mount Vernon: At Home in Revolutionary America*, 219. See also "The Atlantic"—Net Worth of the U.S. Presidents.

13. Smith, *Patriarch: George Washington and the New American Nation*, 301–02.

14. Vibul Vadakan, "The Asphyxiating and Exsanguinating Death of President George Washington," *Permanente Journal* 8, no. 2 (Spring 2004): 1.

15. John C. Fitzpatrick, ed., *The Diaries of George Washington 1748–1799*, vol. IV (Cranbury, NJ: The Scholar's Bookshelf, 2005), 320.

16. Among the various accounts are those by Tobias Lear, George Washington Custis, and most importantly, Dr. James Craik and Dr. Elisha Dick.

17. Vadakan, "The Asphyxiating and Exsanguinating Death of President George Washington," 6. Over a period of ten hours, approximately 125 ounces, or 3.75 liters, of blood was drawn from Washington. Even at the time, questions were raised over just how much blood was drawn from Washington. Dr. James Brickell strongly disagreed with the treatment. His disagreement though was apparently kept private until the early twentieth century. Ibid, 5.

18. Ibid., 3.

19. Account retold in Vadakan, "The Asphyxiating and Exsanguinating Death of President George Washington," 3.

20. Ibid., 5.

21. White McKenzie Wallenborn, *The Papers of George Washington—Articles.*

22. Arthur H. Shaffer, *The Politics of History: Writing the History of the American Revolution, 1783–1815* (New Brunswick, NJ: Transaction Publishers, 2009), 139.

23. Ibid.

24. Gerald E. Kahler, *The Long Farewell: Americans Mourn the Death of George Washington* (Charlottesville: University of Virginia Press, 2008), 1.

25. Gerald Kahler has compiled an extensive—although not complete—list of funeral rites held in memory of George Washington between December 1799 and March 1800. The list is found in his book *The Long Farewell*, as an appendix.

26. Washington Irving, *Life of George Washington*, ed. Jess Stein (Tarrytown, NY: Sleepy Hollow Restorations, 1975), 684.

27. Ibid., 685.

28. Ibid.

29. George Washington, *A Collection,* ed. William B. Allen (Indianapolis, IN: Liberty Classics, 1988), 667.

30. Dalzell and Dalzell, *George Washington's Mount Vernon: At Home in Revolutionary America*, 217.

Chapter 8

1. Wood writes that Weems is "the author of the most popular biography of George Washington ever written." Gordon S. Wood, *Empire of Liberty: A History of the Early Republic, 1789–1815* (Oxford: Oxford University Press, 2009), 353.

2. Edward G. Lengel, *Inventing George Washington, America's Founder, in Myth & Memory* (New York: Harper, 2011), 20.

3. Ibid., 22.

4 Samuel Eliot Morison, *The Intellectual Life of Colonial New England* (New York: New York University Press, 1956), 177.

5. As quoted in Jill Lepore, "His Highness George Washington Scales New Heights," *New Yorker,* September 27, 2010: 2.

6. Abigail was not the only member of the family who considered some of the adulation thrust on Washington a bit beyond normal. Her husband, John, commented in 1777 to his colleagues in the Continental Congress, "I have been distressed to see some members of this house disposed to idolize an image which their own hands have molten. I speak here of the superstitious veneration that is sometimes paid to General Washington." This statement was recorded by his colleague Benjamin Rush. George W. Corner, ed., *The Autobiography of Benjamin Rush: His "Travels Through Life" together with his* Commonplace Book *for 1789–1813* (Princeton, NJ: Princeton University Press, 1948), 141.

7. As quoted in Lengel, *Inventing George Washington, America's Founder, in Myth & Memory*, 23.

8. For a concise overview of this man, see the footnote in Albert J. Beveridge, *The Life of John Marshall,* vol. III (Boston, MA: Houghton Mifflin Company, 1919), 231. The history of traveling salesmen had a long and distinguished history in the United States by the time Mason Weems wrote about Washington. During the early colonial period in the seventeenth century, itinerant salesmen would often be the best source of news, entertainment, and access to the various goods, such as books, that were not readily attainable otherwise. Therefore, Weems fits nicely into the background of the potent traveling salesman who had a ready audience.

9. Lengel, *Inventing George Washington, America's Founder, in Myth & Memory,* 26.

10. Arthur H. Shaffer, *The Politics of History: Writing the History of the American Revolution, 1783–1815* (New Brunswick, NJ: Transaction Publishers, 2009), 139.

11. Wood, *Empire of Liberty: A History of the Early Republic, 1789–1815,* 354.

12. Ibid., 566.

13. Shaffer, *The Politics of History: Writing the History of the American Revolution,* 139.

14. Wood, *Empire of Liberty: A History of the Early Republic, 1789–1815,* 565.

15. Ibid., 7.

16. Ibid., 14.

17. Elizabeth Stevenson, ed., *A Henry Adams Reader* (Garden City, NY: Doubleday Anchor Books, 1958), 101.

18. David Dirck Van Tassel, "Recording America's Past: American Historical Writing, 1607–1889" (PhD diss., University of Wisconsin, 1955), 67.

19. John S. Bassett, *The Middle Group of American Historians* (New York: Macmillan Company, 1917), 13.

20. Ibid., 14.

21. Van Tassel, "Recording America's Past: American Historical Writing, 1607–1889," 67.

22. Shaffer, *The Politics of History: Writing the History of the American Revolution, 1783–1815,* 42.

23. Ibid., 42.

24. Ibid., 19–20.

25. As quoted in Robert L. Brunhouse , "David Ramsay, 1749–1815: Selections from His Writings," *Transactions of the American Philosophical Society* 55, no. 4, New Series (1965), 31.

26. Brunhouse, "David Ramsay, 1749–1815: Selections from His Writings," 19.

27. David Ramsay, *The History of the American Revolution,* ed. Lester H. Cohen, vol. 1 (Indianapolis, IN: Liberty Fund, 1990), xv.

28. Ibid., xvii-xviii.

29. Ibid., xvi.

30. Ibid., xvii.

31. Ibid., xxiii.

32. Brunhouse, "David Ramsay, 1749–1815: Selections from His Writings," 45.

33. Ibid.

34. Ibid., 46.

35. Elmer Douglass Johnson, "David Ramsay: Historian or Plagiarist?" *South Carolina Historical Magazine* 57, no. 4 (October 1956), 192.

36. Ibid.

37. Ibid.

38. Brunhouse, "David Ramsay, 1749–1815 Selections from His Writings," 46.

39. Johnson, "David Ramsay: Historian or Plagiarist?" 198.

40. Quoted in Johnson from the *Edinburgh Review*, Johnson, "David Ramsay: Historian or Plagiarist?" 196.

Chapter 9

1. Clare Cushman, ed., *The Supreme Court Justices: Illustrated Biographies, 1789–1995* (Washington, D.C.: Congressional Quarterly, 1995), 61.

2. Albert J. Beveridge, *The Life of John Marshall*, vol. III (Boston, MA: Houghton Mifflin Company, 1919), 154.

3 See footnote (#42) in Lawrence B. Custer, "Bushrod Washington and John Marshall: A Preliminary Inquiry," *American Journal of Legal History* 4, no. 1 (January 1960), 43.

4. David Dirck Van Tassel, "Recording America's Past: American Historical Writing, 1607–1889" (PhD diss., University of Wisconsin, 1955), 178.

5 "His reverence for Washington was such that any biography he undertook would be respectful and probably laudatory." Leonard Baker, *John Marshall: A Life in Law* (New York: Macmillan Publishing Company, 1974), 438.

6. A quote from Charles Kendall Adams in William A. Foran, "John Marshall as a Historian," *American Historical Review* 43, no. 1 (October 1937), 51.

7. Beveridge, *The Life of John Marshall*, 225.

8. Ibid.

9. Ibid., 224.

10. Ibid., 226.

11. Ibid.

12. Ibid.

13. See the footnote in Beveridge, *The Life of John Marshall*, 228.

14. Ibid.

15. Ibid., 230.

16. Ibid., 234.

17. Baker, *John Marshall: A Life in Law*, 439.

18. Beveridge, *The Life of John Marshall*, 235.

19. Ibid., 236.

20. Bushrod to Wayne, quoted in Beveridge, *The Life of John Marshall*, 227.

21. Charles F. Hobson et al., eds., *The Papers of John Marshall*, vol. VI (Chapel Hill: University of North Carolina Press, 1990), 244.

22 Ibid., 253.

23. See footnote in Beveridge, *The Life of John Marshall*, 231.

24. Quoted in Beveridge, *The Life of John Marshall*, 232.

25. Ibid., 233.

26. David Leslie Annis, "Mr. Bushrod Washington, Supreme Court Justice on the Marshall Court" (PhD diss., University of Notre Dame, 1974), 109.

27. Arthur H. Shaffer, *The Politics of History: Writing the History of the American Revolution, 1783–1815* (New Brunswick, NJ: Transaction Publishers, 2009), 83.

28. Hobson, ed., *The Papers of John Marshall*, 265.

29 Beveridge, *The Life of John Marshall*, 240.

30 As quoted in Hobson, ed., *The Papers of John Marshall*, 303.

31. Hobson, ed., *The Papers of John Marshall*, 265.

32. Ibid., 264.

33. Ibid., 253.

34. Ibid., 253–254.

35. Ibid., 248. This amount was far short of the original anticipated amount.

36. Beveridge, *The Life of John Marshall*, 250.

37. Ibid., 242.

38. Ibid.

39. William A. Foran, "John Marshall as a Historian," *American Historical Review* 43, no. 1 (October 1937), 53.

40. As Foran writes, Marshall's supporters argue that "he was but following accepted historiographical custom." Foran, "John Marshall as a Historian," 62.

41. Hobson, ed., *The Papers of John Marshall*, 258.

42. Some of Marshall's more recent biographers have seemed to return to the notion of "live and let live" regarding Marshall's indiscretions. Leonard Baker in 1974 wrote that Marshall, far from plagiarism, simply drew on "published sources." Indeed, Baker terms Marshall's efforts as producing "a readable and comprehensive account." Finally, Baker states that "All subsequent biographers of Washington must begin with Marshall's as a source." Baker, *John Marshall: A Life in Law*, 442.

43. "Of the original octavo edition, two volumes were published in 1804, the third and fourth in 1805, and the last appeared in 1807." A second edition, with a fifth volume added appeared in 1807. "In 1824 Marshall detached the first volume of his work and published it separately." In 1832 a revised edition appeared

without the first volume, and finally in 1838, three years after Marshall's death an abridged one-volume edition appeared for use in schools. Foran, "John Marshall as a Historian," 52–53.

44. Perhaps no contemporary observer or participant of the period put such a fine boundary on Marshall's work as John Adams. Adams understood more than most the enormity of Marshall's task because he knew Washington was more than an individual. He himself was the story of America. That is to say, there was—and is—no objective way to separate Washington from what he did and how he acted. Just as when Washington died, the sorrow was as much for his "starring role" in the drama of the United States as for the man himself.

45. Foran, 51.

46. Ibid., 52.

47. Hobson, ed., *The Papers of John Marshall*, 538–542.

48 Annis, "Mr. Bushrod Washington, Supreme Court Justice on the Marshall Court," 105.

49. Ibid., 19.

50. Ibid., 20.

51. Ibid., 22.

52. Ibid., 23.

53. Horace Binney, *Bushrod Washington* (Philadelphia: Privately Published, 1858), 6.

54. Ibid., 7

55. Cushman, ed., *The Supreme Court Justices: Illustrated Biographies,* 51.

56. Annis, "Mr. Bushrod Washington, Supreme Court Justice on the Marshall Court," 28.

57. Ibid., 33.

58. Ibid.

59. Ibid., 36.

60. Ibid., 37.

61. Ibid., 38.

62. Ibid.

63. James Wilson, *Collected Works of James Wilson,* eds. Kermit L. Hall and Mark David Hall, vol. I (Indianapolis, IN: Liberty Fund, 2007), xiv.

64. Ibid.

65. Ibid., xv.

66. Annis, "Mr. Bushrod Washington, Supreme Court Justice on the Marshall Court," 55.

67. Theodore J. Crackel, ed., *The Papers of George Washington Digital Edition* (Charlottesville: University of Virginia Press, Rotunda, 2008).

68. Cushman, ed., *The Supreme Court Justices: Illustrated Biographies,* 54.

69. Annis, "Mr. Bushrod Washington, Supreme Court Justice on the Marshall Court," 102.

Chapter 10

1. Van Wyck Brooks, *The Flowering of New England* (New York: E. P. Dutton & Co., 1952), 125.

2. Garry Wills, *Henry Adams and the Making of America* (New York: Houghton Mifflin Company, 2005), 33.

3. Wills, *Henry Adams and the Making of America*, 34.

4. While Harvard was the first American institution to acknowledge the discipline of history, it was not far from being one of the first in the world to do so. "History was an ancient intellectual practice, but not one, until the early nineteenth century—Gottingen was the forerunner—with a firm university teaching base, apart from a scattering of endowed professorships." John Burrow, *A History of Histories: Epics, Chronicles, Romances and Inquiries from Herodotus and Thucydides to the Twentieth Century* (New York: Alfred A. Knopf, 2008), 426.

5. Michael Kraus, *The Writing of American History* (Norman: University of Oklahoma Press, 1953), 108.

6. Ibid., 114.

7. Lester J. Cappon, "American Historical Editors Before Jared Sparks: 'They Will Plant a Forest....'" *William and Mary Quarterly* 30, no. 3, Third Series (July 1973), 376.

8. Ibid., 375.

9. Fred Shelley, "Ebenezer Hazard: America's First Historical Editor," *William and Mary Quarterly* 12, no. 1 (January 1955), 398.

10. Jared Sparks, *The Life of George Washington* (Boston: Ferdinand Andrews, 1839), vi.

11. The Morristown NHP collection is one part of the larger Sparks' letters collection nationwide. The largest portion of the Sparks literary bequest is at Harvard.

12. Jared Sparks, letter (Morristown National Historical Park, Lloyd W. Smith Collection, Rare Books, letters of Jared Sparks.

13. Quoted in Herbert Baxter Adams, *The Life and Writings of Jared Sparks: Comprising Selections From His Journals and Correspondence,* vol. 1 (New York: Houghton, Mifflin and Company, 1893), 406.

14. Ibid., 392–393.

15. Quoted in Adams, *The Life and Writings of Jared Sparks,* 407.

16. Sparks often sought out survivors from the Revolutionary period for their reminiscences. In 1832, Sparks wrote to Robert Gilmore about Charles Carroll—the last surviving signer of the Declaration of Independence. Carroll would die late in 1832 at age 95. Sparks wrote, "If Mr. Carroll is in a humor to talk of revolutionary matters, I wish you to find out from him all he remembers of the cabal against Washington, particularly the *names* of those, who were unfavorably disposed towards him in Congress. I know that Sam Adams and R. H. Lee were among the leaders, and Mr. Carroll will perhaps recollect others, as he was zealous and active on Washington's side." Jared Sparks, 1832, Letter to Robert Gilmore, Historical Manuscript Collection, Mount Vernon Ladies' Association, George Washington's Mount Vernon Estate, Museum & Gardens, Mount Vernon, VA.

17. Adams, 219.

18. Ibid.

19. Kraus, *The Writing of American History*, 91.

20. Adams, *The Life and Writings of Jared Sparks,* 227.

21. As quoted in Kraus, *The Writing of American History*, 89.

22. Throughout his life, Sparks was known as an autograph collector and dealer. A short paragraph from an 1832 letter shows Sparks commenting on his avocation and on his friend and colleague Sprague: "Your autographs have not been forgotten. The Saratoga list has been before me ever since. Some of them I shall be able to supply, particularly those of Revolutionary note. I do not think I can make out more than half a dozen of the signers of the Declaration. Sprague, you know, grasps at everything. He is as voracious as a shark, and has exhausted my treasures a good deal. But I shall keep you in mind. In two, or three, or four weeks I shall be in Baltimore, and shall take with me a parcel of autographs for you, and among others one from the present King of France, Mad. de Stael, and Necker." Jared Sparks, 1832, Letter to Robert Gilmore. Historical Manuscript Collection, Mount Vernon Ladies' Association, George Washington's Mount Vernon Estate, Museum & Gardens, Mount Vernon, VA.

23. Adams, *The Life and Writings of Jared Sparks,* 389.

24. Ibid., 390.

25. Ibid., 402.

26. Ibid., 403.

27. Ibid., 404.

28. Ibid., 405.

29. Quoted in Adams, *The Life and Writings of Jared Sparks,* 408.

30. Jared Sparks, letter, Morristown National Historical Park, Lloyd W. Smith Collection, Rare Books, letters of Jared Sparks.

31. Ibid.

32. Ibid.

33. Ibid.

34. Ibid.

35. Ibid.

36. Ibid.

37. Ibid.

38. Ibid.

39. Ibid.

40. Ibid.

41. Ibid.

42. John S. Bassett, *The Middle Group of American Historians* (New York: Macmillan Company, 1917), 80.

43. Jared Sparks, letter, Morristown National Historical Park, Lloyd W. Smith Collection, Rare Books, letters of Jared Sparks.

44 Adams, *The Life and Writings of Jared Sparks,* 266.

45. Jared Sparks, letter, Morristown National Historical Park, Lloyd W. Smith Collection, Rare Books, letters of Jared Sparks.

46. Ibid.

47. Galen Broeker, "Jared Sparks, Robert Peel and the State Paper Office," *American Quarterly* 13, no. 2, part 1 (Summer 1961), 140.

48. Ibid.

49. Ibid., 144.

50. Ibid., 145.

51 Adams, *The Life and Writings of Jared Sparks,* 60.

52. Ibid., 130.

53. In a letter to Robert Gilmore in 1832, Sparks alludes to the status of the Morris biography: "Gouverneur Morris's book is all in the printer's hands, and will be published in two or three weeks. It is in three volumes; the first a memoir; the two others selections from his correspondence and other writings. There is interesting matter on the French Revolution. I have disposed of the work to publishers, who will doubtless send copies to Baltimore." Jared Sparks, 1832, Letter to Robert Gilmore, Historical Manuscript Collection, Mount Vernon Ladies' Association, George Washington's Mount Vernon Estate, Museum & Gardens, Mount Vernon, VA.

54. Stephen William Schuster IV, "To Build a Monument: Jared Sparks and *The Writings of*

George Washington" (PhD diss., Texas Christian University, 1977), 126.

55. Ibid.

56. Saying Sparks spared no expense is not an exaggeration. Writing to George C. Washington in 1835, Sparks stated, "Every dollar I have in the world is involved in the publication of Washington's Writing, which, since the printing was begun, on account of the necessary investments and the slowness of returns, have not yielded enough for my daily support; although the prospect is fair, that I shall in the end realize a reasonable compensation. As a pecuniary arrangement, the undertaking has been to me unfortunate. There are few employments in which I could not, with the same time and labor, have made a great deal more money." Jared Sparks, 1835, Letter to George C. Washington, Historical Manuscript Collection, Mount Vernon Ladies' Association, George Washington's Mount Vernon Estate, Museum & Gardens, Mount Vernon, VA.

57. One of those commissions was for the Ford mansion in Morristown, New Jersey, Washington's Headquarters during the terrible winter of 1779–1780. This is the first known depiction of the house, which later became the first National Historical Park in the United States; 2013 marks the eightieth anniversary of the Ford mansion's contribution to the American historic preservation movement.

58. Schuster, "To Build a Monument," 140.

59. Ibid., 146.

60. Ibid., 141.

61. Sparks had made sure that the transfer did not violate the terms of the contract with Bushrod Washington on the removal of the material from Sparks' possession. Sparks wrote to Congressman Washington on September 5, 1834:

Before I can be authorized to deliver General Washington's papers to the United States, it is necessary for me to have a direct order to that effect from you. On the other side is a form, which I wish you would copy, and sign, and return to me.

Mr. Forsyth has forwarded papers to Mr. [?], District Attorney, specifying the forms of delivery of the manuscripts, to which I cannot agree. I have written an explanation of the matter to Mr. Forsyth. Whatever forms of transfer may be prescribed, it must leave me in precisely the same relation to the papers in which I stood before the purchase of Congress. That purchase cannot in any manner effect my contract. I presume Mr. Forsyth will see the thing in its proper light.

Jared Sparks, 1834, Letter to George C. Washington, Historical Manuscript Collection, Mount Vernon Ladies' Association, George Washington's Mount Vernon Estate, Museum & Gardens, Mount Vernon, VA.

Chapter 11

1. Stephen William Schuster IV, "To Build a Monument: Jared Sparks and *The Writings of George Washington"* (PhD diss., Texas Christian University, 1977), 159.

2. Ibid., 162.

3. Ibid., 165.

4. Ibid., 168.

5. Ibid., 169–170.

6. Philip Allingham, "Nineteenth-Century British and American Copyright Law." The Victorian Web, 1.

7. Ibid.

8. Ibid.

9. The cumbersome process for a foreign writer to obtain a copyright, when it worked, involved five steps:

1. The author needed to deposit a copy of the title page with the authorities in Washington.

2. The author had to have the work published in Great Britain.

3. Within ten days of publication in the United Kingdom, the author had to have an American edition issued, and copies deposited at appropriate offices on both sides of the Atlantic.

4. The author needed to deposit a copy of the work within a month of British publication.

5. The author could, though not a requirement, register the work at Stationer's Hall in London after United Kingdom publication.

While this is not totally impossible, the process did little to encourage cross-cultural literary cooperation. Allingham, "Nineteenth-Century British and American Copyright Law," 3.

10. Ibid., 2.

11. Cathy N. Davidson, *Revolution and the Word: The Rise of the Novel in America* (Oxford: Oxford University Press, 1986), 35.

12. Russell Blaine Nye, *The Cultural Life of the New Nation, 1776–1830* (New York: Harper & Row, 1960), 249.

13. Allingham, "Nineteenth-Century British and American Copyright Law," 2.

14. Herbert Baxter Adams, *The Life and Writings of Jared Sparks: Comprising Selections From His Journals and Correspondence,* vol. 2 (New York: Houghton, Mifflin and Company, 1893), 362.

15. Schuster, "To Build a Monument: Jared Sparks and *The Writings of George Washington*," 171.

16. Adams, *The Life and Writings of Jared Sparks*, 2, 368–369. Sparks left the following account of his first term approach: "It has been thought best to confine the instructions to the history of the American Revolution from 1763 to 1783. I have adopted Botta's history as a text-book, because I can procure no other; all the other histories of the same period being out of print. Once a week I shall read to the class written lectures; that is, one of the three weekly exercises will be of this sort. My object is to communicate instruction in all the exercises, and not merely to discipline the students in the habits of study, which has been done sufficiently in the early part of their college life." Ibid., 375.

Chapter 12

1. Near the end of the controversy, Reed himself wrote "I printed the Washington letters from the original, the only variations being occasional corrections of grammar and spelling and the omission of one or two sentences, evidently the result of oversight on my part." So, even Reed himself, who did not accuse Sparks of misconduct, edited in a manner much as Sparks had done. As quoted in a footnote in Herbert Baxter Adams, *The Life and Writings of Jared Sparks: Comprising Selections from His Journals and Correspondence*, vol. 2. (New York: Houghton, Mifflin and Company, 1893), 495.

2. Stephen William Schuster IV, "To Build a Monument: Jared Sparks and *The Writings of George Washington*" (PhD diss., Texas Christian University, 1977), 173–174.

3. Ibid., 175.

4. As quoted in a footnote in Adams, *The Life and Writings of Jared Sparks*, 494.

5. As quoted in Adams, *The Life and Writings of Jared Sparks*, 503.

6. Sparks was without doubt a major impetus to the historical profession in its infancy. Sparks generated enthusiasm and reciprocal desire in like-minded scholars wherever he went, especially in Europe. This indeed was the case in England, which is why the Lord Mahon attack is uniquely so galling. Mahon chose to critique Sparks not just in an editorial; rather, he chose to attack in the pages of his own book as an appendix. Mahon had been inspired to finish his *History of England* due in part to Sparks' studies in England. Mahon was encouraged by

his good friend Robert Southey in an August 13, 1832, letter:

"When Jared Sparks was in England about five years ago, our State Papers relating to America during the war were examined in consequence of his inquiries. It was then thought that our own story would bear telling and ought to be told, and a circuitous application was made to me to know whether I would undertake it. I declined the proposal, because a great part of my life had been passed in preparing for other subjects, and if they were left unfinished that labor would be lost. But the American War is a fine subject, and treated as you would treat it, with the same perfect fairness as the Succession War, its history would vindicate the honor of this country, at the same time that it rendered full justice to the opposite cause."

A finer support of objective history would be hard to find. As quoted in a footnote in Adams, *The Life and Writings of Jared Sparks*, 480.

7. As quoted in Adams, *The Life and Writings of Jared Sparks*, 481.

8. Schuster, "To Build a Monument: Jared Sparks and *The Writings of George Washington*," 180.

9. Adams, *The Life and Writings of Jared Sparks*, 276. It should also be remembered what Sparks wrote at the beginning of his work: "In preparing the manuscripts for the press, I have been obliged to use a latitude of discretion, rendered unavoidable by the mode in which the papers have been preserved. They are uniformly copied into volumes, and this task appears to have been performed, except in the Revolutionary correspondence, by incompetent or very careless transcribers. Gross blunders constantly occur, which not infrequently destroy the sense, and which never could have existed in the original drafts. In these cases, I have of course considered it a duty, appertaining to the function of a faithful editor, to hazard such corrections as the construction of the sentence manifestly warranted, or a cool judgment dictated." Ibid., 273.

10. Sparks continued his defense to Mahon:

I have shown first, that in every instance in which you have supposed facts to be suppressed or concealed, these facts are to be found in other parts of the work, or in other works long well known to the public; secondly, that you have frequently selected short sentences, or fragments of sentences, and conjectured some special design for their omission, when in reality they were included in a paragraph, or larger portion of a letter, omitted for reasons in no man-

ner relating to the purport of these sentences; thirdly, that your main charge of a personal motive prompting me to protect Washington's dignity and the good name of the people of New England, at the expense of historical justice, is not sustained by facts, reasonable inferences, or probability.... In making a selection from a large mass of papers left by Washington, extending over a long period and extremely various in their character, an editor could not expect to escape from occasional errors of judgment and opinion. Such errors are fair subjects of criticism; but when you assail motives, and thus call in question the editor's fidelity and rectitude, you give a wide range to a critic's privilege. I trust my sensibility to what I esteem your unfounded animadversions has not betrayed me beyond the proper line of courtesy, nor diminished the respect which I have been accustomed to entertain for you as an author and a man.
As quoted in Adams, *The Life and Writings of Jared Sparks,* 491.

11. Herbert Baxter Adams, *The Life and Writings of Jared Sparks: Comprising Selections From His Journals and Correspondence,* vol. 2 (New York: Houghton, Mifflin and Company, 1893), 271.

12. As quoted in Adams, *The Life and Writings of Jared Sparks,* 501.

13. As quoted in Adams, *The Life and Writings of Jared Sparks,* 493.

14. As quoted in Adams, *The Life and Writings of Jared Sparks,* 493.

15. As quoted in Adams, *The Life and Writings of Jared Sparks,* 494.

16. As quoted in Adams, *The Life and Writings of Jared Sparks,* 502–503.

17. Schuster, "To Build a Monument: Jared Sparks and *The Writings of George Washington*," 186.

18. As quoted in Adams, *The Life and Writings of Jared Sparks,* 504.

19. Schuster, "To Build a Monument: Jared Sparks and *The Writings of George Washington*," 133.

20. Ibid.

21. Ibid., 134.

22. Justice Story wrote: "I have some doubt whether the antiquarians and devout admirers of Washington will not object to your emendations of the style. To correct the grammatical errors (it seems to me) will be deemed by every person an appropriate duty of the editor. But the change of words merely to express the thought more appropriately, or the change of the form of the sentence merely to make it read

more clearly, or, in a literary sense, more correctly, will perhaps be deemed a liberty not required, and very unfair, in the opinion of some, to *veritable* character of the documents themselves." As quoted in Adams, *The Life and Writings of Jared Sparks,* 283.

23. As quoted in Garry Wills, *Henry Adams and the Making of America* (New York: Houghton Mifflin Company, 2005), 34.

24. Ibid.

Conclusion

1. The title of this section comes from the printed version of a lecture given by J. G. A. Pocock at the University of London in 2003. The title of the lecture and of the printed version is "The Politics of Historiography." Pocock describes his approach as meaning in the first place an enquiry within the theory of politics into what it means to have a history; into what those words mean, into what manner of *Lebensform* ... 'we' must be to have one, into what this 'history' we supposedly have must be, and into what it means to this 'us' to have or not to have ... history.
J. G. A. Pocock, "The Politics of Historiography," *Historical Research* 78, no. 199 (February 2005), 2.

2. Roger Sandall, "Objects 101," *The New Criterion* 30 (November 2011), 78.

3. As quoted in John Burrow, *A History of Histories Epics: Chronicles, Romances and Inquiries from Herodotus and Thucydides to the Twentieth Century* (New York: Alfred A. Knopf, 2008), 425.

4. Pocock, "The Politics of Historiography," 9.

5. Ibid., 6.

6. Ibid., 8.

7. Ibid.

8. Ibid., 12–13.

9. John H. Arnold, *History: A Very Short Introduction* (Oxford: Oxford University Press, 2000), 92–93.

Epilogue

1. As quoted in John Burrow, *A History of Histories Epics: Chronicles, Romances and Inquiries from Herodotus and Thucydides to the Twentieth Century* (New York: Alfred A. Knopf, 2008), 432.

2. Ibid., 435.

3. Richard Arthur Firda, "German Philosophy of History and Literature in the North American Review: 1815–1860," *Journal of the History of Ideas* 32, no. 1 (January-March 1971), 133.

4. Ibid., 134.

5. Ibid.

6. Ibid.

7. Ibid., 135.

8. Ibid., 136.

9. Dirus Goldstein, as quoted in Garry Wills, *Henry Adams and the Making of America* (New York: Houghton Mifflin Company, 2005), 36.

10. Firda, "German Philosophy of History and Literature in the North American Review: 1815–1860," 142.

Appendix 5

1. Herbert Baxter Adams, *The Life and Writings of Jared Sparks: Comprising Selections From His Journals and Correspondence,* vol. 2 (New York: Houghton, Mifflin and Company, 1893), 594–595.

Bibliography

......

There are so many books and articles dealing with the topics, people, themes, and events of this work that listing them would entail a separate volume. Likewise, it would be nearly impossible to individually track down and study all of the possible sources that could have been referenced in the research and writing of the present work. This is by no means an attempt to absolve the author from not having consulted them. Rather, it is a warning to readers that the amount of information available beyond that listed below is staggering. The topic is extremely rich in opportunity for study because most of the figures involved are so well known and so important to the founding and early development of the United States. Yet, rarely has the attempt been made to bring together just those elements pertaining to the writing of history in the colonial and early national period outside of the academic treatise. With the above qualifying statement on resource material, the following bibliography represents those texts the author relied on in the preparation of this work.

Adams, Herbert Baxter. *The Life and Writings of Jared Sparks: Comprising Selections from His Journals and Correspondence.* 2 vols. New York: Houghton, Mifflin and Company, 1893.

Annis, David Leslie. "Mr. Bushrod Washington, Supreme Court Justice on the Marshall Court." PhD diss., University of Notre Dame, 1974.

Arnold, John H. *History: A Very Short Introduction.* Oxford: Oxford University Press, 2000.

Austen, Jane. *Northanger Abbey and Persuasion, The Novels of Jane Austen. The Text Based on Collation of the Early Editions by R.W. Chapman.* Oxford: Oxford University Press, n.d.

Bailyn, Bernard. *The Ideological Origins of the American Revolution.* Cambridge: Belknap Press of Harvard University Press, 1992.

Baker, Leonard. *John Marshall: A Life in Law.* New York: Macmillan Publishing Company, 1974.

Bassett, John Spencer. *The Middle Group of American Historians.* New York: MacMillan Company, 1917.

Becker, Carl L. *The Heavenly City of the Eighteenth-Century Philosophers.* New Haven, CT: Yale University Press, 1960.

Beveridge, Albert J. *The Life of John Marshall.* Vol. III, *Conflict and Construction, 1800–1815.* New York: Houghton Mifflin Company, 1919.

Binney, Horace. *Bushrod Washington.* Philadelphia: Privately Published, 1858.

Boyd, Julian P., ed. *The Papers of Thomas Jefferson.* Vol. I, *1760–1776.* Princeton: Princeton University Press, 1950.

Brooks, Van Wyck. *The Flowering of New England.* New York: E. P. Dutton & Co., 1952.

Burke, Peter. *Vico.* Oxford: Oxford University Press, 1985.

Burnett, Edmund C., ed. *Letters of Members of the Continental Congress.* 8 vols. Gloucester, MA: Peter Smith, 1963.

Burrow, John. *A History of Histories: Epics, Chronicles, Romances and Inquiries from Herodotus and Thucydides to the Twentieth Century.* New York: Alfred A. Knopf, 2008.

Burstein, Andrew. *The Inner Jefferson: Portrait of a Grieving Optimist.* Charlottesville: University Press of Virginia, 1995.

Bushman, Richard L. *The Refinement of America: Persons, Houses, Cities.* New York: Alfred A. Knopf, 1992.

Cannon, John, R. H. C. Davis, William Doyle, and Jack P. Greene, eds. *The Blackwell Dictionary of Historians.* Oxford: Basil Blackwell, 1988.

Cappon, Lester J., ed. *The Adams-Jefferson Letters: The Complete Correspondence Between Thomas Jefferson and Abigail and John Adams.* Chapel Hill: University of North Carolina Press, 1987.

Carr, Edward Hallett. *What Is History?* New York: Alfred A. Knopf, 1964.

Cohen, Lester H. "The Course of Human Events: American Historical Writing in the Revolutionary Era." PhD diss., Yale University, 1974.

Colbourn, Trevor. *The Lamp of Experience: Whig History and the Intellectual Origins of the American Revolution.* Indianapolis, IN: Liberty Fund, 1998.

Corner, George W., ed. *The Autobiography of Benjamin Rush: His "Travels Through Life" together with His* Commonplace Book *for 1789–1813.* Princeton, NJ: Princeton University Press, 1948.

Cushman, Clare, ed. *The Supreme Court Justices: Illustrated Biographies, 1789–1995.* Washington, D.C.: Congressional Quarterly, 1995.

Dalzell, Robert F., Jr., and Lee Baldwin Dalzell. *George Washington's Mount Vernon: At Home in Revolutionary America.* Oxford: Oxford University Press, 1998.

Davidson, Cathy N. *Revolution and the Word: The Rise of the Novel in America.* Oxford: Oxford University Press, 1986.

Elliott, Emory. *Revolutionary Writers: Literature and Authority in the New Republic, 1725–1810.* Oxford: Oxford University Press, 1982.

Ellis, Joseph J. *After the Revolution: Profiles of Early American Culture.* New York: W. W. Norton and Company, 1979.

Emerson, Everett, ed. *Major Writers of Early American Literature.* Madison: University of Wisconsin Press, 1976.

Emerson, Ralph Waldo. *Essays & Lectures, Nature; Addresses, and Lectures, Essays: First and Second Series, Representative Men, English Traits, the Conduct of Life.* New York: The Library of America, 1983.

Evans, Richard J. *In Defense of History.* New York: W. W. Norton and Company, 1999.

Gay, Peter. *The Enlightenment: An Interpretation. The Science of Freedom.* New York: W. W. Norton and Company, 1977.

Gibson, Alan. *Interpreting the Founding: Guide to the Enduring Debates Over the Origins and Foundations of the American Republic.* Lawrence: University of Kansas Press, 2006.

Gunn, Giles, ed. *Early American Writing.* New York: Penguin Books, 1994.

Harris, Sharon M., ed. *Women's Early American Historical Narratives.* New York: Penguin Books, 2003.

Heath, Duncan, and Judy Boreham. *Introducing Romanticism.* New York: Totem Books, 2000.

Hobson, Charles F., Fredrika J. Teute, and Laura S. Gwilliam, eds. *The Papers of John Marshall.* Vol. VI, *Correspondence, Papers, and Selected Judicial Opinions November 1800–March 1807.* Chapel Hill: University of North Carolina Press, 1990.

Home, Henry, Lord Kames. *Sketches of the History of Man.* Book 1, edited by James A. Harris. Indianapolis, IN: Liberty Fund, 2007.

Irving, Washington. *Life of George Washington.* Edited by Jess Stein. Tarrytown, NY: Sleepy Hollow Restorations, 1975.

Jefferson, Thomas. *Writings.* New York: Library of America, 1984.

Kahler, Gerald E. *The Long Farewell: Americans Mourn the Death of George Washington.*

Charlottesville: University of Virginia Press, 2008.

Kamrath, Mark L. *The Historicism of Charles Brockden Brown: Radical History and the Early Republic.* Kent, OH: Kent State University Press, 2010.

Koch, Adrienne, ed. *The American Enlightenment: The Shaping of the American Experiment and a Free Society.* New York: George Braziller, 1965.

Kramer, Samuel Noah. *History Begins at Sumer: Twenty-Seven "Firsts" in Man's Recorded History.* Garden City, NJ: Doubleday Anchor Books, 1959.

Kraus, Michael. *The Writing of American History.* Norman: University of Oklahoma Press, 1953.

Leisy, Ernest E. *The American Historical Novel.* Norman: University of Oklahoma Press, 1970.

Lengel, Edward G. *Inventing George Washington America's Founder, in Myth & Memory.* New York: Harper, 2011.

Madison, James. *Writings.* New York: Library of America, 1999.

Mahan, Harold Eugene. "More Than a historian: Benson J. Lossing and Historical Writing in the United States, 1830–1890." PhD diss., University of Wisconsin, 1992.

Marshall, John. *The Life of George Washington Special School Edition.* Edited by Robert Faulkner and Paul Carrese. Indianapolis, IN: Liberty Fund, 2000.

_____. *Writings.* New York: Library of America, 2010.

Martin, Joseph Plumb. *A Narrative of Some of the Adventures, Dangers and Sufferings of a Revolutionary Soldier, Interspersed with Anecdotes of Incidents That Occurred Within His Own Observation.* Edited by George F. Scheer. Boston: Eastern Acorn Press, 1979.

McIlwain, Charles Howard. *The American Revolution: A Constitutional Interpretation.* Ithaca, NY: Cornell University Press, 1958.

Melville, Herman. *Pierre or The Ambiguities, Israel Potter: His Fifty Years of Exile, The Piazza Tales, The Confidence-Man: His Masquerade, Uncollected Prose, Billy Budd, Sailor: An Inside Narrative.* New York: Library of America, 1984.

Morison, Samuel Eliot. *The Intellectual Life of New England.* New York: New York University Press, 1956.

Newmyer, R. Kent. *Supreme Court Justice Joseph Story: Statesman of the Old Republic.* Chapel Hill: University of North Carolina Press, 1985.

Nye, Russel Blaine. *The Cultural Life of the New Nation, 1776–1830.* New York: Harper & Row, 1960.

Ramsay, David. *The History of the American Revolution.* Edited by Lester H. Cohen. 2 vols. Indianapolis, IN: Liberty Fund, 1990.

Sandoz, Ellis, ed. *Political Sermons of the American Founding Era, 1730–1805.* Indianapolis, IN: Liberty Fund, 1990.

Schuster, Stephen William, IV. "To Build a Monument: Jared Sparks and *The Writings of George Washington*." PhD diss., Texas Christian University, 1977.

Shaffer, Arthur H. *The Politics of History: Writing the History of the American Revolution, 1783–1815.* New Brunswick, NJ: Transaction Publishers, 2009.

Skemp, Sheila L. *Judith Sargent Murray: A Brief Biography with Documents.* New York: Bedford Books, 1998.

Smith, Richard Norton. *Patriarch: George Washington and the New American Nation.* New York: Houghton Mifflin Company, 1993.

Sparks, Jared. *The Life of George Washington.* Boston: Ferdinand Andrews, 1839.

Spiller, Robert E., Willard Thorp, Thomas H. Johnson, et al., eds. *Literary History of the United States.* London: Macmillan Company, 1969.

Stevenson, Elizabeth, ed. *A Henry Adams Reader.* Garden City, NJ: Doubleday Anchor Books, 1958.

Toynbee, Arnold J. *Greek Historical Thought from Homer to the Age of Heraclius.* New York: Mentor, ND.

Tyler, Moses Coit. *The Literary History of the American Revolution.* Vol. I, *1763–1776.* New York: Frederick Ungar Publishing Co., 1966.

Vico, Giambattista. *New Science.* Translated by David Marsh. London: Penguin Books, 1999.

Walsh, W. H. *Philosophy of History, An Introduction.* New York: Harper & Row, 1967.

Warren, Mercy Otis. *History of the Rise, Progress and Termination of the American Revolution Interspersed with Biographical, Political and Moral Observations.* Edited by Lester H. Cohen. 2 vols. Indianapolis, IN: Liberty Fund, 1994.

Washington, George. *A Collection.* Edited by William B. Allen. Indianapolis, IN: Liberty Classics, 1988.

Wills, Garry. *Henry Adams and the Making of America*. New York: Houghton Mifflin Company, 2005.

Wilson, James. *Collected Works of James Wilson*. Edited by Kermit L. Hall and Mark David Hall. 2 vols. Indianapolis, IN: Liberty Fund, 2007.

Womersley, David, ed. *Liberty and American Experience in the Eighteenth Century*. Indianapolis, IN: Liberty Fund, 2006.

Wood, Gordon S. *Empire of Liberty: A History of the Early Republic, 1789–1815*. Oxford: Oxford University Press, 2009.

Websites

Allingham, Philip V. "Nineteenth-Century British and American Copyright Law." Accessed October 20, 2011. http://www.victorianweb.org/authors/dickens/pva/pva74.html.

Barrett, William P. "In Pictures: 10 Richest U.S. Presidents." Accessed October 27, 2011. http://www.forbes.com/2010/07/14/george-washington-hoover-jfk-obama-personal-finance-10-richest-presidents_slide_5.html.

Lengel, Edward G., ed. "The Papers of George Washington Digital Edition." Accessed January 8, 2010. http://rotunda.upress.virginia.edu/founders/GEWN-06–02–02-0411.

Lepore, Jill. "His Highness: George Washington Scales New Heights." Accessed October 25, 2011. http://www.newyorker.com/arts/critics/atlarge/2010/09/27/100927crat_atlarge_lepore.

Library of Congress. "Letters of Delegates to Congress: Volume 6, January 1, 1777–April 30, 1777. Benjamin Rush's Notes of Debates." Accessed February 8, 2012. http://memory.loc.gov/cgi-bin/query/r?ammen/hlaw:@field%28DOCID+@lit%28D8dg006203%29%29.

McIntyre, Douglas A., Michael B. Sauter, and Ashley C. Allen. "The Net Worth of the U.S. Presidents: From Washington to Obama." Accessed October 25, 2011. http://www.theatlantic.com/business/archive/2010/05/the-net-worth-of-the-us-presidents-from-washington-to-obama/57020.

Wallenborn, White McKenzie. "George Washington's Terminal Illness: A Modern Medical Analysis of the Last Illness and Death of George Washington." Accessed December 15, 2011. http://gwpapers.virginia.edu/articles/wallenborn.html.

Articles

Andrews, Charles M. Review of "Jared Sparks and Alexis de Tocqueville." *Annals of the American Academy of Political and Social Science* 13 (May 1899), 111–112.

Bauer, Ralph. "Colonial Discourse and Early American Literary History: Ercilla, the Inca Garcilaso, and Joel Barlow's Conception of a New World Epic." *Early American Literature* 30, no. 3 (1995), 203–232.

Berthold, Dennis. "Charles Brockden Brown, *Edgar Huntly*, and the Origins of the American Picturesque." *William and Mary Quarterly* 41, no. 1, Third Series (January 1984), 62–84.

Broeker, Galen. "Jared Sparks, Robert Peel and the State Paper Office." *American Quarterly* 13, no. 2, Part 1 (Summer, 1961), 140–152.

Brown, Ralph H. "St. George Tucker Versus Jedidiah Morse on the Subject of Williamsburg." *William and Mary Quarterly* 20, no. 4, Second Series (October 1940), 487–491.

Brunhouse, Robert L. "David Ramsay, 1749–1815: Selections from His Writings." *Transactions of the American Philosophical Society* 55, no. 4, New Series (1965), 1–250.

Cappon, Lester J. "American Historical Editors Before Jared Sparks: 'They Will Plant a Forest....'" *William and Mary Quarterly* 30, no. 3, Third Series (July 1973), 376–400.

Chacko, David, and Alexander Kulcsar. "Israel Potter: Genesis of a Legend." *William and Mary Quarterly* 41, no. 3, Third Series (July 1984), 365–389.

Custer, Lawrence B. "Bushrod Washington and John Marshall: A Preliminary Inquiry." *American Journal of Legal History* 4, no. 1 (January 1960), 34–48.

Firda, Richard Arthur. "German Philosophy of History and Literature in the *North American Review*: 1815–1860." *Journal of the History of Ideas* 32, no. 1 (January-March 1971), 133–142.

Foran, William A. "John Marshall as a Historian." *American Historical Review* 43, no. 1 (October 1937), 51–64.

Jackson, Leon. "Jedidiah Morse and the Transformation of Print Culture in New England, 1784–1826." *Early American Literature* 34, no. 1 (1999), 2–31.

Johnson, Elmer Douglass. "David Ramsay: Historian or Plagiarist?" *South Carolina Historical Magazine* 57, no. 4 (October 1956), 189–198.

Lizanich, Christine M. "'The March of This Government': Joel Barlow's Unwritten History of the United States." *William and Mary Quarterly* 33, no. 2, Third Series (April 1976), 315–330.

Maxfield, Ezra Kempton. "The Tom Barlow Manuscript of the Columbiad." *New England Quarterly* 11, no. 4 (December 1938), 834–842.

Pocock, J. G. A. "The Politics of Historiography." *Historical Research* 78, no. 199 (February 2005), 1–14.

Pryce-Jones, David. "The Past Is a Foreign Country." *New Criterion* 30 (September 2011) 90–92.

Sandall, Roger. "Objects 101." *New Criterion* 30 (November 2011) 78–80.

Shaffer, Arthur. "John Daly Burk's 'History of Virginia' and the Development of American National History." *Virginia Magazine of History and Biography* 77, no. 3 (July, 1969), 336–346.

Sheldon, Richard N. "Editing a Historical Manuscript: Jared Sparks, Douglas Southall Freeman, and the Battle of Brandywine." *William and Mary Quarterly* 36, no. 2, Third Series (April 1979), 255–263.

Shelley, Fred. "Ebenezer Hazard: America's First Historical Editor." *William and Mary Quarterly* 12, no. 1, Third Series (January 1955), 44–73.

Stearns, Malcolm, Jr. "The Utopian College of Jared Sparks." *New England Quarterly* 15, no. 3 (September 1942), 512–515.

Vadakan, Vibul. "The Asphyxiating and Exsanguinating Death of President George Washington." *Permanente Journal* 8, no. 2 (Spring 2004), 1–7.

Webster, Charles K. "Some Early Applications from American Historians to Use the British Archives." *Journal of Modern History* 1, no. 3 (September 1929), 416–419.

Zunder, Theodore A. "Joel Barlow and George Washington." *Modern Language Notes* 44, no. 4 (April 1929), 254–256.

Index

••••••